The Great Clowns of American Television

The Great Clowns of American Television

by
Karin Adir

McFarland & Company, Inc., Publishers
Jefferson, North Carolina, and London

British Library Cataloguing-in-Publication data available.

Library of Congress Cataloguing-in-Publication Data

Adir, Karin, 1952–
   The great clowns of American television.

   Bibliography: p. 251.
   Includes index.
   1. Television personalities—United States—Biography.
2. Comedians—United States—Biography. I. Title.
PN1992.4.A2A62   1988   791.45′028′0922 [B]   88-42642

ISBN 0-89950-300-4 (lib. bdg.; 50# acid-free natural paper)

Printed in the United States of America.

McFarland & Company, Inc., Publishers
   Box 611, Jefferson, North Carolina 28640

For my parents,
for their love and support.
For Michael, for being there.
And for clowns, everywhere.

Contents

Introduction

Why *The Great Clowns of American Television?* Surely their presence on our small screens over the past 35 years has placed these men and women squarely in the eye of the American public; we have our memories of their talents and routines etched in our memories.

But it is not enough. There are whole generations that have never seen Sid Caesar become an automobile tire, never seen Red Skelton stick his thumbs in his armpits and intone, "Two theagulls . . .," never journeyed with Ernie Kovacs to a surrealistic world of his warped imagination.

Television is a new medium, a radical medium. It has changed the lives of nearly all on planet Earth, far more so than movies or radio. The clowns of this medium were perhaps more beloved than any others. They brought the joy of laughter into our homes, they relaxed us after a hard day's work, they allowed the whole family to share something wonderful and entertaining.

Who are these people who worked so hard to lift our spirits, to transport us on their wild flights of fancy? Where did they come from, by whom were they inspired? Were they funny offscreen as well as on? How did they approach their craft, as tyrant or thrall? What characters did they create, what skills of pantomime did they draw on? And what was the secret behind their mysterious gift of timing, the most crucial element in comedy?

As a performing theater clown for many years in Europe and the United States, I have read numerous books on the lives and works of the great cinema clowns. There are dozens of biographies of Chaplin, many others on Keaton, Lloyd, Sennett, the Marx Brothers, W.C. Fields, to name a few. But when, after viewing the videotapes of the works of Caesar and Kovacs I searched for written material on television clowns, I found only a paucity of such works. Memories fade swiftly; if events are not recorded they could be lost forever.

Here then is a collection of clowns and funny men and women. If your personal favorite has been omitted, apologies are in order; perhaps he or she will turn up in the next volume. It should be noted that it has been a labor of love for me to delve into the lives and labors of those herein, and as such this book has been done in a spirit of delight and admiration.

Karin Adir
New York City

Lucille Ball

Since the advent of American television, the undisputed queen of comedy has been Lucille Ball. She has set the standard for sit-com comediennes, bombarded us with wacky schemes and impossibly funny dilemmas, and taken us for a roller-coaster ride of hysteria with her "Lucy" character. With enormous eyes and carrot-pink hair, Lucy has proved that one can be beautiful, feminine—and funny. Lucille Ball paid her dues to an industry that for many years ignored her, exploited her, or did not fully utilize her prodigious talents. It took television and the toilings of devoted writers, producers, and a certain Cuban for her to develop her innate comic abilities and give free rein to an unabashed love of making people laugh.

Lucy was an exaggerated version of Everywoman: desperate to be noticed; vain; conniving (though never malicious); celebrity-mad; proud; loving; jealous and more. Her appeal to America in the fifties (and ever since during the show's syndication), was that the average family could identify with her. Often wearing roomy smocks and a scarf wrapped around her admittedly dyed hair, Lucy was no longer a glamorous Hollywood actress, but a typical (if somewhat crazed) American housewife. And while it is important not to confuse Lucy with her portrayer Lucille Ball, there is no doubt that she was Lucille's greatest creation and sustained her through more than two decades on television. Endless imitations of the "I Love Lucy" format have surfaced in the years since the show's inception, but there has been only one Lucy.

America's future starlet and zany comedienne was born Lucille Desiree to parents Henry Dunnell and Desiree (known as DeeDee) Hunt Ball on August 6, 1911. She grew up in Celeron, New York, a small town near Jamestown, which is itself about 60 miles south of Buffalo on the southern shore of Lake Chautauqua. Lucy's maternal grandfather, Fred C. Hunt, was the portly son of a well-to-do family

1

that owned the only hotel in Jamestown. He possessed a strong socialist streak, and shocked the local populace by marrying one of the hotel maids, Florabelle Orchutt. Lucy's father, Henry, was an electrical lineman. When Lucy was a baby he moved his family out to Butte, Montana, where he went to work for the Anaconda copper mines. After three years in the cold Montana weather he contracted pneumonia. The three Balls headed back to Jamestown (with DeeDee five months' pregnant with Lucy's brother Fred), but they were forced to halt their travels in Michigan to stay with friends. Henry was too sick to continue, and died there of typhoid at age 23.

DeeDee went back to live with her family and in 1920 married Ed Peterson. She left Lucille and young Fred in the care of Peterson's mother while she followed her new husband to Detroit, where he had found work. Peterson's mother was an austere spoilsport who covered all the mirrors in the house in an effort to deter vanity. Little Lucy missed her mother terribly, but fortunately DeeDee returned before long. Years later Lucille's mother recalled this lonely time in her daughter's childhood. "When I married this second guy [Peterson], he wanted to go to Detroit to work. He was quite a gambler and drank a bit, and he said he'd give up all those things if I went with him. So I left the children. I didn't stay long because he didn't stick to his promises." They were divorced a year later.

DeeDee returned to Jamestown, and her children, and supported them by working in a dress shop. She also assumed responsibility for Cleo Van Marter, the orphaned daughter of her sister. Lucy's cousin Cleo remained her closest friend and confidante in the years to come, and she often referred to Cleo as her sister.

It seems that young Lucille was stagestruck at an early age; she was always taking part in school and local amateur efforts. At the age of 15 she convinced her mother to allow her to journey to New York City alone to attend the John Murray Anderson School of Drama. Apparently she made less than a startling impression there, as Mr. Anderson himself communicated in a note to her mother: "Lucy's wasting her time and mine. She's too shy and reticent to put her best foot forward." It may have been that Miss Ball was, like most of her classmates, too much in awe of the school's star pupil, Bette Davis.

But Lucy held tenaciously onto her dream of stardom and began auditioning for shows. Unfortunately, she had few skills to offer besides her beauty and youth and showgirl legs. She was fired from several shows, including Flo Ziegfeld's "Rio Rita," for lack of ability. To support herself she worked as a secretary and a soda jerk, but mostly she starved. Years later she would describe her search for "one-doughnut" men, those who would order two pastries but eat only one, leaving her to quickly appropriate the other. Hoping to turn her luck around, she even changed her name for a while to Diane Belmont (after the racecourse) and dyed her hair blonde. Things began to look up when she found work as a model, first as The Chesterfield Girl in billboard advertisements, and then for famed dress designer Hattie Carnegie. With her 5'6½", 125-pound frame, she was the perfect size for a dress model. One day in the Carnegie showroom, however, Lucy was struck with rheumatoid arthritis in both her legs. It was so severe that she had to go home to Jamestown to recuperate. She was unable to walk for over two years and spent nearly another year in therapy.

In 1933 she was again ready to seek her fortune in New York. She and her friend Gert Kratzert arrived by bus and got a room together at 72nd Street and Broadway. Lucy was soon back at her old job modeling at Hattie Carnegie's. Fortunately, she would not have to model much longer. She happened to meet an agent who was seeking girls with modeling experience to form the chorus for *Roman Scandals,* an Eddie Cantor film being shot in Hollywood. Lucy did not have to be asked twice. On July 19, 1933, she and six other beauties got off the train from New York for what, Lucy thought, would probably amount to six weeks' work, after which she would return to the East.

With her large blue eyes and pouting lips, the 22-year-old Ball was perfect starlet material. She went under contract to Goldwyn, then Columbia, and finally RKO studios. For her first 18 films, beginning with *Broadway Thru a Keyhole* (20th Century/United Artists, 1933) through *The Three Musketeers* (RKO, 1935) she appeared as an extra or a bit player, usually glamorously decked out, hardly more than ornamentation. She did get to appear in movies with some of the greats of the era, including Eddie Cantor in the aforementioned *Roman Scandals* (Goldwyn/UA, 1933) and again in *Kid Millions,* which also costarred Ann Sothern and Ethel Merman (Goldwyn/UA, 1934); Anna Sten in the ill-fated Goldwyn vehicle *Nana* (1934); Spencer Tracy in *Bottoms Up* (Fox, 1934); Loretta Young in *Bulldog Drummond Strikes Back* (Goldwyn/UA, 1934); and the world's most exciting dance team, Fred Astaire and Ginger Rogers, in *Top Hat* (RKO, 1935). For the last, she was fortunate enough to have one line

Lucille Ball, Hollywood star, circa 1950.

of dialogue, although most of her time on film was spent with her back to the camera.

At RKO she was given small parts in dozens of second-rate movies. She played chorus girls, actresses, dancers, daughters, sisters, and girlfriends, but never a lead. It was not until the splendid *Stage Door* (RKO, 1937), when she co-starred with Katharine Hepburn and Ginger Rogers, that she began to receive some notice.

Soon after *Stage Door* Lucille was cast in a series of comedies and had her first leading role co-starring with Joe (*Wanna Buy a Duck?*) Penner in *Go Chase Yourself* (RKO, 1938). She also made two Annabel pictures with Jack Oakie, *The Affairs of Annabel* (RKO, 1938) and *Annabel Takes a Tour* (RKO, 1938), in which she starred as a willful actress with an overzealous publicity agent. She also had a small role in the Marx Brothers' *Room Service* (RKO, 1938), as an actress whom Groucho, as an itinerant Broadway producer, has promised to star in his next show.

Life in Hollywood was lonely for the beautiful, hard-working starlet, and in 1935 Lucy, now that she had a contract with RKO, sent for her family to join her. DeeDee, Grandpa Fred, brother Freddy and cousin Cleo all turned up to start life over in Hollywood at the house Lucy had bought at 1344 Ogden Drive. Although only 24 and receiving a starting salary of only $75 a week (which was more than many were earning in the depths of the Depression), Lucy was supporting her whole family. Family and filial ties have always been the most important things in the comedienne's life, as her devotion to her own children years later would prove.

Finally, by the late thirties and early forties Lucy was receiving some challenging, starring roles. In *Five Came Back* (RKO, 1939) she played one of the survivors of a plane crash in South America. As usual, her role was the hard-bitten tootsie with a fresh mouth. In Rodgers and Hart's light-hearted musical *Too Many Girls* (RKO, 1940), she portrayed a spoiled heiress who has four football heroes as bodyguards. The film, directed by Broadway great George Abbott, was also notable in that one of her co-stars was a dark, handsome Cuban named Desi Arnaz.

Two years later Miss Ball enjoyed perhaps the best role of her career in *The Big Street* (RKO, 1942), with Henry Fonda. In this Damon Runyon story she again played the tough dame, this time a nightclub singer who is left paralyzed by her gangster boyfriend. Fonda, as a busboy, befriends her and eventually takes her to Florida to recuperate. It is only when she is dying that she realizes who her true friends are. As Lucy herself would say about her film roles: "I would never try to play a 'lady' role. I was the cheap chorus girl, the clothes horse, the career girl, the prostitute, the other woman."

Soon after, she appeared in another light musical, *Du Barry Was a Lady* (MGM, 1943), with Red Skelton and Gene Kelly. Though her voice had to be dubbed for the songs by Cole Porter, Lucy proved to be a first-rate musical performer. It was during the filming of *Du Barry* that the hairdresser told her her hair should match her fiery soul, and gave her what would become her trademark red hair.

At MGM the burgeoning comedienne became friendly with one of the finest silent film clowns, Buster Keaton. Watching her work, the former star (by the time he was working at MGM Keaton was considered a washed-up has-been) felt she had great comedic pos-sibilities. He imparted probably the best advice she would ever receive: Never trust anybody else with your props or your writers. She took this advice seriously, and in later years it served her very well.

Lucy was also gaining experience in the medium of radio. On February 16, 1938, *Variety* reported on her appearance on a popular comedy show:

> Lucille Ball rattled off some corking comedy last Sunday night as guestee for Phil Baker. Her material was only so-so, but her tim-ing and knock-'em-dead emphasis on the tags italicized the humor. Her withering style of always-belittlin' was particularly well suited to go with Baker's fooling.

As far as romance went, the glamorous redhead played it cool in Hollywood. Her frequent escort was producer Al Hall, who was a good deal older than she, and for a short time it was reported that Lucille was engaged to actor Broderick Crawford. But the course of her life changed when she fell for a darkly handsome Cuban nearly six years her junior on the set of *Too Many Girls*.

Her future husband, comedy partner and producer was born Desiderio Alberto Arnaz y de Acha on March 2, 1917, in Santiago de Cuba, the town where his father, also named Desiderio, was mayor. His family were wealthy compared to the average Cuban household, and though Desiderio Sr. was well-liked by the local populace, they were forced to flee to Miami in the 1933 revolution. Having left all their wealth behind, the Arnaz family struggled to survive in Florida. Sixteen-year-old Desi attended school there and eventually drifted into show business as a singer and guitarist. Upon graduation from high school he went to join the Xavier Cugat Orchestra in New York, where he often stole food from the kitchen of the Waldorf-Astoria between sets to survive. This was the era when Latin music was beginning to be a craze in the United States, and Desi arrived on the scene just in time to capitalize on the popularity of the samba, the rumba, the cha-cha and the conga. Leaving Cugat, he formed his own band which began to get bookings in Miami and New York. It was while performing at a New York club called La Conga in 1939 that he was spotted by George Abbott, who cast him in *Too Many Girls* as Manolito, a Latin American football player.

When the movie rights to the show were bought by RKO, Desi

went West with the rest of the cast, except for the lead, played by Marcy Westcott, who was replaced by Lucille Ball. Their attraction was immediate and compelling, but both had fiery tempers and suffered from uncontrollable jealousy, triggered all the more by the long separations they were forced to endure. Lucille had her film career, and Desi went back to touring with an orchestra.

During these forced separations their telephone and telegram bills were enormous, as seen in these touching wires Desi sent in the fall of 1940:

DARLING JUST ARRIVING IN NEW YORK. I LOVED YOUR NOTE AND I ADORE YOU. LOADS AND LOADS OF KISSES. DESI

DARLING IT WAS WONDERFUL TALKING TO YOU TO-NIGHT BUT AWFUL WHEN I HUNG UP AND WAS LEFT ALONE. I LOVE YOU DEAR AND MISS YOU SO VERY MUCH. TAKE CARE OF YOURSELF AND BE GOOD. LOADS OF KISSES. DESI

BABY DARLING I RECEIVED YOUR WIRE AND LOVED IT. I'M WRITING YOU A BIG LONG LETTER TOMORROW. I MISS YOU SO TERRIBLY AND LOVE YOU SO VERY MUCH THE DAYS DON'T SEEM TO GO BY. HOPE TO GET OUT OF THE NEW SHOW AND NOT HAVE TO BE AWAY FROM YOU AGAIN. MILLIONS OF KISSES AND ALL MY LOVE. DESI

SWEETHEART IT IS WONDERFUL TO KNOW EXACTLY WHAT ONE WANTS. THESE FEW WEEKS AWAY FROM YOU HAVE BEEN VERY SAD AND PAINFUL BUT THEY HAVE SHOWED ME THAT I WANT YOU AND YOU ALWAYS. SO MAYBE IT WAS WORTH IT. I LOVE YOU VERY MUCH AND I WANT TO SEE YOU VERY SOON. DESI.

On November 30, 1940, Lucy and Desi were married by Justice of the Peace Joseph P. O'Brien at the Byram River Beagle Club in Greenwich, Connecticut. The witnesses were Desi's business manager and his agent. Right after the ceremony they had to rush back to New York for Desi to do the second show at the Roxy Theater (he had already missed the first).

Shortly thereafter the newlyweds headed back to California, where they soon bought a small ranch, Desilu, in the San Fernando Valley.

Although Desi made a few second-rate pictures in Hollywood, he did not become the next Valentino. He went back on the road with his Latin orchestra until joining the U.S. Army in 1943. Lucy, meanwhile, continued to star in a number of MGM comedies including *Best Foot Forward* and *Thousands Cheer* (both 1943), *Without Love* (with Tracy and Hepburn, 1945), and *The Ziegfeld Follies of 1946.*

Due to their long separations during this period, Lucy filed for divorce in 1944 but did not complete the proceedings and the two were reconciled. In 1949 they were remarried at the Valley Church in Canoga Park, California, in deference to Desi's religion. Beginning in July 1948 Lucy starred in a radio situation comedy for CBS with Richard Denning entitled "My Favorite Husband." In it, she played Liz Cugat (later Americanized to Cooper), an ex-debutante housewife married to a former playboy who is now "fifth vice-president of the bank." The show's writers were Bob Carroll, Jr., and Madelyn Pugh, and soon after Jess Oppenheimer joined them as head writer, producer and director. This was the start of a long and rewarding partnership the three writers were to enjoy with their female lead. Although the "Lucy" character was not yet developed in all her zaniness, Liz Cooper did manage to get into some tight jams and exasperate her husband; indeed, many of the scripts for "My Favorite Husband" were reworked to become episodes of "I Love Lucy." The show was popular enough to place near the top of the radio ratings for the 1949–50 season.

By 1950, however, thanks to Milton Berle's phenomenal success on television, that new medium was garnering excitement. CBS wanted to move "My Favorite Husband" into television with the same cast and writers. Lucy, however, knowing that her marriage was in danger of collapsing due to forced absences from her husband, insisted that Desi be her co-star. The CBS brass did not think American audiences would find the Arnazes believable as husband and wife, even though in real life they *were* husband and wife. In order to prove their abilities as a comic team, Desi and Lucy took a vaudeville-style act on the road, which met with tremendous success.

And so it was decided. Desi would play the Latin bandleader Ricky Ricardo and Lucy his wife, who was always trying to worm her way into show business. Another couple was needed as a comic foil and Lucy wanted Gale Gordon and Bea Benederat, who had had supporting roles on "My Favorite Husband," but they were not available. Instead William Frawley, a gruff character actor from Burlington,

Iowa, was cast as neighbor and landlord Fred Mertz. Frawley had appeared on Broadway, in vaudeville and in over 100 film roles but by 1951 was out of work and eager to play the role of the impecunious older man.

Vivian Vance, engaged to play the role of his wife, Ethel, was 19 years Frawley's junior, a casting conundrum that irritated her (to have audiences think she could be married to such an old man) and created tension and rivalry between her and her television husband. Vance was a distinguished stage actress from Albuquerque, New Mexico, who had gotten her big break on Broadway in the 1937 E.Y. Harburg/Howard Lindsay musical "Hooray for What!" starring Ed Wynn. In 1941 she appeared in Danny Kaye's "Let's Face It," and after entertaining troops abroad she returned to star in the John van Druten play "Voice of the Turtle." In 1945, while appearing in a road company production of the play in Chicago, Vance suffered a complete nervous breakdown, and she retreated to New Mexico for three years.

Shortly after coming out of "retirement" she was asked to reprise her role in "Turtle" at a production being directed by Mel Ferrer at the La Jolla Playhouse. It was there that Desi first saw her perform (Lucy was not present, as she had given birth to their first child, Lucie Desiree, 11 days earlier) and knew that he had found his Ethel Mertz.

Studio space in which to shoot the show was not as easy to find as the actors. Having settled down in their ranch in Chatsworth, and after finally having a baby after many years of trying (Lucy was 40 years old when Lucie was born), the Arnazes were not eager to move to New York and do the show live, as the network wished. At that time the coaxial cable linking the East and West coasts was not in use, so naturally the network wanted the East Coast, with a greater concentration of population, to get the show live and send a kinescope out to the rest of the country. Desi insisted that the show be done on film, even trading away some of his and Lucy's salary to get Bill Paley, the head of CBS, to agree. Desi also managed to procure all rights to the programs after they were aired. The network did not foresee the phenomenal amount of revenue "I Love Lucy" would generate in the decades to come through re-runs, especially as it was thought that the show would last no more than a few weeks.

A studio suitable for filming a television show had to be found, not an easy feat in Los Angeles in 1951. The task was made even more

difficult because Lucy and Desi wanted to shoot in front of a live audience in order to give the show more immediacy and spontaneity.
Due to zoning laws and fire regulations it was generally prohibited
to allow an audience into the regular film studios. However, after
much wrangling with the local authorities, Desi rented space at
General Service Studios and outfitted them with bleachers for the
audience.

Karl Freund was hired as Director of Photography. The
German-born cinematographer had won an Academy Award for the
1937 film *The Good Earth* and had also shot Lucille in *Du Barry Was
a Lady.* He agreed to take the job in television for the sheer challenge
(it could not have been the money, for they could afford to pay him
only scale at first) of lighting a set where three or four cameras were
being used simultaneously in front of a live audience, the show being
done as a stage play with no retakes except in emergencies. (Known
as the "Desilu" method, this set-up became increasingly popular with
the networks and eventually was used for dozens of television shows,
including "Make Room for Daddy" and "The Andy Griffith Show.")

At last the technical complications were ironed out, and the
filming of the first episode of "I Love Lucy" began. The Ricardo
household was set in apartment 3-B at 623 East 68th Street in New
York City. Ricky Ricardo, a singer and orchestra leader at the
Tropicana Club (later, when Ricky became more successful, it was
changed to the Ricky Ricardo Babalu Club), and his wife, the former
Lucille McGillicuddy, lived upstairs from their friends and landlord,
former vaudeville performers Fred and Ethel Mertz. On Monday,
October 15, 1951, "I Love Lucy" made its debut at 9:00 P.M. on the
CBS network. The first program aired, "The Girls Want to Go to a
Nightclub," was not the first one filmed. Broadcasting of the initial
episode, "Lucy Thinks Ricky Is Trying to Murder Her," had to be
delayed due to technical difficulties.

Several of the shows of the first few seasons were based upon
previous scripts done for "My Favorite Husband." For instance, in
"The Seance," which aired November 26, 1951, Lucy, having taken
up numerology and horoscopes, tries, with the help of a ouija board
and Ethel pretending to be a seance-holding medium, to convince a
producer to hire Ricky. On the "My Favorite Husband" episode of
December 12, 1948, the Cugats have their rent raised by a landlord
who is so hen-pecked that he obeys the orders of his dead wife, communicated by a ouija board. In this case it is their friend Corey who

Lucy attempts to play "Glowworm" on her saxophone so she can be part of Ricky's act.

is dressed up as a fortune-teller to tell the landlord that his late wife has changed her mind and decided not to raise the rent after all.

Many of the shows centered on Lucy's desire to get into show business, especially at Ricky's nightclub. In "Lucy Fakes an Illness," which aired January 28, 1952, Lucy decides to stage a complete nervous breakdown because once again Ricky will not hire her for his new act. Consulting a medical encyclopedia, she settles on three symptoms: She pretends to be Tallulah Bankhead, she develops amnesia and she reverts to her childhood by riding around the apartment on a tricycle. Alerted by Fred that it is all an act, Ricky brings home an actor friend (played by Hal March) to impersonate a doctor, who informs the patient that she is indeed very ill, having contracted "the gobloots," a disease that has entered the country "on the hind legs of the boo-shoo bird." Lucy, now convinced that she is really dying, pulls the face that the show's writers referred to as "the spider" (because she had first done it years earlier while playing the role of a spider in a commercial based on Little Miss Muffet), pulling her lips back and away from her teeth. She also added a back-of-the-throat growl which was thereafter known to the writers as the "Gobloots" sound.

Other shorthand notations were used by the writers to connote certain looks and gestures for Lucy to do. The "light bulb" referred to that magic moment when the conniving Lucy would come up with yet another impossible scheme, and it was almost possible for the audience to see the machinations going on in her head, like a clock encased in clear plastic.

"The Credentials" look indicated an indignant, how-dare-you! gape which originated in "The Saxophone" (the second episode of the second season), in which Lucy again tries to get into Ricky's act, this time by dressing up as a be-bop jazz musician and claiming she can play the saxophone. "What are your credentials?" demands Ricky. Mortified, she gives "the look."

The writers also had code names for Lucy crying, known as "Lucy Puddles Up," and for when her schemes were discovered and revealed by Ricky, called "Foiled Again."

Of the 35 episodes of the first season (not including the pilot), probably the most classic is number 30, "Lucy Does a TV Commercial," which aired May 5, 1952. In this hilarious sequence, Lucy has maneuvered her way into doing a television commercial for a health tonic known as "Vitameatavegamin":

> Hello friends. I'm your Vitameatavegamin girl. Are you tired, rundown, listless? Do you poop out at parties? Are you unpopular? The answer to all your problems is in this little bottle: Vitameatavegamin. Vitameatavegamin contains vitamins, meat, vegetables, and minerals. Yes, with Vitameatavegamin, you can spoon your way to health. All you do is take a tablespoon after every meal. It's so tasty, too. Just like candy. So why don't you join the thousands of happy, peppy people and get a great big bottle of Vitameatavegamin tomorrow. That's Vita . . . Meata . . . Vegamin.

During the course of the commercial Lucy has to partake of the nutritional benefits of the elixir (in actuality apple pectin was used), not knowing that it contained 23 percent alcohol. The more she rehearses, the more convoluted her delivery becomes, and the name Vitameatavegamin becomes impossible for her to pronounce. Her drunken speech was a tour de force performance.

The first episode of the 1952 season, which aired on September 15, was "Job Switching," and it too became a classic "Lucy" show. In order to prove that the other sex has an easier life, Lucy and Ethel change household roles with Ricky and Fred. The women will go out and seek employment and bring home the paycheck, while the men stay at home to cook and clean. Untrained in any job skills, the girls lie about their abilities to an interviewer at an employment agency and get jobs in a candy factory. Lucy is assigned the job of chocolate dipper, forming the viscous concoction into little balls. She has no idea of how to go about it, but watches the technique of the dipper next to her (played by real-life candy maker Amanda Milligan). Attempting to swat a fly with her chocolate-covered hands, she gets into a sticky fight with her co-worker.

Next, Lucy and Ethel are put on the candy-wrapping assembly line. At first, the slow pace of the conveyor belt makes their task seem easy. But as the belt speeds up they are driven to hiding the candy in their blouses, hats and mouths.

The men, meanwhile, have not fared much better. Ricky has flooded the kitchen with rice while attempting to make his favorite dish, *arroz con pollo* (in real life, Desi's favorite too) and Fred bakes a seven-layer cake that looks like a squashed pork-pie hat. In the end, all agree that they should return to their former roles, and the husbands apologize by presenting their wives with—five-pound boxes of chocolate.

The second year of "I Love Lucy" was also momentous in that it produced offspring. In May 1952 Lucille Ball Arnaz found out that she was pregnant with her second child. After some initial trepidation, the writers and producers received permission from CBS, sponsor Philip Morris and the Biow ad agency for Lucy Ricardo to give birth as well. As it turned out, Lucy's pregnancy was the greatest thing ever to happen to the show, adding variety and a new perspective. In order to give real-life Lucy enough time to rest before the birth of her baby, everyone's vacation was cut short and the production schedule pushed up.

On December 12, 1952, "Lucy Is Enceinte" (French for pregnant, which the CBS censor would not allow) aired. It had been filmed nearly two months earlier, when Lucy was not yet obviously with child. In the story, Lucy has a hard time finding the right opportunity to break the news to Ricky. She finally slips him a note during his nightclub act, and when he realizes its impact they dissolve into tears.

Because Lucille Ball knew in advance that she would be having her child by cesarean section, it was not impossible to time the birth of the television baby to occur simultaneously. It had been decided that no matter what sex the real-life baby was, its television counterpart would be a boy, in order not to confuse or wound the feelings of little Lucie Desiree. As it turned out, they were both boys: Desiderio Arnaz y Ball IV and Little Ricky Ricardo made their entrance into the world on January 19, 1953. Two million more people watched "I Love Lucy" on that fateful night than tuned in to see the hero of World War II be inaugurated as President the following evening. The show captured an enormous 71.8 percent of the viewing public.

The excitement generated by the birth of Little Ricky and the continued excellence of the scripts turned out by Jess Oppenheimer, Madelyn Pugh and Bob Carroll, Jr., ensured "I Love Lucy" first place in the ratings for the 1952/53 season (in 1951/52 it had placed third after "Arthur Godfrey's Talent Scouts" and the "Texaco Star Theater" with Milton Berle). Phenomenally, it stayed in the number one spot until 1957, with the exception of the 1955/56 season when it was edged into the number two space by "The $64,000 Question." In 1952 and 1953 "I Love Lucy" was given an Emmy for Best Situation Comedy and Lucy won for Best Comedienne in 1952.

In 1953 Lucy got into a jam that was scarier and more lifelike than those created by her writers. She was called before the House Un-American Activities Committee to answer charges that she was a Communist sympathizer. During those days of the Cold War most public figures were under scrutiny for their political views, but in Lucy's case there was evidence that she had indeed been allied with certain socialist causes. It seems that her crusty old grandfather, Fred C. Hunt, had persuaded Lucille and her brother to register for the 1936 election with the intention of voting for the Communist Party. Whether she actually did vote according to her grandfather's wishes may never be known, but for her whole life she had heard her mother's father defend the rights of the working man and the politics of Eugene V. Debs. Apparently Grandpa also had a few Communist Party meetings at the house he shared with Lucille at 1344 North Ogden Drive without her knowledge or consent. When all this evidence was presented to the House committee, it took a lot of fast talking and a certain amount of acting by Lucy to convince them that she was a dizzy, non-political actress who did whatever her grandfather asked her to. In any case, the comedienne's youthful tendencies towards socialism seemed to have dissipated as she earned high salaries and eventually became head of the multimillion dollar corporation of Desilu.

After some initial nervousness that the Red-paranoid American public would desert their favorite television star, as had happened with many other stellar personalities, it became obvious that her fans would continue to be devoted and adoring. It seems that laughter can overcome even misguided patriotism.

The third and fourth seasons of "I Love Lucy" continued with the same formula that had proved so successful: Lucy getting into trouble with the help of Ethel and (sometimes) Fred and trying to keep Ricky from finding out. In the middle of the fourth season, however, in order to introduce new dimensions and possibilities, the writers had Ricky get a movie contract in Hollywood, and the Ricardos and Mertzes packed up the car and drove out to California. Life in Hollywood gave Lucy the chance to chase after celebrities like Bill Holden in "L.A. at Last!" which aired on February 7, 1955. It included a hilarious sequence in which Lucy, trying to disguise herself after having splattered a pie on Holden at the Brown Derby restaurant, caught her putty nose on fire while lighting a cigarette.

Other celebrities who made appearances on the show were Cornel Wilde, Rock Hudson, Van Johnson, Harpo Marx (in which he and Lucy recreated the brilliant "mirror routine" from *Duck Soup*), Richard Widmark (Lucy falls into his walled garden while seeking a souvenir grapefruit from his tree; she ends up getting stuck in his house and having to hide under a bearskin rug when Widmark and his pal Ricky Ricardo come in).

At the opening of the 1955/56 fifth season the Ricardos have not yet returned to New York, giving Lucy the chance to meet John Wayne (after having stolen the cement block with his footprints from in front of Grauman's Chinese Theatre) before the two couples return to New York via train. It also marked the addition of two

As usual, Lucy's high jinks get her into hot water.

writers to the show's staff, the "two Bobs," Schiller and Weiskopf, to add new energy to the Lucy-weary Oppenheimer, Pugh and Carroll.

It seems that travel settings were good for the show's ratings, for no sooner had the Ricardos and Mertzes returned from the West Coast than they were off to Europe, this time for a tour with Ricky's band. Their tour took them to London, Scotland, Paris (where the celebrity-mad redhead got to meet Charles Boyer), Switzerland, Italy and Monte Carlo. Probably the most memorable episode in Europe occurred when the foursome were in Rome. In "Lucy's

Italian Movie" she is offered a role in *Bitter Grapes,* the new film by Italian film director Vittorio Fellipi. In order to research what she thinks will be her role, she goes to the nearby town of Turo to make wine by stomping grapes with her feet. Unfortunately she and her co-worker in the vat, played by real-life grape-stomper Teresa Tirelli, end up brawling in the sticky mess. According to Bart Andrews in his Lucille Ball anthology, *The "I Love Lucy" Book,* it was not all make-believe:

> Teresa Tirelli, the Italian grape-stomper, was not an 'actress and spoke little English. Therefore, it was not always easy to explain direction. Lucy, as always, wanted the fight scene to be as realistic as possible, but, on the night of the filming, March 8, 1956, she had no idea that Miss Tirelli would suddenly become a "method" ac-tress, determined to make the fight scene a brawling war. Lucille Ball explains: "I didn't want the scene to be a little tug-of-war. I wanted it to look as real as possible. But since we hadn't worked with the grapes in the vat during rehearsals, I had no idea what I was in store for. Once the fight started, the lady was bent on drowning me. At one point, she literally held my head under water, and I had to fight to get my breath back. A lot of that was edited out of the final print. Looking back, of course, I'm glad it happened that way because the scene was so good."[1]

The sixth season of "I Love Lucy" introduced Keith Thibodeaux as Little Ricky. The young actor had won some talent contests for his prodigious abilities on the drums. Since there was a certain physical resemblance between him and Desi, and since it seemed only natural that the bongo/conga drum-playing Arnaz would sire a whiz on per-cussion, little Keith was given the role as television's favorite son.

The 1956/57 season again provided Lucy with a chance to gawk at celebrities when she caused Bob Hope to get beaned by a baseball and when she became Orson Welles' assistant in his magic act. The Ricardos and the Mertzes also took to the road again when they went to Florida and to Cuba so that Ricky could introduce his wife and son to his relatives (and where Lucy inadvertently called patriarch Uncle Alberto a fat pig in Spanish and ruined his fine cigars).

In the second half of the season, in order to keep the spirit of the show fresh, the writers finally had the Ricardos move out of their small Manhattan apartment to a house in the countryside of West-port, Connecticut. The Mertzes, at first distraught at being left behind, are provided with their own guest cottage and are on hand as often as before. Living in the country gave Lucy a whole new set of challenges, from raising chickens to impressing the new neighbors. The longest laugh ever recorded on "I Love Lucy," 65 seconds, came during "Lucy Does the Tango," which aired on March 11, 1957. Lucy has hidden dozens of store-bought eggs in her shirt, so that Ricky will not know that the chickens in which they have invested so much time and money are not laying. When he insists upon rehearsing the tango sequence that they will be doing for the PTA show, the eggs are all broken against her body. Lucy milked the gag for all it was worth, and as she had insisted upon using hard-boiled eggs during rehearsal, her "take" was spontaneous—and hilarious.

Seen from today's feminist perspective, the character of Lucy Ricardo had a long way to go on the road towards liberation. She was the epitome of the frustrated housewife, and as though to add insult to injury was portrayed as being inept at any jobs, on or offstage, that she did manage to get. The Lucy/Ricky household was not a 50/50 proposition: To get her way Lucy had to resort to feminine wiles, whining, trickery and elaborate schemes. This, of course, was the basis for the show's comedy, which is precisely why it is unfair to judge "I Love Lucy" from today's more egalitarian outlook. It is interesting to compare Lucy's predicament with some of the female roles in today's successful situation comedies. The Phylicia Rashad role in "The Cosby Show" is a lawyer and mother of five who shares all decision-making with her doctor-husband. On "Family Ties," Meredith Baxter Birney similarly plays a sort of "supermom" as an architect and mother of four who also shares the responsibilities of the household with her husband. On television, at least, women do seem to have come a long way.

For the real-life Lucy and Desi, their success with the television show was taking a toll on their private lives. Desi worked hard as the star and executive producer of the number one–rated show, and as president of Desilu. Lucy had two children and a career. During the weeks when "I Love Lucy" was on hiatus, the pair made personal appearances and movies. In the summer of 1953 they shot *The Long, Long Trailer* for MGM, and in 1955 they teamed up again for *Forever Darling*, this time produced by their own Zanra (Arnaz spelled backwards) Productions, with Lucy's old boyfriend Al Hall directing.

To slow down from such a hectic schedule, the "I Love Lucy" format was changed for the 1957–58 season. The 30-minute comedy was transformed into the 60-minute "Lucy-Desi Comedy Hour," a

Lucy and Desi, for a while the most famous couple in America, on- and offscreen.

series of specials that appeared about once a month. The first episode, "Lucy Takes a Cruise to Havana," which explains, via flashback, how the Ricardos met, was so good that Desi wrangled 15 more minutes in which to present it, possibly making it the sole 75-minute show in American television history.

In 1957 Desi negotiated the purchase of the former RKO studios where he and Lucy had once been employees. He raised part of the money needed for the acquisition by selling off the rerun rights to "I Love Lucy" to CBS for $5 million. This gave Desilu a total of 33 sound stages and more than 14 acres in downtown Hollywood as well as RKO's extensive library of stock footage. It also increased Desi's workload proportionally.

By the time the last "Lucy-Desi Comedy Hour" was shown on April 1, 1960 ("Lucy Meets the Mustache," co-starring Ernie Kovacs and Edie Adams), the Ball-Arnaz marriage was faltering beyond repair. Desi's drinking, womanizing and long days at the studio taking care of business did not leave much time for his redhaired wife. Lucy explained in an interview a few years later: "It wasn't the industry and our working that broke us up, but the pressure had a lot to do with it. He was a very sick man. I was living with hope for many years. When the children got to an age when they were noticing the unhappiness, it was time to move away. That helped me make up my mind . . . that, and the end of our performing commitments together."[2]

Years later Desi also gave an interviewer his view of their disintegrating marriage: "The more we fought, the less sex we had, the more seeking others, the more jealousy, the more separations, the more drinking, which led right back to more fights, less sex and more seeking others. Add to this the herculean effort we had to make to maintain the imaginary bliss of Lucy and Ricky, and our lives became a nightmare. . . . As fate would have it, the very last scene [of theirs together] called for a long clinch and a kiss-and-make-up ending. As we got to it, we looked at each other, embraced and kissed." They knew it would be the last time, on- or off-camera.

After filming their last show together, Lucy threw herself into a whirlwind of activity, possibly in an attempt to be too busy to dwell on her failed marriage. During the summer she appeared in the movie *The Facts of Life* with Bob Hope. In the fall of 1960 she and her two children moved to New York, where she began rehearsals for the musical "Wildcat." The show, produced by Desilu, was written by N. Richard Nash, with music and lyrics by Cy Coleman and Carolyn Leigh, and introduced the hit song "Hey Look Me Over." Directed and choreographed by Michael Kidd, Lucy was featured as Wildcat Jackson, a tomboyish oil prospector who arrives in the West with her crippled sister. The role was a far cry from Lucy Ricardo, and audiences flocked to Broadway's Alvin Theater to see their favorite television comedienne.

After six months with "Wildcat," Lucy's physical condition required her to leave the show (at one point she fainted on stage due to total exhaustion). Her mental condition also debilitated when her final divorce from Desi came through in May 1961.

But Lucy was not destined to remain a divorcée for long. During the run of "Wildcat" she was introduced to stand-up comic Gary Morton. The romance began immediately, and when she left New York to return to California, he soon followed. Eighteen months later, on October 19, 1961, they were married by the Reverend Norman Vincent Peale at Marble Collegiate Church on Fifth Avenue in New York. Gary continued to do his act in nightclubs and even appeared on the "Ed Sullivan Show." Eventually, however, he devoted himself exclusively to Lucy's career, with the exception of portraying a Milton Berle–type comic in Bob Fosse's 1974 film, *Lenny*.

In the fall of 1962 Lucy teamed up once more with Vivian Vance in a situation comedy, this time without husbands. "The Lucy Show" featured the comedienne as Lucy Carmichael, a widow with a daughter (Candy Moore) and a son (Jimmy Garrett) who share a house with a divorcée (Vance) and her son (Ralph Hart). Because it was necessary for the Lucy character to have a male authority figure around to defy and exasperate, Gale Gordon was called upon to play Theodore J. Mooney, president of the local bank. For the show's first three seasons, from 1962 to 1965, the story was set in Danfield, Connecticut, and centered on the male-less household's problems, particularly concerning money. For the second version of the show, which ran from 1965 to 1968, the action was moved to San Francisco, where Mrs. Carmichael was now the harebrained secretary to Mr. Mooney. Vivian Vance, tired of the rigors of weekly television, did not return for the 1965 season.

The show's producer was Desi Arnaz, who, as president of Desilu, made sure that many of the old staff of "I Love Lucy" were on hand once again to provide the laughs. In November 1962, however, Desi stepped down as head of Desilu. Lucy elected to retain control of the company, rather than sell out. She paid her ex-husband $2.5 million for 300,500 shares of the company, bringing her holdings to 600,650 shares. From then on she was forced to be a businesswoman as well as a clown, and she soon had the ailing Desilu's finances under control.

"The Lucy Show" appeared on CBS on Monday nights from 8:30 to 9:00 and was immediately successful. Even without her Cuban husband, all America wanted to see what shenanigans the so-called "typical housewife" could get into. "The Lucy Show" was among the top ten–rated shows for its entire run and was nominated for several Emmy awards. As in "I Love Lucy," there were celebrity guest stars, including Jack Benny, Bob Hope, Danny Kaye, Arthur Godfrey, Danny Thomas, Dean Martin and George Burns.

In 1967 Miss Ball sold Desilu to Gulf and Western for $17 million. For the 1968 season "The Lucy Show" became "Here's Lucy" with a new format, cast, and writers. Once again co-starring Gale Gordon, this time as president of the Unique Employment Agency and brother-in-law to widow Lucy Carter. Lucy's two children were played by their real-life counterparts, Lucie Arnaz and Desi Arnaz, Jr. Set in Los Angeles, this Lucy gets into hot water as a part-time employee for her brother-in-law. Although the first season's scripts (supervised by head writers Milt Josefsberg and Bob O'Brien) were not much very inspired, subsequent seasons started to regain that old Lucy panache.

For the first episode of the 1970–71 season, in a script penned by former "Lucy" writers Bob Carroll and Madelyn Pugh Martin, Lucy Carter mistakes Richard Burton for a plumber and gets Elizabeth Taylor's 69-carat ring stuck on her finger. In a hilarious sequence that was a throwback to the best slapstick days of "I Love Lucy," Taylor addresses a press conference for an unveiling of the ring while standing in front of a curtain, while Lucy's diamond-laden arm masquerades as her own from behind the drape.

Subsequent seasons of "Here's Lucy" featured fewer stories involving Lucy's children, and in 1971 Desi Jr. left the show. Celebrities continued to be an important part of the action, however. In one lovely episode, "Lucy and Jack Benny's Biography," the legendary comic dictates his life story to Lucy, his temporary secretary, and in a series of flashbacks she plays all of the women in his life. Sammy Davis, Jr., Danny Kaye, Ginger Rogers (Lucy's friend and advisor from their RKO days), and even Helen Hayes, all made guest appearances. Vivian Vance also occasionally came back for an onscreen reunion with her old partner-in-crime.

For the 1972–73 season the writers had to incorporate a new twist into their storyline: While skiing in Snowmass, Colorado, Lucille Ball had broken her leg, and the doctors had warned that the cast would have to remain on for quite some time. All 24 episodes featured Lucy in bed, in a cast, or in a wheelchair. Desi Jr. even returned to the show to shift some of the focus away from his incapacitated mother.

By the time of the 1973–74 season, the evidence was clear: After 25 years the show's writers were simply running out of inventive stories for their hapless heroine. She had been in every jam, every sticky situation, insulted nearly every celebrity in almost every fashion. Ahead was only repetition—it was time to stop. Lucy returned briefly to films, where she had begun, to play the irrepressible auntie in *Mame,* co-starring Robert Preston and Bea Arthur, but the reviews were lukewarm at best. American had grown too used to seeing her as the Lucy character to believe her as the eccentric sophisticate.

Nevertheless, Miss Ball has never really retired; it is clear that she enjoys working too much. She has appeared on a number of specials over the years and even tackled dramatic acting again in the 1985 television movie *Stone Pillow* about the trials of a homeless woman. The septuagenarian actress was inspired by the success of "The Golden Girls" to return in another version of the Lucy Ricardo/Carmichael/Carter character in the fall 1986 television season with a series entitled "Life with Lucy," reuniting her once again with her old nemesis, Gale Gordon.

As the grand dowager of television comedy, Lucille Ball is a survivor. A self-confessed mediocre ad-libber, she was always clever enough to surround herself with great writers, producers and directors, and to count on their guidance. She was the great anomaly: the beautiful clown. Her Lucy character will endure, possibly forever, in reruns around the nation and the world, showing the genius of a comedic actress in a role created for her tremendous talents. We have laughed with Lucy, occasionally cried with her, always been touched by the universality of her plight, and, most of all, loved her.

Milton Berle

No other comedian in the history of modern entertainment has relied as much on the adulation of his public, the response of laughter, and the rapt attention of his audience as Milton Berle. Spanning the seven decades of his life on stage and screen, the personal communication between artist and admirer has been his life's blood—the anima of his existence. Not to laugh at a Berle joke is to provoke a personal affront. This interplay between audience and performer gives Berle's act an exuberance and vitality all its own. Although it has been imitated by scores of comedians, no one can approach Berle's mastery of timing, his mental encyclopedia of gags, and his innate sense of intimacy with his audience.

One cannot think about the days of early television and not reflect on the Milton Berle phenomenon. Directly responsible for thrusting that mysterious black box into the homes of millions of Americans, he was, literally, as Walter Winchell dubbed him, "Mr. Television." In 1948, Berle and television were synonymous; his popularity came like an explosion, the force of which today's audience, jaded with their choices of sit-coms, car chases and nighttime soap operas, cannot fathom.

Since his early days in vaudeville, Berle's image has been that of the brash, aggressive smart aleck, the big city boy who could put down a heckler with his incisor-sharp tongue and a lightning-fast comeback. He tried varying that formula over the years — on occasion being the nice guy, or the victim, but ultimately he found that he could not desert the image he had created, that a comedian must remain true to the persona with which the audience identifies — and he returned to being America's favorite ad-libber and self-proclaimed egotist.

Unlike Sid Caesar or Jackie Gleason, who endeared themselves to their public by appearing to be regular guys with whom the average man in the street could identify, Berle was always larger than life, always a show-business personality. He could be insulting without being offensive, but he was not the kind of fellow one could imagine being on the bowling team, or hanging out at the local tavern. Detached from the ways and lifestyles of the average man, Berle lived and breathed (and does to this day) only to amuse, a modus vivendi instilled in him from early childhood.

Milton Berlinger was born July 12, 1908, in the Harlem section of New York City, to Moses and Sarah Glantz Berlinger. Preceded by three brothers, Philip, Frank and Jacob, and followed by the only girl, Rosalind, little Milton soon showed theatrical talent and thus became the apple of his mother's eye. Sarah, known as Sadie, was the perfect stage mother, a woman who would have loved to be on the stage herself (in the days when actresses were only slightly more respectable than prostitutes). She realized her frustrated ambitions through her darling Milton. The boy's talent was not only fortuitous, but providential as well, for Milton's father had never been adept at supporting his family. From the time Milton won a Charlie Chaplin look-alike contest (a popular entertainment of the era) at the age of five, Sarah knew that there were real possibilities to be explored to make money in show business. She began to schlep her youngest son, the child prodigy, to all casting calls and auditions for silent films in production in the New York area, generally at Fort Lee in the New Jersey Palisades. Her tenaciousness paid off, and Milton appeared in silents with many of the great stars of the day: Pearl White, Mabel Normand, John Bunny, Flora Finch, and even with the greatest silent film star of all time, Charlie Chaplin, in *Tillie's Punctured Romance* (1914).

From silent movies the next logical step was vaudeville. Joining a number of "kid acts" managed by impresario E.W. Wolf, Milton sang and danced and was known for his rather precocious impression of Eddie Cantor. When the group went on tour to Philadelphia and nearby towns, Sarah went with her son and brought along baby Rosalind, leaving the three older boys in the care of their father. The young entertainer's wages provided much-needed income for the Berlinger family back in New York.

On April 5, 1920, famed Broadway producers the Shubert brothers mounted a revival of the 1900 musical "Florodora," and Milton made his Broadway debut as a member of "Baby Sextette" (meant to portray the performers of yet another "Florodora" revival that would take place in 1940!) in the six-boy, six-girl ensemble.

According to Berle's autobiography,[1] his mother sent him out on stage on opening night with firm instructions to start off the dance routine on the wrong foot, which would of course keep him out of step with the rest of the Sextette for the entire number. This bold move brought down the house, the audience laughing hysterically at the kid who could not, it seemed, keep in step. The producers, at first irate, decided to keep the wrong step gag in the show. Milton Berle's career as a ham and an ad-libber was on its way.

"Florodora" ran for another nine months, on Broadway and on tour. After these productions closed, Milton teamed up with a young actress, Elizabeth Kennedy, in a comic sketch called "Broadway Bound," the appeal of which lay in the kick audiences got from seeing kids behave like grown-ups. For this act the marquee changed from Berlinger to Berle, and the rest of the family also adopted the shorter appellation. Sarah even went so far as to change her first name to the more glamorous "Sandra."

"Kennedy and Berle" were given a warm reception at New York's Palace Theater, and "Broadway Bound" toured on vaudeville circuits around the country. Between shows Milton did the homework assigned to him by the Professional Children's School, where he was an average student.

A spurt of growth during his teen years precluded Milton's carrying on as a juvenile performer and dictated that he leave the cute, "kid show" shenanigans of "Kennedy and Berle," so he went solo. After testing his 12-minute act (composed of songs, impressions, corny jokes, card tricks and some soft shoe routines) in the provinces, the 16-year-old showman (showboy?) opened at the Loew's State Theater on December 29, 1924. From then on, nothing could keep this enthusiastic clown away from an audience. No matter how small the size of the crowd, Berle would entertain. In theaters, clubs and benefits Berle was and would remain as comfortable in front of an audience as most people are in their kitchens. It was during these early years that the brash young comic was honing his act and gathering a valuable repertoire that would sustain him throughout his career.

The jokes came from a myriad of sources — begged, borrowed or stolen — but contrary to popular opinion, most were original. It was not until 1932 that Berle became known as "The Thief of Bad Gags," when he and comic Richy Craig, Jr., waged a mock battle over material, and not incidentally garnered some publicity. For the rest of his career, Berle embellished and enlarged his notoriety as a joke stealer with such lines as "I went to see [name any comedian] the other night, and I laughed so hard I dropped my pencil!" or "I wish I'd said that—and I will!" Berle also came under fire from others, including Joe E. Lewis: "He's lifted more material than a pushcart boy in the garment center," and Red Buttons: "Many good things have come out of Milton's mouth—my act, Jessel's, and others'."

Jokes are in the public domain, but to get laughs a comic has to have an effective delivery, proper timing, and the right sort of persona. In the introduction to his 1939 booklet on comedy, "Laughingly Yours,"[2] Berle explained his view on the "ownership" of jokes:

WARNING

To those who may have heard some of these stories before.

Jokes are like folk lore, difficult to define, a part that is neither written nor exact, and an origin buried in a multiplicity of sources.

In the following volume the humorous phrases are only my interpretation of these age-old classics of wit, perhaps refurbished with a new adjective or adverb but in essence the same salient form of comedy heard by our grandparents and their grandparents as long back as written history provided for witticism.

So, remember, nothing that's funny is ever new. Or vice versa!

In 1929 Berle made his debut on an experimental television system, the United States Television Corporation, owned by Frank Sanabria. Berle and Trixie Friganza, his co-star at the Palace Theater in Chicago, were asked to do some short bits in a crude forerunner of a television studio. The lighting and camera work were primitive, as was the make-up. Milton's lips were coated with black lipstick. "I looked like Theda Bara or Pola Negri or Nita Naldi," he said. There was no studio audience, so of course Berle's jokes got no response, and the number of people watching on television sets was probably fewer than two dozen. This early experience with an empty studio may have accounted for Berle's insistence on a live audience when he went on the air in 1948. His second appearance on experimental television took place, again in Chicago, in 1933, when he was asked to substitute for Sally Rand (and her strategically placed fans) at the World's Fair because she was considered too risqué for the fair's family audience.

Besides making his television debut in 1929, Berle also made his film debut, appearing in a short called *Popping the Cork*. In it the 21-year-old entertainer sang "Here's Looking at You" to a bevy of beautiful girls, and the film showed a thin, darkly handsome young man with the breezy confidence of a show business veteran many years his senior. His one facial flaw, his nose, seemed to be magnified on film, however. Overly long, it detracted from his otherwise magnetic good looks, and Berle made sure to have it corrected by a plastic surgeon before embarking on a Hollywood career. His new nose caused such a stir that even Groucho Marx was heard to remark, "Who did it? Gutzon Borglum?"

In 1930 Berle made his debut in yet another medium, one that would carry his inexhaustible personality into the homes of millions of Americans. He appeared on the "Rudy Vallee–Fleischmann Radio Hour," and the audience loved him. Although hamming it up on radio prevented him from being seen by the home listeners, Berle's infectious enthusiasm and rapid-fire delivery kept the pace moving and the laughs coming. Over the years Berle would host a number of radio programs, and although the nonvisual nature of the medium kept him from becoming a superstar of the airwaves, he was popular and enjoyed by many.

Milton's major source of income at this time continued to be vaudeville and, in time, nightclubs. He toured the country constantly, almost always accompanied by Mama, playing the best theaters from New York to Los Angeles. He was more than just a comic or a master of ceremonies. Berle became known for barging into the acts of those he introduced: jugglers, acrobats, singers, actors — it made no difference, Berle was always ready to jump in with a barb, a gag, a spoof. On March 11, 1933, the *New York Times* summed him up in its review with "Milton Berle is still on duty as the Master of Ceremonies for the Capitol stage show. He is quite at home, whether he is dancing, singing or regaling his audience with jokes." In October of that year he was hailed as an "exhilarating personality" by the New York *Daily Mirror* after appearing as emcee at the Paramount Theater. But not all critics were enamored of the fast-talking jokester; Chicago critic Lloyd Lewis called him "a blab-mouthed, satyr-eyed kid who toys with physiology, pathology and pruriency, tossing them about with all the freedom of a delinquent boy."

On September 9, 1932, Berle appeared in his first "legit" production on the Broadway stage when he opened at the Broadway Theater in "The Earl Carroll Vanities," directed by newcomer Vincente Minnelli. In the show's funniest sketch, Berle, playing a coarse gangster, discovers his wife in bed with a refined Englishman. The show closed after only 87 performances, putting an end to Berle's $1500-a-week salary. The experience was not a total loss, however, for the show allowed young Milton the opportunity to indulge his increasing appetite for female pulchritude; there was an entire chorus line of gorgeous girls in the show. As a handsome, up-and-coming young bachelor, Milton was eager to partake of the sins of the flesh, not an easy task with one's mother always in the vicinity. Berle relied on his mother to such an extent (there is no doubt that Sarah was his most ardent admirer, trusted adviser and personal claque) that he was unwilling to go against her wishes by settling down with one woman, so he continued to play the field.

On August 28, 1934, Milton opened in "Saluta," a musical comedy, at Broadway's Imperial Theater. "Saluta" was a satire that poked fun at Mussolini's Blackshirts, and in it Berle played "Windy" Walker, a nightclub emcee who is persuaded by gangsters to go to Italy and stage an opera in competition with Il Duce's official productions. Brooks Atkinson of the *New York Times* gave Milton a less than whole-hearted endorsement by reporting, "He runs the whole gamut from vulgarity to grossness [with] immense enthusiasm and no discrimination." With its convoluted plot and uninspired score, "Saluta" closed after only 39 performances.

Immediately after its closing, however, Berle was booked for the road tour of "Life Begins at 8:40," taking over the role originated by Bert Lahr on Broadway. This show marked the beginning of a long-standing feud between the famed "Cowardly Lion" and the brash young comic, occasioned for the most part by Lahr's jealousies and insecurities. It was simply fate that, as far as versatility was concerned, both comedians had much in common, and a lot of the material Lahr performed was tailored to Berle's talents as well. Lahr took it personally and never forgave his replacement in "Life Begins at 8:40."

In 1936 Milton Berle was signed by the Gillette Corporation as master of ceremonies for its new radio program, "Gillette Original Community Sing" on WABC. The show was a big success and eventually had the largest radio hook-up in the country—104 stations. The "Community Sing" was just that, with the studio audience following the lyrics that were projected onto a screen, and between songs were

Young Berle sought his fortune in the movies, but it eluded him there.

musical and comedy acts, introduced and kidded by Berle. This was the first time Berle's name became a household word in America's heartland, wherever the airwaves carried the musical refrains and Berle's exuberant brand of clowning.

In 1937 Berle made what he hoped would be the first step towards a major Hollywood career. Unfortunately it did not turn out that way. He was given a two-year contract by RKO Pictures for the handsome salary of $3000 a week. What he was not given was a decent script or character to play. In *New Faces of 1937* he reprised one of the "Lahr" sketches from "Life Begins at 8:40," and he appeared in another clunker called *Radio City Revels*.

If he was not being given good projects to work on, Milton did not allow that to hamper his private life. He was young, handsome, talented, and in Hollywood: home to bevies of beautiful starlets (even if Mama was on the scene as well). Berle threw himself into the California social scene that included partying and dating a variety of lovely ladies, although not becoming serious about any of them.

He also continued to work in vaudeville and, increasingly, nightclubs (it is ironic that although Berle had worked many of the biggest and most prestigious watering holes in the nation, he does not drink at all). After Berle appeared at Chicago's swank nitery, Chez Paree, in December 1938, *Variety* reported: "Berle is dynamite. Today he stands as the most glib comic on any stage, and a guarantee to entertain. His running patter is loaded with solid laughs and his songs are put over well enough. Berle has tried and gotten away with every possible trick, including sleight of hand, card manipulation and even risley work [foot juggling]. Only hoofing is not in the Berle catalog, but he's getting a bit too heavy for that. He was on the floor for two hours at the opening show and didn't tire himself or his audience. When he called for the finale, this usually cold mob nearly broke its mitts trying to get him to continue his clowning."

The late thirties and early forties were particularly busy times for the outgoing comic, and there was nothing in the world of show business that he would not attempt. He appeared in two plays in 1939, "Blessed Event" at the Maplewood Theater in New Jersey, and back on Broadway for "See My Lawyer," a bright comedy that also starred Gary Merrill and Teddy Hart (nephew of composer Lorenz Hart). "See My Lawyer" was produced by Mr. Broadway himself, George Abbott. Berle was so eager to appear in the show, even though he was playing the straight role, that he agreed to work for only $200 a week, as opposed to the $5000 or more he was getting in vaudeville or nightclubs at the time. Only Mama was unhappy—all the actors were getting laughs except for her Milton.

In addition to treading the boards, Berle was also appearing each week as the emcee on "Stop-Me-If-You've-Heard-This-One," a radio joke show sponsored by Quaker Oats on WNBC. *Variety* was lukewarm about this endeavor, saying that the show "highlighted an old fault of Berle's, the tendency to stress personal insults in his ad libbing. . . . Berle's chief drawback in the past has been his tendency to get too fresh. It's a dangerous type of humor. . . ."

Besides "See My Lawyer" every night and the radio show once a week, Berle was also doing his act in the late show of "The Georgia Hale Revue" at the International Casino, a well-known nightclub. In fact, on Saturday nights the comic was so busy that the curtain for "See My Lawyer" had to be held until 9:15 to accommodate Mr. Berle's frenetic schedule.

In 1940 Berle returned to Hollywood, hoping once again that this time would be his big break in films. But the studio bosses still did not see him as star material, and again he was cast in a series of second-rate movies. Some of the nonclassics he appeared in were *Tall, Dark and Handsome, Sun Valley Serenade, Rise and Shine, A Gentleman at Heart, Over My Dead Body, Whispering Ghosts,* and *Margin for Error,* an anti–Nazi opus in which he played a Jewish cop.

Between films the tireless Berle managed to return to the stage. When he wowed audiences at the Oriental Theater in Chicago, *Variety* reported:

> For general all-round clowning and fast gagging Milton Berle is tops in the comedian parade. . . . He has a solid following in this town, and is worthy of it, being an indefatigable worker and having a sure sense of popular entertainment. He can keep going at a remarkable pace throughout and is never at a loss for a gag to fit into any situation. For his wind-up he comes back to the trick of parodying popular songs for a running gag story of his sad experiences with a married femme. It typifies the sure fire approach that Berle has to popular vaudeville taste.
>
> After years of talking about his mother, Berle brings her to the stage this week and does a nifty job of making the interlude solidly entertaining as well as sentimental.

After enjoying years of being a young bachelor on the town, Milton Berle was finally caught in the ties of matrimony by a breathtakingly beautiful blonde chorine, Joyce Mathews. Her father, James Mathews, had been a boy wizard on Wall Street and had retired with a fortune at the age of 32. Though she was only 23, Joyce had previously been married to 41-year-old Colonel Gonzalo Gomez, son of the former president of Venezuela. After enduring ten days of physical abuse from the hot-tempered Latin, Joyce left him and they were divorced in 1940, when she met Milton. Although he was instantly smitten, it was no easy matter for the comedian to rebel against his mother's will, but at last the free-wheeling 33-year-old bachelor had met a woman he did not dare lose, and they were married on December 4, 1942. It was the beginning of a long and problematic relationship. Joyce never stopped hoping to have a major career of her own, but was handicapped by a demanding husband and her own minor talent. She also had a hard time keeping up with her nightclub-hopping mate on his night-owl jaunts, as well as the eternal presence of her mother-in-law. For his part, Berle was jealous of any time she spent on her own career and was often amazed and irate at Joyce's prodigious ability to spend money.

Though they seemed to love one another genuinely, the comic and the beauty had a hard time living together. In an effort to cement their relationship they adopted their daughter Victoria, but their devotion to little Vicki was not enough to overcome the stresses of their divergent outlooks on life, marriage and work, and they were divorced in 1947. In 1949 they were remarried, partly for the sake of their daughter, as well as a clear case of "we can't live together and we can't live apart." But the second time around was no less tumultuous than the first, and the differences that divided them were still the same.

Milton and Joyce were divorced for the second time in 1950, with Joyce receiving $2,500 a month in alimony. An interesting postscript to the life of Joyce Mathews was the scandal she created on July 15, 1951, when she slashed her wrists in Billy Rose's apartment in an effort to force the diminutive showman to divorce his wife, Olympic swimmer Eleanor Holm, and marry her. Apparently the ruse worked, as she and Rose were married, and not just once, but as with Berle, twice.

After having failed once again to take Hollywood by storm, Berle and his bride returned to New York, where he opened in "Ziegfeld Follies of 1943" at Broadway's Winter Garden Theater on April 1. He was the first performer ever to receive above-title billing in a Ziegfeld production. Co-starring with Ilona Massey and Arthur Treacher, Berle contributed to the evening's entertainment by doing his usual shtick of interrupting other acts, as well as appearing in an amusing sketch of "J. Pierpont Armour," a wartime meat baron who keeps his valuable war-rationed steaks in a vault and withdraws them only while under the protection of his machine gun–toting armed guards. The show ran for 553 performances, outlasting any of the great Ziegfeld's former "Follies."

During and after the "Ziegfeld Follies of 1943," Berle continued to be a popular attraction on radio. The first "Milton Berle Show," sponsored by Ballantine Beer (it was not made public that the star of the show did not drink) was a variety show that foreshadowed the work he would later do on television, and Berle also hosted two unusual programs: "Let Yourself Go," in which contestants and celebrity guests acted out their secret desires; and "Kiss and Make Up," with Berle as the judge of people's petty complaints (a less serious forerunner of today's "People's Court"), e.g., the case of Mrs. Kissel vs. Myers Laundry and "who put the holes in Mr. Kissel's shorts?"

In addition to the radio and stage work he was doing, Berle also wrote a newspaper column called "True Confessions" for *Variety* (later the column was syndicated under the title "The Berle-ing Point"). His breezy writing style was similar to his rapid-fire delivery on stage, as is shown in the following from *Variety*, January 6, 1943:

> I was born 34 years ago. . . . The stork was very busy that day . . . so I was delivered by a gopher . . . that's why I'm so down to earth. . . . It was a rough trip . . . we were grounded twice . . . when we got to the hospital, the windows were closed so I was delivered through the coal chute, which later developed into my black-face act. When my mother first saw me, she started to laugh . . . she hasn't stopped since (as you no doubt know) . . . the first day I was there the nurse picked me up and kissed me. . . . I started to cry like a baby . . . at that age did I know what I was doing? . . . Who'd have thought that the nurse would grow up to become Sophie Tucker. . . .
>
> My first love was Clara Kimball Young . . . she was Young and I was younger . . . it was a case of puppy love so I bought her a puppy . . . we broke up. . . . I wasn't strong enough to carry a torch, so I carried a firefly. . . . I used to write her love letters in the sand . . . what a job putting it in a mailbox.

As a nightclub act Berle was in a class by himself, with all the other comics striving to command an equal amount of attention and fees. In 1946 Berle played for 44 weeks at the popular New York club The Carnival, and was paid $7,500 per week plus a percentage of the gross profits over $42,000, giving him on average another $2,500. This $9,500 salary was the highest ever paid to a nightclub performer.

As if nightclubs, a newspaper column, radio and films were not

Berle fills in as one of the men from Texaco who work from Maine to Mexico.

enough for the effervescent comedian, Berle reportedly never turned down a request to do a benefit. All charities could count on him to turn up for their causes; indeed, sometimes they couldn't keep him away. A sampling of the numerous benefits he appeared at over the years includes Beth-El Hospital, Broadway Saranac Relief Fund, the Damon Runyon Cancer Fund (for this charity Berle hosted the first telethon), Hadassah, the Shoe, Brace and Limb Fund for Crippled Children, the *Evening Journal* and *New York American* Christmas Fund, United Jewish Appeal, City of Hope, New York Arthritis and Rheumatism Foundation, B'nai B'rith, New York Committee of the

National Council to Combat Blindness, and innumerable war bond drives and shows for servicemen during World War II.

In the fall of 1948 Milton Berle's career found its true niche, and the beaver-toothed comic was firmly entrenched as the nation's number one superstar. Texaco decided to sponsor a program on the new medium of television (radio wit Fred Allen dubbed it "a medium rarely well done") during the summer of 1948. Each week of the show featured a different host, including Harry Richman, Georgie Price, Henny Youngman, Morey Amsterdam, Jack Carter, and Peter Donald.

When the decision was made to keep the show going through the fall season, the first host of the summer, Milton Berle, was chosen to stay on permanently. He in turn provided the basic format of the show: a one-hour variety bill with a live studio audience, very much like the vaudeville that had nurtured his talent for many years. *Variety* instantly dubbed his latest venture as "vaudeo," and it soon became obvious that Berle and television were made for each other.

From the moment he stepped onto the stage of NBC's Studio 6B at Rockefeller Center at 8 P.M. on Tuesday, September 21, 1948, an almost electric connection was made between the viewers and the madcap, energetic Berle. From then on Tuesday was Berle night, and restaurants and theaters suffered from lack of patronage on that evening. One theater manager in Ohio put up a poster in his lobby that read, "Closed Tuesday. I want to see Berle too!" In New York a laundromat owner installed a television in his establishment and advertised, "Watch Berle while your clothes whirl!" Large cities reported a noticeable drop in water pressure from 9:00 to 9:05, when rapt viewers were finally able to tear themselves away from their sets (these were the days when television advertisements were actually part of the action of the show). The "Texaco Star Theater," as the show was called, was the only program not preempted in order to report the returns of the Dewey-Truman presidential race on November 2, 1948.

The show began with the sound of a fire alarm and the opening song in homage to the sponsor ("We are the men of Texaco, we work from Maine to Mexico, there's nothing like that Texaco of ours!. . . .") and sung by the four Texacomen dressed as mechanics. Berle would then make an outrageously flamboyant entrance, often parading through the studio audience. How he was introduced, by one of the Texacomen, gave a clue as to his forthcoming costumed buffoonery, i.e., if he was introduced as the man "who just returned from Washington after paying his income tax," Berle would enter dressed as an impoverished tramp, or stripped down to his underwear and dressed in a barrel. When introduced as "the man who just drove in from his vacation in Miami," Berle came in on a dogsled, dressed in furs (a comment on the unseasonable weather in the Florida city). It was not unusual for Berle to wreak havoc with the hapless members of his studio audience. On one memorable occasion, when introduced as "the man whose jokes are prehistoric," Berle entered from the back of the theater dressed as a caveman, complete with dummy cavewoman. On his way·up to the stage he sat in people's laps, took their handbags or mink coats, tied them up, and knocked over a television camera. But that was all part of the fun and excitement of live television, and of Milton Berle.

After his arrival onstage came the monologue. But first the entertainer would have to respond to the whooping laughter that emanated from the theater's balcony, emitted, of course, by none other than his greatest fan, Sandra Berle. "Watch it lady, some day you may have children of your own!" was a favorite, if ironic, gag. Then came the jokes, fast and furiously. "I was sick this week. I was in bed with 104 . . . it was mighty crowded. . . . I went to see the doctor . . . he wasn't in, so I took a turn for the nurse. . . . She was a melancholy baby—she had a head like a melon and a face like a collie." Milton's older brother Frank was often the butt of the jokes: "My brother is money mad, he gets mad if I don't give him any money." "Ever since he's been old enough to work, hasn't." "He should get a job so we'll know what kind of work he's out of." "Frank's afraid to sleep—he's afraid to dream he's working." In actuality Frank Berle worked diligently as manager for his younger brother.

If a joke failed to get the desired laugh, there were always the old standbys: "My mother's not here tonight," or "Your name and address please" (to an applauder). As usual with Berle, the actual hilarity of the jokes was less impressive than the magnificent timing and finesse with which they were delivered.

After the monologue Berle would introduce a specialty act, generally acrobats, jugglers or dancers. As a master of ceremonies he was unfailingly generous, always predisposing the audience to show their appreciation for these guest artists. Berle's accolades were always magnanimous: "Please welcome the very great, the very talented, the very wonderful. . ." he would intone while adding his

Berle as Carmen Miranda—drag comes to Middle America.

own applause to the audience's. Whether he was truly sincere in his praise was beside the point; his intros gave a feeling of warmth and enthusiasm for his guests. After the visiting troupe had completed most of its act, Berle was famous for moseying onto the scene and into their performance. He was juggled on the feet of risley men, flipped into the air by acrobats, precariously teetered on unicycles, all the while cracking mile-a-minute jokes to and doing "takes" for his viewers.

When it came to the dancers, Berle joined in with gusto. Though he was no Fred Astaire (with his penchant for drag he was probably closer to *Adele* Astaire), he was good enough to fake it with the best of them. His body English carried him far as he jumped and tapped and fell down—and got laughs.

Milton's guest stars over the years were varied and spectacular. Repeat guests included Henny Youngman, Martha Raye and Ethel Merman. Respected actors like Peter Lorre, Basil Rathbone and Tallulah Bankhead joined in the fun and seemed to enjoy every minute. Frank Sinatra came on and did an impression of "Uncle Miltie," including Berle's famous lisp, "I thwear awl kiwl you, awl kiwl you a miwlion times!" and the nonsensical walk on the insides of his shoes. Vaudeville veterans such as Bill Robinson, Smith and Dale, and "Peg-Leg" Bates brought their acts to the small screen for the first time on "Texaco Star Theater."

From the beginning Berle was a one-man crusade to break down any possible color barrier on television. Pearl Bailey, Jackie Robinson, Cab Calloway, and Nat "King" Cole were among the tremendously talented black artists who appeared on the show. When Milton casually put his arm around Lena Horne's shoulders while thanking her for appearing, letters poured into NBC from outraged viewers across the country.

The sketches Berle did with his guest stars ranged from the merely outrageous to the flamboyantly chaotic: Berle as a crusty sea dog (with Basil Rathbone) in "Captain Horatio Hornberler," or in drag as a cancan dancer with Martha Raye in "Follies Berlegers," or with Martin and Lewis as comic book heroes Buck Rogers, Superman and Flash Gordon. During the comedy sketches Berle was the patsy for the mayhem of slapstick. His clothes were ripped from his body, cream pies were shoved into his face, and as a running gag for many years someone would appear, yelling "Make-Up!" to clobber him right in the kisser with an oversized powder puff.

Probably the most distinctive device of Berle's was his prodigious use of drag on screen. Using the art form and comedic effect employed by almost all cultures since time immemorial, Berle donned women's apparel and daubed his face with lipstick, rouge and mascara with just the right combination of pastiche and lunacy. Whether it was his popular impersonation of Carmen Miranda, or of a slightly sleazy Cleopatra, audiences roared to see the six foot, 185-pound (or more, as Berle's weight tended to fluctuate during his years on television, but by the mid-fifties he had slimmed down considerably) funnyman with the deep voice in high heels and exaggerated bust.

Midway through the program Berle would introduce Sid Stone as "the young fellow you're likely to meet on any street in the U.S.A." Stone portrayed the epitome of the sly pitchman, with one eye on a potential sucker and one looking out for the long arm of the law. Setting up a small table, rolling up the sleeves of his shirt and jacket, loosening his tie, Stone would begin his pitch: "You say you're not satisfied? You say you want more for your money? Well, I'll tell you what I'm gonna do." No matter what the subject of his discourse, he always came around to selling the products of the sponsor, Texaco oil and gas. Sometimes Stone's pitch went on for ten minutes or more, but since this was the only commercial interruption of the show, and since Stone himself was fairly amusing, audiences did not seem to mind.

For the first year of "Texaco Star Theater" there were no writers; Berle simply relied on his computer-like memory to call forth the thousands of jokes he had accumulated, through theft, borrowing, or originality, in vaudeville. He even kept (and still has) a joke file that reputedly held upwards of 300,000 jokes on all subjects, from aardvarks to zippers. Sketches, too, often had a strong vaudevillian feeling, which was not surprising in that many of them were culled straight from the stage and thrust before the television lights. A piece called "Hotel Hokum" was done on "Texaco Star Theater," for instance, but had previously appeared in Berle's 1939 book, *Laughingly Yours.*

HOTEL CLERK (BERLE):	Don't tell me you're checking out!
2ND GUEST:	We couldn't stand it any longer....
CLERK:	What's the matter?
2ND GUEST:	Mental cruelty.... You know that beautiful girl that lives in the room next to mine? Well, we were separated by a wall . . . you know what a wall is, don't you?
CLERK:	Yeah . . . a hunk of cement that separates you from a good time.... Won't you give us one more chance?
2ND GUEST:	Listen, we wouldn't stay here another night if—Besides the rooms are too small. It's so tiny I had to use a folding

	toothbrush. Last night when those two mosquitos checked in, I was positive I'd have to check out. (*He leaves*)
3RD GUEST:	And my room is so small that I had to write letters in shorthand. (*He leaves*)
4TH GUEST:	Listen, my room is so small that I had a headache and the guy in the next room took the aspirin.
CLERK:	Of course I admit that your room wasn't much bigger than a cigar box with windows but—
4TH GUEST:	(*Interrupts*) Why, I had to go out of the room to change the expression on my face.
CLERK:	But can't you be reasonable?
4TH GUEST:	Reasonable? The last straw was when you asked me to take a bath in a Dixie cup. (*He leaves*)[3]

From the very beginning of "Texaco Star Theater," Milton Berle contributed not only all of the comic material, but he oversaw the entire production of the show. Not one detail escaped his scrutiny—choreography, lighting, costumes, direction. He wore a towel around his neck (he had a monstrous fear of drafts) and a whistle in his mouth (to save his voice; unfortunately some members of the crew saw it as an instrument of tyranny). From Wednesday morning's think session until the show went out live the following Tuesday, Berle was a whirlwind of activity.

After the show Berle and his aides would repair to Lindy's restaurant to unwind, discuss the successes and failures of that evening's show, and consume copious amounts of corned beef and pastrami while kibitzing with the other comics who hung out at the deli until all hours of the morning. "I tried to do everything," he says, "and I had to do everything, 'cause I knew just as much about television as the next person. . . . 'Fix that light, fix that fresnel, fix that lico, push up camera three,' I was doing everything. . . . I was a pain in the ass, to myself and possibly to crews, actors, lights and electricians because I was working under pressure. . . . You had to get the show on at 8 o'clock, when that bell rang 'bong, bong' and the four schmucks walked out. . . . As I look back to 35 years ago I think that my performance could have been even better, but I was worried so much about the overall performance. . . . I was worried about everybody else but me."[4]

But the work paid off. His was the number one rated show in all of the rating systems, and Berle was personally responsible for millions of Americans going out to buy their first television set. The joke (which has been variously ascribed to several comics, including Joe E. Lewis and Fred Allen) was "Berle is responsible for selling hundreds of sets. I sold mine, my uncle sold his. . . ." Even Berle's radio show profited by his television success; now that audiences were able to see him weekly, it was easier for them to imagine his antics on radio, and his Hooper rating on that medium improved tremendously.

A number of products came on the market to cash in on Berle's phenomenal success. They included puppets, a trick car, a children's magnetic game, and a make-up kit with a red wig, three mustaches, two noses, false teeth, an eye patch, black, red, tan and white make-up, a Milton Berle button, a Milton Berle biography and make-up instructions.

Berle was in his element more so on television than he had been either on films or radio. Radio had been limiting to him not only because of its nonvisual nature, but also because of its tightly scripted situations. There was less opportunity for a free-spirited comedian to cut up and improvise on radio than there was on the early days of television. Today, of course, with television programming being many times more expensive than it was in the late forties or early fifties, there is little or no chance of departing from the script, but on the first year of "Texaco Star Theater" the cost of a single show, including the star's salary, came to $15,000. One *minute* of air time costs more than that today. Improvising became the norm rather than the exception for Berle and his guests, generally playing havoc with the show's timing. Although the sketches and acts were carefully timed during rehearsal, so many unexpected shenanigans could take place during the broadcast that Berle was forced either to hurry up and finish (and more than one sketch was simply cut off in midstory) or use up leftover time at the end of the show.

On one such occasion the "Uncle Miltie" moniker was born. With time to kill at the end of the show, and the floor manager making desperate "elongate" motions with his hands, Berle implored all the children who were watching to listen to their Uncle Miltie and go to bed. From that moment on he became Uncle Miltie to millions of Americans, young and old. Even the competition over on the Dumont network paid homage to the title, when Bishop Fulton Sheen began his emission one evening by saying, "Good evening, this is Uncle Fultie."

Unlike the other great clowns who came to television, Berle never maintained a stable of characters to return to week after week. Caesar had the German Professor, Skelton had Clem Kadiddlehopper, Freddie the Freeloader and others, Gleason the Poor Soul and Ralph Kramden. For these great names, having a group of characters to return to kept them from becoming boring to their audience. It probably never occurred to Berle and his healthy ego that audiences might become tired of watching him week after week. By keeping the "Texaco Star Theater" fast-paced with surprises, slapstick and good-natured chaos, Berle felt that the addition of extra characters would be constricting. As he has stated, "I did non sequiturs. I was in drag, but not every week. I used to do slapstick, with pies and everything, but not every week. . . . I never did play one character. . . . It was not loose enough for me."[5]

Similarly, Berle did not go in for pantomime as did his television peers. "I was a verbal comedian," he explains. "I tell jokes and stories, they didn't. . . . The most difficult thing is to just stand there and talk, and get laughs. It is quite difficult to do pantomime, but not as tough as telling jokes. I took the hard way and they took the easy way, and they did it very well."[6]

There is little doubt that it was the live transmission of the "Texaco Star Theater" that gave it a certain *éclat*. Other very early shows were being done on film, but Texaco went out live before millions of Americans every Tuesday. "In those days," says Berle, "back in '48 and '49 and the early fifties, we had live audiences; you got what you saw, you saw what you got. *We did not have a second chance.* You couldn't take it over like they do with tape. . . . We didn't have any tape, no cue cards, no teleprompter and no giggler—no laugh machine. I can't stand that. In the monologue, when I forgot a joke I'd remember what I did at Loew's State. If a joke died, out came all those 'savers,' the protecting lines. They are standards and clichés now—'Are you here for entertainment or revenge?' 'Which joke are you working on?' 'Here's another joke you may not care for.' They come in handy when you need them."[7]

No matter the secret of success of Milton Berle and the "Texaco Star Theater," NBC knew it was onto a good thing. In 1951 Berle was offered a 30-year exclusive contract with the network for $200,000 a year. The offer was made both to keep him tied to NBC, and as a trade-off, for he had wanted to start filming the shows for posterity (and the value of residuals). The network felt that was too expensive, so he was given this "lifetime" contract with a tremendous raise in salary, in fact the highest paid to any television performer.

The year 1951 was also propitious for Milton for romantic reasons. He met an attractive divorcée, Ruth Cosgrove (née Rosenthal), from Patterson, New Jersey, who made him forget the trials and tribulations of being married to Joyce. Although not as stunning as Joyce had been, Ruth was smart, independent, and she refused to let Berle's star-sized ego dictate to her. After dating for two years, the pair were married on December 9, 1953. They have remained a steadfast and loving couple, as well as devoted parents to Billy, the son they adopted in 1961.

In 1952 the format of the "Texaco Star Theater" was changed. This was due to the rise of other comedic talents, such as Lucille Ball and Red Skelton, and the competition for ratings. Berle was no longer the only funny person on the small screen, so new writers were brought in by the network in an effort to bring a fresh approach to the show. Goodman Ace, a successful radio writer, was hired to head a new writing team that included Selma Diamond, Jay Burton, Aaron Ruben and Arnold Auerbach. "Goody" Ace was told by Berle to make sure that the jokes were "lappy," that is, overt enough to fall into the audience's lap. Ace saw to it that there were fundamental changes made in the show's rhythm; no longer was it to be a vaudeville-style free-for-all; a more structured situation comedy was to take its place. Berle would no longer be seen as the aggressive smart-aleck who insulted people; rather, he would become the insulted; he would play the harried star of a television variety show who has to put up with the egocentricities of his staff and guest stars. Actress Ruth Gilbert joined the show as Max, Berle's adoring secretary, and in 1953 Arnold Stang, the weak-chinned character actor who specialized in playing wimps, was cast as Francis the Stagehand. Sid Stone was replaced as pitchman by the sweet-faced ventriloquist Jimmy Nelson and his dummies Danny O'Day and Farfel the Dog.

The following year Buick became the show's new sponsor, and the "Buick Berle Show" was born for the 1953 season. Goodman Ace and the more structured format were retained, and although the show was still funny and fresh, the star would have preferred a return to the wacky, no-holds-barred formula of 1948. The writers had changed Berle from brash to lovable, and the audience was not buying it. The ratings had gone from first place with a whopping 61.6 percent of the viewing Nielsen audience in 1950, to finishing thirteenth with 34.6 percent of the viewers in 1954/55. Still respectable, but no longer phenomenal.

After the season finale on June 14, 1955, Buick deserted Berle as sponsor and went over to Jackie Gleason. Berle signed with Whirlpool and Sunbeam to do "The Milton Berle Show," in color and from California. The show limped along from September 1955 to June 1956 (the final show featured a young, shy, rock and roll singer named Elvis Presley), when it was cancelled, partially due to the competition on CBS, Milton's old friend Phil Silvers as Sergeant Bilko in "You'll Never Get Rich." After eight continuous years on television, "Mr. Television" was reaching the end of his heyday.

But Mr. Berle was not idle. He is a man who needs a steady diet of applause and laughter to survive. After a two-year hiatus, Berle returned to television in October 1958 as the master of ceremonies of the "Kraft Music Hall." Typically, he greeted his return with a joke, "I haven't heard so much applause since I announced I was quitting." For this show he went back to being the "old" Berle, although in a more sophisticated guise; no more pies in the face, no more drag. One particularly delightful show featured Berle trading quips with the aging poet and Lincoln biographer, Carl Sandburg. "I bet some of the jokes that I tell would amuse Mr. Lincoln," proposed the comedian. "Well," answered the poet, "he knew nearly all the ancient jokes of mankind. [Pause] Of course, as everybody knows, some of yours go back to Noah and the ark."

After the demise of "Kraft Music Hall" in May 1959, Berle, ever eager to continue working (and under exclusive contract to NBC), accepted the job of host for "Jackpot Bowling," broadcast Monday evenings at 10:30. A rather ignominious comedown for the great clown, and for five years afterwards he had no show on television. In 1966, however, having obtained a release from his NBC contract in exchange for a considerable reduction in salary, he returned in a new "Milton Berle Show" on ABC, broadcast on Friday evenings from 9:00 to 10:00. This new show attempted to attract the burgeoning youth market, so pop singers Bobby Rydell and Donna Loren were engaged as regulars, along with a group of go-go dancers. There was also the addition of Irving Benson, a dour-faced actor who played "Sidney Spritzer," a heckler who sat in the audience. Some of the heckling routines between him and Berle dated back to vaudeville:

BERLE: I ride so well I actually become part of the horse.
SPRITZER: I know which part.

BERLE: This is not the intermission, it's the show.
SPRITZER: You could have fooled me.
BERLE: Don't be funny.
SPRITZER: Just because you gave it up why should I?

SPRITZER: How long will you stay in Hollywood?
BERLE: As long as my public wants me.
SPRITZER: Just passing through, huh?

BERLE: Does your wife enjoy having a dum-dum around the house?
SPRITZER: Sure, stop by anytime.

The "Milton Berle Show" on ABC ran until January 1967, when it was killed in the ratings by "The Man from U.N.C.L.E." on NBC. It was the last series of the garrulous clown, although he did appear regularly as the host of the variety spectacular "Hollywood Palace" during the sixties. Berle also appeared as a guest star on dozens of shows, from "Batman" to "I Dream of Jeannie," to "Saturday Night Live." He also appeared over the years in many television dramas, including "Family Business" on American Playhouse and "Doyle Against the House" on the "Dick Powell Show," for which he was nominated for an Emmy. In all of his dramatic endeavors Berle exhibited a masterly sense of the art of acting, great sensitivity, and generally fine performances.

Although Milton's beloved mother Sarah, who became Sandra, died in 1952, he has remained guided by her indomitable spirit as much in his seventies as he was as a small boy being taken to casting calls for silent pictures. Berle has never slowed down, never resisted entertaining an audience of one or many millions. As his wife Ruth has put it, "The world's greatest love affair is not Romeo and Juliet — but Milton and show business."

In June 1985, Berle underwent quadruple heart bypass surgery, and, typically, was joking and mugging for the nurses only days after the operation. Whether in a dress, a caveman's furs, a tuxedo or a hospital gown, the man is simply dauntless. For television comedians, he was the trail-blazer and the standard-bearer. He still thrives on giggles, titters and belly laughs, still comes alive to the sound of two hands clapping. The song Berle sang to close his show for many

years succinctly encapsulates how much this great clown has always
needed to be loved and appreciated by a room full of strangers:

> There's just one place for me
> And that's near you.
> It's been a thrill for me to be near you.
> If I've brought you just one smile
> Then you've made this night worthwhile
> I love you all and I love
> Being near you!

Carol Burnett

Carol Burnett is one of the most popular performers on television today. She has consistently encouraged her audiences to sense that she could be their sister, friend or neighbor. As a clown she has captured their hearts, and as a comic actress she has brought them laughter and pleasure. From her beginnings as a gawky young singer/entertainer to her evolution into a sequined, begowned hostess of her own show, she has maintained a healthy, resilient attitude towards comedy and life.

Being a comedienne is not one of the simpler tasks of the entertainment world, and it never has been. A woman walks a fine line between what is considered tasteless and unfeminine, and what is humorous and appealing. Burnett never had the goofy image of an Imogene Coca or a Martha Raye, nor did she approach the cool good looks of a Lucille Ball or a Carole Lombard. It was necessary for her to forge a comic personality for herself without becoming grotesque or banal, a task which she, with the help of an able writing and producing staff, accomplished capably during her 11-year reign on television.

The star of "The Carol Burnett Show" sprang from the most humble beginnings imaginable. She was born on April 26, 1933, in San Antonio, Texas, to Jody and Louise Creighton Burnett. Jody had migrated from Arkansas to Texas, where he occasionally had work as manager of a movie theater. When little Carol was two, her parents moved to Los Angeles, leaving her in the care of her maternal grandmother, Mae White, whom she called Nana. Mrs. White was a formidable character, a Christian Scientist who had had six husbands (and bragged that she never loved any of them) and who, when she died at the age of 82, left a 40-year-old boyfriend.

In 1940 Carol and her grandmother joined her parents in California. The Burnetts' marriage was not a happy one, and they continued to separate and reunite for several years. Carol and Nana moved into an apartment across the hall from her parents, a one-bedroom dwelling with a Murphy bed encased in the wall. Although her living arrangements may have seemed unsettling to those who knew of them, Carol's childhood was generally a happy one; she was a good student and had friends to play with. In 1945 her mother gave birth to her half sister, Christine, who had been fathered by one of Louise's boyfriends, an actor.

Jody had not been successful in finding much work in Los Angeles, and his failure to provide for his family led him into alcoholism. Never an abusive drunk, he seemed to become even gentler and quieter when inebriated. In 1954 he died of tuberculosis and the effects of alcoholism. Louise, who had done some writing for fan magazines and for one of the movie studios, also began to drink. Four years later she too died of alcoholism.

Carol continued to be a good student at Hollywood High School, where she was proficient at athletics, especially running, and where she contributed to the school newspaper. Her interest in journalism led her to UCLA, where she began to major in English ("I wanted to be Brenda Starr," she has said). Part of her curriculum included an acting class, and it was there that the bug bit. While doing a scene for her class she inadvertently got a laugh, and a new world opened. "The first time I ever forgot I was homely, was the first time I heard an audience laugh," she later reminisced. Soon thereafter she switched her major from English to theater.

At the end of her junior year fate took a hand in Carol Burnett's future theatrical career. She and her boyfriend and fellow student, Don Saroyan, a cousin of the writer William, were invited to do a scene from "Annie Get Your Gun" for an end-of-the-semester party being thrown by a member of the faculty. Attending this affair was a middle-aged businessman from San Diego, who was obviously impressed by their talents. This businessman had made his fortune in the construction industry and was willing to financially assist Burnett and Saroyan in their dream of going to New York and appearing on the stage. Loaning them each $1,000, he exacted several promises in return for his generosity: that the loan would be repaid five years hence; that the money would be used only to further their careers; that if successful, they would in the future help other young and struggling performers; and that they would never reveal the name of their benefactor. All of these conditions were later fulfilled.

A month later, in August 1954, Carol Burnett was on her way to New York. Her grandmother was skeptical of such a move and made Carol promise to return by Christmas if she was not a star by then. She also made her granddaughter promise that should she become a success on television, she would be sure and send a signal that all was well.

Having heard that the Algonquin Hotel was home to many of New York's leading performers and literati, she checked into the midtown establishment. Realizing that her $1,000 nest egg was not going to last long with the hotel's rate of nine dollars a night, she soon moved into the Rehearsal Club, a boardinghouse for young ladies with theatrical aspirations, on West 53rd Street. The lodging had been the subject of the classic film *Stage Door*, with Ginger Rogers and Katharine Hepburn, but the important thing to Carol was that a room and two meals a day cost only $18 a week.

In order not to keep spending her savings, Carol got a job as a hatcheck girl at Susan Palmer's restaurant on 49th Street, where she was soon earning up to $30 a week in tips. Her nighttime employment left her days free to see agents and casting directors and attend auditions, but little materialized for the girl with the big teeth and gawky figure. She was still unclear as to where she would fit into the broad spectrum of performers. At one point she went backstage and introduced herself to Eddie Foy, Jr., star of Broadway's "Pajama Game," and asked him for advice on how to break into show business. "What do you want to do, kid, wanna be in the chorus?" Foy asked. "Oh, no," she replied. "I'm not good enough. . . . I want to play leads."

As is often the case, Burnett was caught up in the classic catch-22 of the aspiring actor: Agents would not give her work until she had more experience, and she could not get any experience if the agents would not submit her for work. In an effort to overcome this conundrum, Burnett, as secretary of the Rehearsal Club, organized a variety show with the girls who resided there, directed by Don Saroyan, who had also come East. In the show Carol did a spoof of the Eartha Kitt hit "Monotonous." Kitt did her version in a sexy outfit and a chaise lounge. Burnett did hers in curlers and an old bathrobe. The Rehearsal Club was an establishment with enough prestige to attract a number of agents and producers, and both Carol and Don got work in industrial shows ("a week in Chicago plugging aluminum foil," she says). Carol and the darkly handsome Saroyan were married on December 17, 1955, in Yonkers, New York.

From there, Carol was cast as ventriloquist Paul Winchell's girl-friend on his children's show on NBC for 13 weeks. Following that she played Celia, Buddy Hackett's girlfriend in his short-lived sit-com about a hapless newsstand owner entitled "Stanley," which ran on NBC from September 24, 1956, to March 11, 1957. On television she also made appearances on "The Ed Sullivan Show," "Omnibus," and the "Dinah Shore Show." Onstage, she was a hit at the swank nightclub the Blue Angel, on which *Variety* reported on June 12, 1957:

> Carol Burnett looms like a potential in the comedy song field. This redhead has a batch of excellently tailored mate-rial, which coupled with a highly developed flair for comedy, should bring her to important levels after exposure on the cafe circuits.
>
> Miss Burnett's major opus at show caught was a rib of various types of singers. However, her satires run along different paths; they have a bite and sting without being vicious. Her reports on the girls spieling the weather data are laced with humor even though she beats them rather heavily.
>
> Miss Burnett, further, seems to have an excellent horizon in niteries, and with more development, on video. Her native ability to express herself in comedic terms makes her a safe bet in most situations.

Sometime before her appearance at the Blue Angel Carol had a felicitous meeting with talented young pianist and composer Ken Welch. He and his future wife Mitzi and Carol and Don had worked together in a Poconos resort, where Welch had written Carol a song entitled "Destroy Me," in which a dowdy housewife sings a torch song to her unnamed idol, based upon Elvis Presley. For her Blue Angel appearance, Welch and Burnett modified the idea so that it was now sung by an adoring teenager to her heartthrob, Secretary of State John Foster Dulles, chosen for the spoof because of his dis-tinctly unsexy demeanor. Members of the staff of the "Jack Paar Show" caught Burnett's act and arranged for her to sing "I Made a Fool of Myself Over John Foster Dulles" on the show in August 1957. The song which caught the nation's (and the Secretary of State's) at-tention went:

"I Made a Fool of Myself Over John Foster Dulles"
(Words & Music by Ken Welch)

CAROL
(speaking)
It's so nice of you all to come visit me here in prison.
I look forward to Friday—Friday is visiting day.
Would you like to know just why I'm here in prison?
I'm here because I'm classified as a threat to the national security:
"Top Secret, First Class, 4.0, Double A"!
And it happened this way:

(singing)
I made a fool of myself over John Foster Dulles.
Oh, I made a chump of myself over John Foster Dulles.
The first time I saw him 'twas at the U.N.,
I never had been one to swoon over men,
But I swooned, and the drums started pounding, and then
I made a fool of myself over John Foster Dulles!

I knew it was futile to dream, for we never could marry;
Still my heart ripped apart at the seam for the State Secretary.
The next time I saw him he was flying to Spain;
He waved to someone as he boarded the plane;
"Was it me?" cried my heart, and then I went insane,
And I made a fool of myself over John Foster Dulles.

"Get ahold of yourself!" I told myself;
To my heart I cried "Behave!"
"Who are you to John Foster Dulles?"
I asked my heart—and it replied, "His slave!"

Then in somebody's newspaper column—I think Robert Ruark—
I read that John Foster was due at the airport in Newark.
To Jersey by taxi I made a mad race,
I pushed through the crowd 'til we stood face to face,
I grabbed for his sleeve, but I got his briefcase—
At least it was something belonging to John Foster Dulles!

(speaking)
It's so nice of you all to come visit me here in prison.
With good behavior, I should be out in about seven years.
I'm not un-American, and I'm not a spy,
But how can I convince the F.B.I.
(singing)
That I'm simply on fire with desire—for John Foster Dulles?

It appears that Dulles missed seeing the show but requested that it be repeated, which was done a few nights later. The Secretary was enthusiastic about the song and its singer and asked for a copy of the recording.

Carol's career was taking off. Unfortunately, her marriage to Don Saroyan suffered as a result of her success. He just could not compete with the amount of work and critical acclaim she was receiving. Since 1956 their household had included Christine, Carol's younger sister, for Carol's mother in California was too ill to properly care for the young girl. Carol had worked diligently to send Christine to private school.

In 1959 Carol and Don separated. Theirs was a friendly parting of the ways, and Carol did not actually get her divorce until September 25, 1962.

A fairy tale came true for Burnett when she was signed to appear in a musical comedy directed by her hero, "Mister Broadway," George Abbott. "Once Upon a Mattress" was a light and innocent piece based on the story of the princess and the pea. With music by Richard Rodgers' daughter, Mary, the story told of Princess Winnifred ("call me Fred") Woebegone and her plight at the castle of Prince Dauntless and his overbearing mother, Queen Agravain. Opening on May 11, 1959, at the off–Broadway Phoenix Theater (later moving to Broadway, but not before Miss Burnett and other cast members picketed the management to find them a new theater), the show garnered favorable reviews, but with most of the highest accolades reserved for the star. Brooks Atkinson reported on the opening in the *New York Times:*

> Some of [the show] is sung by a breezy comedienne who comes brawling into the story halfway through the first act and gives it a wonderful life for the rest of the evening. She is Carol Burnett. . . . Miss Burnett is a lean, earthy young lady with a metallic voice, an ironic gleam and an unfailing sense of comic gesture. As a singer, she discharges Miss Rodgers' music as though she were firing a field mortar. As a performer, she is bright and entertaining.

Donald Malcolm was even more enthusiastic in the *New Yorker:*

> The greatest single asset of the production, however, is Carol Burnett, the toothy, brash, and bouncing young lady who plays Winnifred. By some private alchemy, whose secret I was unable to

penetrate, she can extract laughter from the most withered comic routines. Her manner of hoisting a weighty bar bell, which has previously taxed the lifting powers of Prince Dauntless, is sufficient to persuade the spectator, at least momentarily, that he is seeing this feeble old stunt for the very first time. If I cannot congratulate Miss Burnett on the production, I can and do congratulate the production on Miss Burnett.

The show ran for 460 performances, closing on July 2, 1960. Carol was kept very busy during this period, for on November 19, 1959, she joined the cast of the "Garry Moore Show" as a regular, where she remained for three seasons. She was hailed as a combination of Bea Lillie, Carole Lombard and Fanny Brice; the *Saturday Evening Post* called her "equally convincing as a slob or a slinky glamour puss." The show contained many comedy sketches, and Burnett was often called upon to play five or six characters during the show's 60 minutes. And she kept her promise to Grandmother White by tugging on her earlobe at the end of the show to signal that everything was all right (she continued to tug on her ear for years after her grandmother's death, in remembrance of the formidable woman who had raised her).

"The Garry Moore Show" gave Carol nationwide exposure, and she learned a lot from Moore himself, but on the eve of the show's third season she told the press: "This season and that will be it. I don't want to be typed, strange as that may sound, and will, if I keep on doing what I'm doing on Garry's show, there will be no preventing it. Let's face it, I'm stage struck, and what I want is to follow along the lines of Mary Martin, or Ethel Merman, or maybe Judy Holliday. Sure, TV is great to me. It put me on the map, and don't think I am ungrateful." Regarding the offers she had received to do her own series, she stated, "It's the same thing all over again, I'd by typed all over again. Sure, it'd be fun, I guess, but what would happen? I'd go two, maybe three years—provided I was lucky—and I'd be something like 'Lucy' or 'Margie' or 'Susie.' No, I'm chicken when it comes to having my own show. I'm interested in making good—on Broadway." Fortunately for millions of devoted viewers, she came to have a change of heart.

After leaving Moore, Carol had time to promote her own projects, including touring a revue around the country, and a joint concert at Carnegie Hall with Julie Andrews written by Mike Nichols. She was also a member of the cast of the short-lived comedy show

"The Entertainers" on CBS with Bob Newhart and Caterina Valente. Burnett had polished her television technique on "The Garry Moore Show," but she acquired something else as well: the show's director/producer, Joe Hamilton. What began as a good working relationship and platonic friendship blossomed into romance. Hamilton had started his career as a singer with the vocal group the Skylarks, appearing regularly on "The Dinah Shore Show" before moving his talents to behind the camera. At the time he and Burnett began their affair he was married to the former Gloria Hartley, and with her had eight children ranging in age from 13 years old to 18 months. Nevertheless, Joe flew to Mexico for a divorce, and in May 1963 Carol and Joe were married in Juarez, flying to Hawaii afterwards for a honeymoon.

On November 12, 1963, Carol starred in the title role of "Calamity Jane," a musical by Sammy Fain and Paul Francis Webster on CBS. Jack Gould in the *New York Times* said, "Miss Burnett's personality compensated for the heavy book and undistinguished songs."

Her ill luck with musical projects continued when she returned to Broadway on May 26, 1964, in "Fade Out—Fade In." With book and lyrics by Comden and Green, music by Jule Styne and direction, once again, by George Abbott, the show must have seemed a sure hit, but it was not to be. Carol played the part of an unpromising chorus girl who is accidentally given the starring role in a new movie (which turns out to be a hit). Co-starring Jack Cassidy, the show was a satire of the machinations of the Hollywood studio system. Carol's best bit was her takeoff on Shirley Temple. On November 14, Carol withdrew from the show (causing its closure), claiming ill health due to spinal injuries incurred in a car accident. The fact that she was well enough to continue her television appearances caused the show's producers to bring her to court to try to get her to finish her contract. After three months Burnett returned to "Fade Out—Fade In," but it was obvious that she was unhappy with the show (she had lost so much weight in those three months that all of her costumes had to be altered). It folded after 271 performances and a great deal of acrimony between Carol and the show's creators and producers.

Her bad experience with "Fade Out—Fade In," especially her being ordered by a court and by Actor's Equity to go back onstage to honor her contract, probably soured Carol on performing in the theater. From then on, until she began to make movies in the 1970s, nearly all her efforts were geared towards television. On February 24, 1963, she did a special entitled "An Evening with Carol Burnett" on CBS. In that year she also appeared as Dean Martin's snoopy secretary in the disastrous film *Who's Been Sleeping in My Bed?*

In 1965 Carol and Joe moved to Hollywood, into the house that had formerly belonged to Betty Grable and Harry James. Carol had given birth to their first child, Carrie Louise, on December 5, 1964, in New York and in the coming years produced Jody Ann (born January 18, 1967) and Erin Kate (born August 14, 1968). Three of Joe's children from his first marriage often lived with them, so Carol had plenty of work being a mother.

On March 22, 1966, Carol (with husband Joe as permanent producer) did a special called "Carol Plus 2" with guests Lucille Ball and Zero Mostel. By 1967, however, it was obvious that American viewing audiences were ready for Carol to have her own, regular show. "The Carol Burnett Show" premiered on CBS on Monday, September 11, 1967, at 10:00 P.M. The 60-minute comedy-variety show had Jim Nabors as its first guest star (he continued the tradition by appearing on her first show every season) and was an immediate hit. During the show's run over the next 11 years, it was nominated every year for an Emmy and won three times.

With Joe Hamilton at the production helm, the writers for the first season were Arnie Rosen, Stan Burns and Mike Marmer, Don Hinkley, Saul Turtletaub, Kenny Solms and Gail Parent, and Bill Angelos and Buz Kohan. In later years there would be several changes in the writers' staff, including Hal Goldman, Al Gordon, Gary Belkin, Roger Beatty, Arnie Kogen, Bill Richmond, Gene Perret, Rudy DeLuca and Barry Levinson, Dick Clair and Jenna McMahon, Barry Herman, Ed Simmons, Ray Jessel, Stan Hart and Larry Sigal, Woody Kling, Tom Patchett, Jay Tarses, Robert Hilliard and others. Gone were the days of the three-man (or -woman) writing staff that was the norm during the "Your Show of Shows" era; now that production budgets were enormous, writing staffs were increased with the view that more is funnier. Sometimes this reasoning was correct, sometimes not. In Carol's case, the writers put together a slick, fast-moving hour of entertainment that had its moments of sublimely funny sketches, and the rest of the time at least managed to amuse and divert its audience.

Burnett was also aided by a supporting cast that in time worked like a fine repertory company, a well-oiled machine for making

Carol and her doppelgänger Vicki Lawrence.

sketches funny. Lyle Waggoner, a handsome, deep-voiced, leading man–type, was on hand as straight man and announcer. Harvey Korman, who had previously been second banana for Danny Kaye, was a fine comedian and character actor known for cracking up at least once during each show. "Harvey and I are as married as two performers can be. He's to me what Carl Reiner, Howard Morris and Imogene Coca were to Sid Caesar. Harvey can play anything," said Burnett. Vicki Lawrence joined the cast after sending a fan letter and her photograph to Carol, revealing her startling resemblance to the star. From then on she was often cast as a relative of Burnett's, either as her mother in the "Eunice's Family" series of sketches, or as the younger sister living with Burnett and Korman (much as Carol's own younger sister, Christine, had lived with her and Don during their years in New York). And of course Tim Conway was available to contribute a touch of insanity to the proceedings.

The hour-long show featured comedy sketches, songs, production numbers, guest stars and a question-and-answer period between Carol and the audience. Much of the material was topical—the first show featured Burnett (in an impersonation reminiscent of her "Fade Out—Fade In" number) as "Shirley Dimples," an aging Hollywood child-star with political pretensions. Movie spoofs included lampooning *The Dolly Sisters* ("The Doily Sisters"), *Love Story* ("Lovely Story"), *Little Miss Markem* ("Little Miss Broadway"), as well as parodies of such classics as *Golden Boy, The African Queen, From Here to Eternity,* and, in a tour de force performance of Burnett's, *Sunset Boulevard*'s Nora Desmond. She also parodied such superstars as Joan Crawford ("Mildred Fierce") and Rita Hayworth ("Golda").

Carol's most famous character, that of a woebegone charwoman, was often reprised, until her desire for playing this Chaplinesque, impoverished woman began to pall. "There's no reason for me dressing up as a charwoman," she said. "Of course, it's very popular, but I don't think I play it well. It feels dead to me. I feel embarrassed doing it."

Probably the best-remembered series of sketches done on the show (even more so when it spun off into its own half-hour sit-com under the title "Mama's Family") were the trials of Eunice, her husband Ed, and Eunice's resident mother. Endowed with nasal, southern twangs, the three of them are locked in a never-ending battle that makes Jean-Paul Sartre's "No Exit" look like a night out on the town. Overbearing Mama, played with age make-up and grey wig by Vicki Lawrence, imposes her will on her daughter and son-in-law with a series of verbal barbs that fall on the ears like fingernails on a blackboard, only far more deadly. She has psychologically battered her daughter, yet Eunice continues in an attempt, however pathetic, to improve her life. Husband Ed, a lumbering slob who works in a hardware store, has no imagination and just wants to tune out the world; instead, he is forced to join in the bickering that occurs constantly between mother and daughter. Occasional guest star Betty White played Eunice's older, more successful sister, who is maliciously able to torture and enrage Eunice with jealousy, all the while seeming that butter would not melt in her Southern-belle mouth.

It has been noted that the tragicomedy and hostility of the "Mama's Family" sequences were pure Tennessee Williams in tone. Eunice is a relative of Blanche Dubois, seeking a more genteel existence amid the boors and back-stabbing in her home. Perhaps the appeal of the comedy lay in the viewer's notion that no matter how unhappy and distraught his or her own family might be, it could not be more vicious and destructively poor than Eunice's. Burnett has

Audiences loved Carol's charwoman character, but she quickly tired of it.

noted that Eunice bore a certain resemblance to her own mother, Louise, particularly when she was under the influence of alcohol. On March 22, 1982, she told *People* magazine: "At times I felt I was portraying my mother. It was like psychodrama. It was sure a lot better than going to a psychiatrist. . . . My mother was a beautiful woman whose problems were alcohol and a frustrating life. . . ."

By the tenth season, the show was beginning to lose much of its creative energy. Harvey Korman, a stalwart cast member who added

No one worked harder than Carol Burnett to make millions love her.

much of the hilarity on the set, left and was replaced by Dick Van Dyke. Van Dyke did not fit into the show's rhythm as well, and the ratings continued to drop. Finally, on March 29, 1978, after 286 shows, "The Carol Burnett Show" performed its farewell in a two-hour retrospective of the show's funniest moments (as well as a recap of Carol's changing hairstyles over the years). The show concluded in typical fashion with Carol singing her familiar theme song, "I'm So Glad We Had This Time Together." In the summer of 1979 Burnett and crew returned to do four shows on ABC, but it was obvious that the magic of previous years could not be recaptured. The comedy sections of the shows were edited together and went into syndication as "Carol Burnett and Friends" in a 30-minute format.

In 1972 Burnett had reentered the world of films with *Pete 'n' Tillie*. In 1978 she played Tulip, the bride's mother, in Robert Altman's *A Wedding*, and in 1980, a health food faddist in his comedy *Health*. In 1981 she appeared as Alan Alda's wife in his film *The Four Seasons*, and in 1982 she portrayed the evil Miss Hannigan in the movie version of the musical "Annie."

In 1982 Carol and Joe Hamilton were divorced. Their marriage had undergone a severe strain during their eldest daughter's drug addiction. Carol and daughter Carrie were brave enough to take their problem before the public in a story in *People* magazine. Carol again faced public scrutiny in a libel case she brought, and won, against *The National Enquirer* for reporting that she had gotten drunk in a Washington, D.C., restaurant. After enduring the effects of her own parents' alcoholism, she has always been abstemious with liquor. In 1982 Burnett starred in *Life of the Party: The Story of Beatrice*, a television movie based on the true-life story of a female alcoholic.

From a struggling, gawky big-voiced girl who tugged on her ear, Carol Burnett worked hard to become a source of pleasure and happiness for millions of Americans. It is to her credit that she achieved all this without losing the innocence and openness that made her so human to her audience. She is self-admittedly "a white bread woman," ordinary, with the kind of face that reminds people of "their aunt, their niece, their cousin, their brother, their mother." She thinks that part of her durability on television has come from this ordinariness. "I'm not a striking beauty, which works in my favor. When somebody is picture perfect, you stare but don't touch. Because they might break. I'm not really slick, either. I still have that tinge of being amateurish. I get embarrassed and can't take a bow that doesn't look like I'm kicking dirt." What a refreshing attitude from one of television's biggest stars!

Sid Caesar

During his television heyday in the fifties, Sid Caesar was a man of huge appetites. His suits had to have the widest shoulders, his steaks had to be the thickest and juiciest, and his television scripts the funniest. Caesar's tremendous vitality and appetite for life were what catapulted him to fame and success, sustained him as one of America's best-loved clowns, and also nearly destroyed him.

One of the most versatile comedians television has ever produced, Sid was equally comfortable doing pantomime, monologues, characters, impersonations, parodies, or situation comedy. He was by turns almost terrifyingly funny, endearingly sweet, or touchingly vulnerable. Above all, he was an expert observer of life with all its idiosyncracies, able to recreate that life on our television screens. He has often stated, "Comedy has to be truth. You take truth and you put a little curlicue at the end." The epitome of a master craftsman, Caesar has justifiably been called "The Chaplin of Television."

Sidney Caesar was born in Yonkers, a suburb of New York City, on September 8, 1922. When the wave of Jewish immigration arrived in New York from Eastern Europe at the turn of the century, most settled in the ghetto on the Lower East Side. They dreamed of making enough money to move to such places as The Bronx, or its nearby neighbor, Yonkers. These places represented an escape from the squalor of the ghetto and an opportunity to join the middle class. This was "the country," almost.

So it was with Sid's parents. His father, Max, had emigrated from Austrian Poland and his mother, Ida, from Odessa, Russia. The origin of the name Caesar is unclear. Very likely it was some immigration official's idea of a joke, giving a poor immigrant (Sid's Uncle Joe) the name of an emperor. Another possibility is that when Joe arrived at Ellis Island the clerk could not pronounce his Austro-Hungarian name, so he asked Joe's occupation. The answer was "tseezer" (tax collector), which became Caesar, and when Joe's brother Max arrived he took the same name.

By dint of hard work and perseverance, Max and Ida came to own the St. Clair Lunch in Yonkers. The St. Clair was what was known as a "one arm joint," i.e., a sort of diner/luncheonette. It catered to the hunger of the local laborers, mostly immigrants themselves, offering early breakfasts through late suppers. In addition, there were a few cheap rooms for rent upstairs.

Sid was the youngest of the Caesar children. His older brothers, Abe and Dave, were eighteen and ten years older than he. As soon as they were able the boys were expected to help out at the luncheonette. As a youngster, Caesar had to fight to get any attention from his busy family. He began to mimic the languages he heard the various groups of workers speaking at the St. Clair. It would take several minutes for a table of Italians, Russians or Poles to realize that what *sounded* like their language being spoken by the little Jewish kid was in fact gibberish. This facility with foreign accents, rhythms and cadences was a talent that would, in later years, astound millions and reduce Sid's audiences to uncontrollable hysteria.

The Caesar family was physically very large, and being in the restaurant business probably contributed to their size. They were not making a fortune, but there was always food to eat. Although as an adult Sid would reach 6'1" and 240 pounds (Abe and Dave were both taller and heavier), as a child he felt like a midget in a world of giants, particularly as his brothers were so much older. Later these feelings of insecurity would take their toll by eroding his confidence and self-worth.

Like nearly everyone else during the Depression, the Caesars had to struggle to make ends meet. They managed to hold onto the St. Clair Lunch but were obligated to move out of their house and into a few of the "rooms-to-let" above the restaurant. There a chance encounter with a musical instrument led to Sid's career in show business. As he tells it, "Someone left an old saxophone in my father's restaurant. With his encouragement, I started to play it and found I liked it — and my first idol was Benny Goodman. I've often been glad that no one ever left a sawed off shotgun. . . ."

By the time Sid graduated from high school he was an accomplished tenor saxophonist and played with a local band at small gigs. In an effort to become a professional musician, he moved into Manhattan. He kept an eye towards classical music and "dropped in" on classes at Juilliard, hoping one day to study at the Paris Conservatory. To earn a living he worked as the doorman at the Capitol, where his imposing size helped to maintain order as well as serve as a status symbol for the movie theater.

Before long he began to get work as a saxophonist, first with Shep Fields' all-saxophone orchestra, and later with the bands of Claude Thornhill, Charlie Spivak and Art Mooney. These associations with the world of jazz may have later contributed to his antic portrayals on television of those doyens of cool, Progress Hornsby and Cool Seas (Mr. Seas was born "in 1927 on february the 68th, while my mother played bongos for Stan Kenton...").

Like many other future stars of his generation, Caesar would take summer jobs at Jewish hotels in the Catskills in order to escape New York's searing summer heat. Unlike these other aspiring comics and musicians, Sid did not have to go through a period of waiting on tables or carrying luggage while trying to get a chance to perform in the hotel's nightclub. Young Sid was already a real saxophone player. During these summers he came to be used more and more as a straight man or stooge to the comic on the bill. Since the comic was more often than not from the burlesque school of comedy, Sid would be the one to take a pie (actually it was a tomato) in the face. This sort of basic humor turned Sid off, and he never used it in his career. But he must have made a favorable impression at the time, for he came to the attention of Don Appel, the social director of Kutscher's Hotel. He and Sid began to develop original comedy material for the hotel's entertainment program.

In the summer of 1942 Appel was hired as social director at the Avon Lodge in Woodridge, New York. He made it a condition of his employment that he be allowed to bring along a "brilliant young comic" named Sid Caesar. It is interesting to note that Sid was already being thought of as a brilliant young comic who played the sax, rather than a brilliant young saxophonist who did comedy.

During that summer, Sid met and fell for the niece of the owner of the hotel. At 19, Florence Levy was a tall, beautiful, blonde, blue-eyed student at Hunter College. They were married the following summer, on July 17, 1943. In the hectic and difficult years to come it would be her intelligence, quiet determination, and patient love that would sustain them through dark periods. He would be the temperamental boy genius of television; she would be the rock that anchored them.

Caesar's wife Florence stuck with him through the good times and the bad.

In the summer of 1942 they were just two young people in love, while World War II raged in Europe and the Far East. By then Sid knew that he would be entering the Coast Guard in the fall, and although that branch of the service was considered comparatively safe, it might have produced an edge of "let us love today for who knows about tomorrow" into their romance. As it turned out, Sid was not posted to guard anything more dangerous than Brooklyn, which made it convenient for him to continue courting Florence.

When not out on patrol, Sid played sax with the base orchestra. It was there that he became acquainted with Vernon Duke, the well-known Broadway composer. Sid and Duke put together a revue of music and comedy sketches called "Six On, Twelve Off," after the hours of the Coast Guard patrol schedule.

Sometime later Duke was assigned to Palm Beach, Florida, to write a recruiting show for the Coast Guard, to be called "Tars and Spars." He requested, and got, Caesar transferred down from Brooklyn to be in the show. The meeting between the young seaman from Yonkers and the civilian director of the show, Max Liebman, proved to be a momentous occasion for the future of television.

Liebman was born in Vienna and came to the United States at an early age. Small and pixie-like, he was a showman and stage director of unusually good taste and consummate artistry. He had written material for vaudeville and by 1934 was social director for Tamiment, a hotel in the Poconos. There, in 1938, he discovered the talents of young Danny Kaye, and the following year brought a show called "The Straw Hat Revue" to Broadway. It featured Kaye, Alfred Drake, and a young, wide-eyed comedienne, Imogene Coca.

As soon as Max arrived at the rehearsals for "Tars and Spars" he began to work with Caesar, helping him to refine and polish the material and timing of his sketches. These included two monologues: a conversation between Donald Duck and a German-gibberish-spouting Hitler, and a more sophisticated satire on World War I airplane movies. The latter piece came to be known as "Wings Over Bombinschissel" and featured the archetypal bad guy German ace versus the all-American good guy hero in a suspense-filled dogfight, with Sid producing the appropriate sound effects. "Wings Over Bombinschissel" was very popular, and Caesar later reprised it in clubs and on films and television.

"Tars and Spars" was a big success and toured the country to entice young men to join the Coast Guard. A movie version was made in Hollywood and showed a young, blond Sid Caesar making his film debut. After being discharged from the Coast Guard Caesar remained in Hollywood for a short time to play a small part in a forgettable film, *The Guilt of Janet Ames*. Coincidentally, the film's star, Janet Blair, would later become one of Sid's television "wives" during the last season of "Caesar's Hour." Feeling that his career in Hollywood was progressing at a snail's pace, Sid and Florence moved back to New York. There he was reunited with Max Liebman, who helped

Sid get together a club act that was a huge success in prestigious niteries like the Copacabana and the Roxy. But Sid was unhappy in clubs, where the audience was easily distracted by waiters, chorus girls, and alcohol. Not realizing it at the time, he was ripe for a more intimate, personal medium.

Caesar made his Broadway debut in a musical comedy revue, "Make Mine Manhattan," in January 1948. The show's most popular sketch featured Caesar as an overbearing Hollywood movie director who comes to New York to shoot a film. He appears to be supremely Anglo-Saxon until he gets into a shouting match with a nosy bystander (David Burns), when his accent degenerates to reveal the immigrant glovemaker he once was. Caesar also appeared in a solo piece as a recalcitrant gumball machine. It was the beginning of a series of portrayals of inanimate and nonhuman objects which he did with breathtaking accuracy. Over the years on television Sid became a whitewall tire, a lion, a dog, a punching bag, a telephone, an elevator, a railroad train, a herd of horses, a piano, a rattlesnake, a soda water bottle, and a fly, to name a few.

By 1948 Max Liebman had become aware of the enormous potential of the little black box called television. In the summer of that year Sylvester "Pat" Weaver, soon to become vice president at NBC-TV, visited Tamiment to see Liebman's Saturday night show. Weaver was so impressed by the quality of the presentation that he proposed to Liebman to bring it to television. His only reservation, he said, was whether they would be able to produce enough material for a different show every week. Liebman's response was to invite Weaver to return week after week to see that the material was always fresh and original at Tamiment. Eventually they struck a deal and the start of a historic era in television entertainment was begun.

The show was "The Admiral Broadway Revue" and was sponsored by Admiral appliance manufacturers. Max brought in two of his talented writers from the Poconos, Mel Tolkin and Lucille Kallen. He also brought in Imogene Coca, pairing her with Sid Caesar for the first time. For the dancing sequences there was a young, talented couple, Marge and Gower Champion.

"The Admiral Broadway Revue" was broadcast live on NBC from 8:00 to 9:00 P.M. and opened on January 28, 1949. Its format was similar to what Max Liebman had been doing at Tamiment: sophisticated comedy, a lot of music and dance, solos, and group efforts.

Liebman was a pioneer and a visionary. He felt that television

Caesar and his mentor, the Austrian-born impresario Max Liebman.

producers should not pander to, nor underestimate, the intelligence of their audiences. He knew that the appeal of the broader comedy of vaudeville and burlesque was beginning to pall with the postwar public, and that they were ready for something more subtle and refined. "The Admiral Broadway Revue" and its later incarnation, "Your Show of Shows," dared produce satires on ballet, opera, or modern art.

The premiere of the Admiral show gave Sid ample opportunity to showcase his talents for the first time on television. In one sketch he displayed his uncanny facility with foreign language double-talk and accents, the skill he had developed in his father's diner. In the piece, a new coffee shop has opened across the street from the (equally new) United Nations. The owner is hoping that his establishment will prove to be popular among the delegates, but his waitress (Coca) remains skeptical. Enter the Persian ambassador (Sid) with his manservant, who places a carpet on the floor for his master to sit on. The proprietor is delighted to see his first customer until the Persian, giving thanks to Allah, consumes food and drink he has brought with him, unable to touch an infidel's comestibles. With thanks (but no money) he takes his servant and carpet and departs. Next enters the very-stiff-upper-lip British consul (Sid); in fact, his lip is so stiff that his English is nearly incomprehensible. With much pomp he recreates the excitement of fox hunting for the hapless restaurateur, but with typically English eccentricity he forgets to order anything and leaves, Tallyho! Last to enter are a group of Russians, Tovaritch Sid as their leader. The decision of what to order for lunch has to be made by committee, with Sid leading the negotiations in his inimitable Russian gibberish, with just enough English interspersed so that the audience understands the gist of his conversation. Finally they decide on "rosbif," but just to be sure, Sid goes to the pay phone to get permission from "Joe" (Stalin). The response from the Kremlin is "nyet," there will be no consuming of roast beef; they had better order *borscht!* After they accuse the owner of getting his borscht out of a can of Campbell's, they depart, conveniently forgetting to pay. It is a tribute to Sid's marvelous talent for gibberish that his English double-talk is as smooth and baffling as his performance in other languages.

On the first Admiral program Caesar also did a reprise of "A Date in Manhattan," a song he had done in "Make Mine Manhattan." It told the story of two nights on the town, one taking place in 1938, when five dollars was more than enough for a guy to take his girl on a really lavish date (taxis, drinks, dinner, a movie and a hansom cab ride through the park), and the same date in 1948 when five dollars did not even cover the cost of one taxi ride. On the first date, with the country still in the depths of the Depression, the cab drivers, waiters and movie ushers were desperate for business, and obsequiously polite. Ten years later, due to wartime prosperity, these same people were rude, sneering and snobbishly able to pick and choose from among their clientele. The song was done in a fast patter style, and although Sid did not possess the world's greatest singing voice, his breezy confidence and superb timing made this piece a joy to behold.

"The Admiral Broadway Revue" ran for 19 weeks, until June 17, 1949. It closed because Admiral, recently having entered into the manufacturing of televisions, had more orders for sets than it could handle, partly due to the success of "The Admiral Broadway Revue." The company chose to put the money it was spending sponsoring the show into expanding its manufacturing capabilities. In effect, the show was cancelled for being too successful.

By September the triumvirate of Caesar, Coca and Liebman was back on the air. "Your Show of Shows" premiered on February 25, 1950, and like "The Admiral Broadway Revue" was broadcast live from the International Theater on New York's Columbus Circle. It was the last 90 minutes of NBC's "Saturday Night Revue," the first hour of which was broadcast from Chicago and hosted by comedian Jack Carter. It was not long before millions of Americans refused to go out on Saturday nights from 9:30 to 11:00 in order to stay home and watch "Your Show of Shows."

This production was an expanded, improved version of "The Admiral Broadway Revue." It had a guest star every week (Burgess Meredith was the first) as well as guest artists from the worlds of opera, ballet, modern dance and classical music.

"Your Show of Shows" was done as a legitimate Broadway-style revue, and more than one critic stated that it was better than anything being offered on the Broadway stage. Programs were even distributed to the studio audience listing that evening's fare.

Two new actors were added to the show, and coincidentally both were hired due to their sizes in relation to Caesar. Max Liebman believed that the straight man of a comedy duo had to be taller than the funnyman. Since Sid was 6'1" this was no easy task. Carl Reiner had been performing as a "top banana" comic himself for several years in New York, and was offered the job since, at 6'2", he met the height requirement; because he was already a great admirer of Caesar, he accepted the number two spot. Howard Morris, on the other hand, was chosen because of his diminutive size. Max wanted someone Caesar could lift easily by the lapels; in Howie's case, he could do it with one hand.

Caesar's size worked for and against him in comedy. Liebman explained: "The thing Caesar has against him is the very size that gives him stamina. . . . [O]ther greats who played the part of little men actually were little men. Caesar plays the downtrodden fellow, but it is difficult to feel sorry for such a big, strong, handsome ox. It's a tribute to . . . his acting is able to overcome this. . . ."[1]

For most of his television career, Sid weighed in at 240 pounds, but he was stocky and barrel-chested rather than fat. Doing a live television show every week obviously kept him busily burning up calories, but his appetite was legendary. A typical day's meals for him might include:

Breakfast:	juice of 4 oranges 2 eggs rasher of bacon kippered herring 3 slices of bread 2 glasses yoghurt
11 A.M.:	egg salad sandwich cherry soda
Lunch:	turkey leg, wing and neck celery tonic
3 P.M.:	4 hot dogs 2 glasses chocolate milk
Dinner:	shrimp cocktail cream of tomato soup sirloin steak home-fried potatoes apple pie yoghurt

In addition to his propensity for eating, his drinking habit grew with his fame and he was known to down a fifth or more of Scotch each day.[2]

Besides Kallen and Tolkin (the latter went on to write for "All in the Family"), other new writers were added to "Your Show of Shows." Some years earlier Don Appel of the Avon Lodge had introduced Sid to a brash, skinny young kid from Brooklyn named Mel Brooks, born Kaminsky. Brooks was devoted to Sid and became his writer, protégé, alter ego and jester. Max Liebman described his first meeting with the future director of *Blazing Saddles* and *Young Frankenstein* as follows: "I first met Mel at the old Broadhurst Theater — Caesar had brought him. Sid introduced us and said to Brooks: 'Do for Max what you just did for me.' And this, believe it or not, is what Mel did: He faced the empty seats and sang:

Hello, hello, hello
I've come to start the show
I'll sing a little, dance a little
I'll do this and I'll do that
And though I'm not much on looks
Please love Mel Brooks!

Whereupon, he got down on one knee and made a Mammy-type gesture."[3] Liebman's reply was "Who is this meshugganah?" Not overly impressed, the producer refused to put Brooks on the payroll as a writer. So Caesar paid him out of his own pocket—$50 a week. When the other writers were stuck for a punch line, joke or gag, Sid would poke his head out of the door of the writers' room and put the problem to Mel who was waiting in the hallway. Brooks would fire off five or six different jokes and save the day. Eventually they put him on salary.

The other writers on "Your Show of Shows" and "Caesar's Hour" seem like a Who's Who of American comedy. There were Tony Webster, who had previously written for Bob and Ray; Joe Stein, who later wrote "Fiddler on the Roof"; Larry Gelbart, the genius behind $M*A*S*H$; the Simon brothers, Danny and Neil; Mike Stewart, who later wrote "Hello Dolly" and "Bye, Bye Birdie"; Carl Reiner, who went on to create "The Dick Van Dyke Show," based upon his experiences working with Caesar; and a teenager named Woody Allen.

Sid, too, contributed much of the show's material, and all of the scripts had to have his approval; he was a tough critic. After all, he was the one who had to go before millions of people and make it come alive. The writers' room was a frenzied, occasionally hostile place, with the writers like baby wolves snapping at each other while vying for the approval of Daddy Wolf Sid.

Caesar was a moody man, noted for his black depressions, long periods of silence, and a violent temper. It he did not like a sketch he was known to pick up a large metal desk and hurl it against the wall, or rip a sink out from its plumbing. He nearly killed Mel Brooks one day by attempting to throw him out of the window on the eighteenth floor of a hotel. At other times he could be overly generous, sweetly shy and totally sane. After killing a deer on a hunting trip he was so upset that from then on the only thing he shot at was empty Halvah cans filled with water. Yet he maintained a large gun collection and was fascinated with military history.

Caesar was not the only one in the writers' room with problems.

Caesar's German Professor. One of the most popular characters on television, the Professor was an authority on everything—and nothing.

All of the writers suffered from mother complexes, father complexes, inferiority, superiority, Oedipus, Electra and you-name-it complexes, and they all devoted at least some portion of their weekly paychecks to the psychiatrist. There was simply no other way to retain one's marbles while working in the pressure-cooker atmosphere of turning out an original, live, 90-minute show week after week.

Their psyches may have suffered, but they came up with the funny stuff. Caesar soon played one of the most popular characters on television—the German Professor (though actually he was from Austria). The Professor went by a variety of names, depending on his field of expertise, which changed weekly. He was a lovable, cantankerous, babyish authority on everything and nothing. The closest Caesar ever came to a tradition tramp-type clown was when the Professor sported an oversized tailcoat and a crumpled top hat and his German accent would have put Von Stroheim to shame. The comic foil was Carl Reiner (who not coincidentally in later years would play a very similar role for Mel Brooks' "2000 Year Old Man"), who would begin these "Airport Interviews" with: "Hello there, this is your roving reporter, Carl Reiner, at LaGuardia Airport awaiting a planeload of eminent visitors, among them the distinguished Viennese authority, — —." The airport interviews generally included the Professor telling a rather involved story with an unexpected ending, such as Professor Ludwig Von Sedative, author of "Wake Up and Sleep!":

> REINER: Doctor, would you explain to the audience in simple language the basis for your theory of sleep?
>
> PROF: Jah. Schleep is vunderbar. Schleep is beautiful. But schleep is not good to you if you is vide awake. . . . I haff a friend vunce, he could schleep anywheres. In der boiler factory, in der foundry, in a shtock yard. He could go on a train and right avay he fall aschleep. Pass all der shtations.
>
> REINER: That's wonderful!
>
> PROF: It vas lousy. He vas der engineer. He wrecked more trains, dot friend of mine.

This "interview" has a curious history. Mel Brooks wrote it but Caesar did not like it. While walking along the street together Brooks tried everything to sell the sketch to his boss, who kept saying no. In desperation the diminutive Brooks hauled off and punched the titanic Caesar in the face. After an uneasy moment Caesar's response was to look down at his minion and say, "I'll let you live." Eventually Caesar did the sketch, figuring that if it meant so much to Brooks that it was worth risking his very life, he would give it a shot. The piece worked.

Over the years the Professor assumed many aliases. Among them were:

> *Ludwig Von Pablum*, child psychologist, author of "How to Raise Your Children — Or I Don't Envy You."

> *Wolfgang Von Forever*, author of "Try Not to Die." (His secret of longevity? "At the age of 75, cut out spicy food.")

> *Ludwig Von Fossil*, archaeologist, author of "Archaeology for Everyone — Or Don't Lift Heavy Rocks."

> *Heinrich Von Heartsick*, marriage consultant, author of "Happy

Though Married" (His advice on how to keep one's wife at home: "Chain her to the radiator" and "Every five or six years tell her you love her.")

Kurt Von Close-up, European filmmaker whose movie used "One million extras, no actors."

Lapse Von Memory, memory expert, author of "I Remember Mama — But I Forget Papa."

Hugo Von Gezundheit, medical authority, author of "The Human Body and How to Avoid It."

One of the funniest Professor episodes featured Sigmund Von Fraidy Katz, authority on mountain climbing and author of "Mountain Climbing—What Do You Need It For?":

REINER: Who was the greatest mountain climber of all time?
PROF: Jim Richardson. [The name Jim Richardson seems to have held some mystic attraction for Caesar and his writers. It was often used to denote the all–American, WASPY, good guy type. During "Caesar's Hour" the movie spoofs were produced by "Sir James Richardson."] He vas der greatest. He made the record you know. He climbed der Matterhorn in two veeks, four days und tvelve hours.
REINER: Is that the record?
PROF: No, he made der record on the vay down. Ten seconds. He vas a shveet guy.
REINER: You still save that rope [tied around Katz's waist] as a token of your great respect for Hans Goodfellow [who was killed in a climbing accident]?
PROF: No. If I didn't have der rope, my pants vould fall down. . . .

When asked for advice in an emergency he replies:

PROF: Vell, as soon as you see der rope breaking . . . scream und keep screaming all der vay down . . . this vay they'll know vhere to find you.
REINER: But, Professor, isn't there anything else you can do?
PROF: Vell, there's the other method. As soon as der rope breaks, you shpread your arms und begin to fly.
REINER: But humans can't fly.
PROF: How do you know? You might be the first vun. Anyvay,

you can alvays go back to screaming. That's alvays vork-
ing for you.
REINER: Was Hans a flyer or a screamer?
PROF: He vas a flying screamer und a crasher, too.

Caesar did not need the rumpled frock coat and squashed top
hat in order to be funny. He was just as inventive and delightful in
a pin stripe business suit (although the shoulders on those suits got
wider and wider). He delivered monologues that were soon a highlight of "Your Show of Shows," transporting audiences without the
use of costumes, props or scenery, just a man in a business suit in
front of a curtain.

It was natural for audiences to identify with Caesar because he
identified with them. His monologues were more often than not on
the most mundane subjects, events that befall everyone: dating, love,
marriage, arguments, vacations, children, and the like. Caesar was
accessible to people. Unlike a wisecracking Bob Hope or an urbane
Jack Benny, Caesar seemed to be like somebody one knew from one's
own neighborhood, office, or bowling team. His monologues revealed the same insecurities and mistakes that plague us all, each of
us believing that we are the only one afflicted with these problems.
As Caesar himself put it: "People think that, out of four and a half
million people, that they're the only ones who do anything stupid.
But we're all the same person. We're all unique but we're all the
same. You can show that through laughter...."[4]

In one monologue on the subject of dieting, he endured the
same agonies as dieters everywhere:

> Look how chubby I am . . . look at my ears, how fat they are. My
> eyeballs don't even fit in their sockets any more. And look at this
> jacket. It used to be a top coat. . . . Yep, today's the day I'm gonna
> do it. . . . I gotta have will power. . . . I gotta be strong . . . and you
> gotta have a lot of strength. . . . So make me a big breakfast 'cause
> I gotta have a lot of strength to go through with this diet! . . .

On occasion the monologues became more fantastic, with Sid
portraying inanimate objects, children or animals. On December 12,
1950, he did a speech written by himself, Kallen, Tolkin and Brooks
on how the world appears to a six-month-old baby:

(Music — "Rockabye Baby")
(Business — Sleeping. Waking Up. Looking Around. Then:)

Gee, it must be late. The sun is coming up. I'm hungry. I think I'd better wake up my parents. Look at them sleeping so soundly. I gave them a pretty rough night. Four times I had the old man walk me. (Laughs a little triumphantly). Look at them sleeping.... But I'm hungry! Well here goes: (Cries a little tentatively. No response. Tries a little louder cry, no response. Lets out a whoop). That did it. Now it's gonna take them ten minutes to decide who'll come over.... Well, he lost again.... What a dummy.... He's gonna feed me the formula.... Now he's gonna test if it's too hot . . . on *my* hand. (Screams) . . . It'll be a miracle if I grow up!... Now he's gonna teach me to walk. (Has trouble with it). Just because the boy next door can walk.... But he's ten years old.... I wonder why daddy is staying home tonight.... Sunday! Today is Sunday! What a day for me! The relatives are coming to visit us.... By the thousands! What a tribe! Here they come! My uncles, my aunts, cousins.... Now I gotta put on a show for them.... Every day something different.... What was that word I said yesterday?... Now I remember! "Gaga." "Gaga." ... Look at them jumping. Look at them making somersaults.... I said a word! Six years from now I'll recite the Gettysburg Address, nobody will listen to me.... Now grandpa's going to take me on his knee. (Being jogged up and down mercilessly. Finally put down.) Now grandma is going to take me on her knee. (Being jogged even more. Finally put down.) Now they're throwing me from one to the other. (Pretty hectic.) It'll be a miracle if I grow up!... Oh, they're leaving — good! Only my little cousins — he's 7, she's 6 — they're staying behind.... They're gonna play. Darts they're playing.... Nice. (Sudden terror.) I'm the target!... It'll be a miracle!

Though Caesar never made a point of his Jewishness while performing, nevertheless it did emerge in some of his inflections and phrasing (most of the writers were Jewish as well), such as "Darts they're playing." The almost Talmudic lament of "It'll be a miracle!" is the sort of thing Jewish mothers wail when their kids are growing up. There is little doubt that this piece had a personal significance for Sid; his first child, Michelle, had been born in 1948.

One of Caesar's greatest monologues was inspired by a visit to a Greek restaurant. He had gone there on a Friday night with some of the show's writers and had seen a fly on the food. Monday morning he announced to the writers' room that he wanted to do a piece about how the fly felt. A distinct stillness greeted this suggestion; the writers were not enthusiastic about creating a sketch around a

fly. But by Saturday night's show, the idea had evolved into a master-
piece of imagination:

> What a house I live in. . . . I was so lucky to find this house. Always
> something to eat. Crumbs on the table, banana peels on the floor,
> lettuce leaves in the sink. . . . Well, I'm hungry. I'll see what there
> is in the sink. (Can't find any crumbs, not even under the toaster.)
> They cleaned up the house. It's disgusting! They must be expecting
> guests. . . . Oh well, why should I aggravate myself? So I'll eat out
> today. It won't kill me. But I hate restaurants. That greasy food! I
> keep slipping off! . . . (Buzzing on over to the restaurant, he meets
> a moth.) He's crazy that guy, eats wool. Blue serge . . . all that dry
> stuff. Yuk. And then every night he throws himself against an elec-
> tric light bulb, knocking his brains out. He's crazy. . . . (Flies on.)
> Well, I gotta get down to the restaurant. (Buzzing.) Hi ya
> Harry. . . . (Lands on the wall.) How ya been? Gee, I haven't seen
> you in a long time, since we were kids. . . . What happened Harry?
> Got married! That's pretty nice. How long ya married? Six weeks,
> that's nice. Got any children? Four and a half million, that's nice.
> 4½ million — all girls! 4½ million girls! . . . I tell you, it must be a
> pleasure to be married, all those children. . . . What's that? 4½
> million children and NOT ONE COMES TO VISIT YOU?
> (Tsking.) Buzz, buzz, buzz. . . . Well, see you around, Harry. (Flies
> off.) (Sees a sign.) Look at that. "Get the new powerful DDT. Kills
> flies instantly." Oh my, there's a lot of hatred in the world.

The genius of Caesar's talent is so awesome that he is as formidable performing silently as he is working verbally. He describes his
style as "a combination of mimicry, pantomime, farce, everything."
It was a technique he developed as a child, when he did not begin
to speak until the age of three. "A lot of people thought I was dumb,"
he says, "but I think I was just inarticulate."[5]

His pantomime, even more than the other facets of his comic
ability (monologues, characters, parodies, etc.), exemplified the basic
Caesar formula of high comedy: Exaggeration and Repetition. If a
gag is mildly amusing once, do it again and again *ad absurdum*. With
another comedian we might just become bored; with Caesar we are
at first dismayed that anyone would have the chutzpah to repeat a gag
a dozen times or more, but by the end we are convulsed with
laughter.

"The Glamour Treatment," done with Imogene Coca on February 14, 1953, begins with the lady at a beauty salon for a complete
treatment: hair, skin, make-up. Sid is the beautician. He prepares to

One of the great partnerships on television, Sid Caesar and Imogene Coca enjoyed a special chemistry together.

pluck her eyebrows, but his hand is shaking badly. Finally he begins, painfully plucking out each hair. On and on he plucks. He presents Coca with a mirror to inspect the results. She is horrified! He has removed the entire eyebrow! Never mind, he assures her, he will repair the damage with make-up. He begins to draw in the eyebrow with a pencil; above the eye, continuing onto the side of the face, slowly on down to the jaw, past the ear and down along the neck. We watch the journey of the eyebrow pencil with breathless disbelief. We cannot wait for Imogene to see what havoc he has wreaked on her face by creating the world's longest eyebrow. She looks in the mirror. Surprise! She loves it!

Exaggeration and repetition are certainly the modus operandi in "Waking Up," a pantomime about a woman getting ready to face the day. Sid impersonates a woman getting up sleepily and stretching. He loads on the face creams and emollients, teases his (her?) hair until it falls out in clumps, and puts on enough make-up to supply a circus. Watching Caesar imitate a woman valiantly pulling on her girdle against all odds is a sight to behold. The dress he dons has not one zipper but dozens. And the jewelry he loads on is so abundant that he can barely stand up. Watching a 6'1", 240-pound man in a suit and tie, with neither props nor make-up, so thoroughly transform himself into a woman by the merest of suggestions, we are left wondering if some sort of mass hypnosis has taken place.

"The Hickenloopers" ("Your Show of Shows") and "The Commuters" ("Caesar's Hour") were situation comedy sketches on domestic life. They reflected the true-to-life husband/wife confrontations of Caesar and his writers, taken to extreme. Mel Tolkin once recalled that his relatives would know whether he and his wife were getting along by watching that week's domestic sketch.

On "Your Show of Shows" Imogene and Sid were featured as Doris and Charlie Hickenlooper, an average middle-class couple who lived in an apartment on Staten Island. The sketch almost invariably began with a certain amount of exposition—Doris on the phone with her mother. Charlie would take the ferry home from work and be tired and irritable, want only to put his feet up and relax. Then the trouble would begin. He would discover, for instance, that Doris had taken in a boarder (Howard Morris in a particularly hilarious portrayal of a trumpet-playing, food-devouring Casper Milquetoast) to save money in order to rent a summer cottage. Or that Doris, desperate to climb the social ladder, had hired a maid, destroying any chance of Charlie's relaxing in a home where he had to be on his best behavior in front of "the help."

The battles between Doris and Charlie were knock-down-drag-out, and no holds barred. The famous Caesar cough, a dry, throat-clearing sound which he emitted throughout the show, was most prevalent during the Hickenlooper sketches. Caesar ascribed the cough to the nervousness of doing live television, but more likely much of it was caused by the bellowing he did as Charlie.

"The Commuters" was an upward socio-economic progression of "The Hickenloopers." Bob and Nan Victor (Sid and the talented comedienne Nanette Fabray) reflected the prosperity of the 1950s. They did not live in an apartment like Doris and Charlie, but in a big, beautiful home in "Springdale," a fictitious, affluent suburb of New York in Westchester or Connecticut. The Victors belonged to the country club, attended community board meetings and frequented expensive restaurants. Their life was the American dream come true. Coca's Doris was more overtly aggressive than Nanette's Nan Victor, who used feminine wiles and charm to get her way, rather than screaming and yelling. Bob and Nan's arguments often were over how to spend money: whether or not to indulge in new furniture, cars, or a fur coat.

"The Commuters" was Sid's idealized version of domestic life. Although the Victors had problems and disagreements, there was a Norman Rockwellish feeling to the scene—a nice house in a nice suburb with nice neighbors and a lovely, impeccably groomed housewife to come home to. The upward ascent of the living standards from the Hickenloopers to the Victors paralleled Caesar's own. In the early fifties he and Florence lived in a five-room apartment in Forest Hills, for which they paid $175 a month. Following his enormous success on television they moved first to a deluxe apartment on Park Avenue, and then bought a large house in Kings Point, Long Island, overlooking Long Island Sound and complete with soda fountain, swimming pool, an impressive art collection (Rouault, Klee, Vlaminck, Cézanne) and a huge Great Dane, Julius.

It is no coincidence that both of Sid's television "wives" on "Caesar Hour" (where Caesar was the producer and chose his own co-stars; Imogene Coca had been asked to join "Your Show of Shows" by Max Liebman), Nanette Fabray and later her replacement, Janet Blair, were both physically quite similar to Florence Caesar. It is as though Caesar was trying to mirror his own life as closely as possible on the television screen. Bob Victor, like Sid, had served in the Coast Guard. Like Sid he had also been forced by circumstances to live with his in-laws in the early days of his marriage. The major difference between the Caesars and the Victors was that the Victors had no children to deal with, while the Caesars had Michelle, Richard, and later, Karen.

Caesar and Coca in one of the great movie spoofs on "Your Show of Shows," *From Here to Obscurity.* Columbia Pictures was so incensed by the parody that it filed suit for plagiarism, but the suit failed.

The most elaborate production numbers on "Your Show of Shows" were the satires. Anything was considered fair game for a takeoff: opera, ballet, silent film, other television shows, movies. The "Caesario Opera Company" usually featured Carl Reiner as the wobbly-voiced tenor hero, Coca as the sultry diva, Caesar as the poor slob, and Howard Morris in all the character roles, from old men to impish children. Since none of them could actually sing opera, popular tunes were insinuated into the score. What may have started out as an aria soon became "Making' Whoopee" or "Just One of Those Things." By the end of the opera everyone was dead, either by assassination or suicide, and as in real opera it could take an interminable amount of time to die, and all the while singing, of course. One of the truly memorable moments in live television occurred when Caesar, while simultaneously singing an "aria" and putting on make-up as the clown "Gallipacci," accidentally drew a mark on his cheek with eye-brow pencil. Not missing a beat, he continued singing and extended the mark into a tic-tac-toe game on his face.

The movie satires of both "Your Show of Shows" and "Caesar's Hour" were showcases for Sid's accomplished talents for acting and impersonation. Columbia Pictures was sufficiently irked with the "Your Show of Shows" parody entitled *From Here to Obscurity* to sue for plagiarism but the suit was unsuccessful. Caesar was the essence of Marlon Brando in *A Trolleycar Named Desire* and *On the Docks*. His evocation of Brando included the nasal voice, the gum-chewing, the slouch, and of course the famous "Method mumble" that was Brando's alone. Foreign films were also spoofed, which provided Sid the opportunity to use his extraordinary talent for gibberish in foreign tongues as a Japanese submarine commander, a French baker, or an Italian peasant.

As innovative and energetic as it was, "Your Show of Shows" finally came to an end. Because the show was still very popular, there was much speculation on the reason for its demise. Some said it was the "goose-that-laid-the-golden-egg" syndrome, that NBC wanted to split up Caesar, Coca and Liebman to produce three hit shows instead of one. Most surmised that Caesar wanted a show that concentrated on comedy without giving up air time to music and dance, as "Your Show of Shows" had. It was also thought that Sid had a hard time sharing the spotlight with anyone, even the unassuming Imogene. In any case, a weeping Coca and a tight-lipped Caesar bid adieu to their faithful audience on June 5, 1954.

By that time Caesar's abuse of alcohol had worsened. In an effort to wean him from Scotch and other spirits, doctors prescribed the sedative chloral hydrate, which he took *with* the booze, a potentially lethal combination. Caesar drank and took drugs (Valium and other sedatives "to unwind") only after working hours. His constitution was still strong enough to withstand the ravaging effects of substance abuse during the daytime, so his performances did not yet suffer. It was at night that the cycle of overeating, overdrinking and general overindulging was constant. Though Caesar extolled the benefits of psychoanalysis to an interviewer from *Look* magazine, in fact the therapy seemed unable to help him cope with his addictions or the many insecurities and jealousies that haunted him.

Nevertheless, the show went on. After the cancellation of "Your Show of Shows," Caesar formed a production company called

"Shellric," after his first two children. When Karen was born in 1956 a "k" was added at the end. On September 27, 1954, Shellric productions unveiled "Caesar's Hour." Caesar himself was the host, assisted by Reiner, Morris and Nanette Fabray. Sid was now in control; there was much less song and dance—the emphasis was on comedy.

One of the delightful inventions of this new enterprise was "The Three Haircuts." In a takeoff of fifties' singing rock groups, Caesar, Reiner and Morris were Casey, Lacey and Dacey Haircut. Outfitted in greasy pompadour wigs (Sid's wig sat so low on his forehead that he resembled Cro-Magnon man), they had ribbon ties and falsetto voices. The lyrics to their songs were moderately asinine and endlessly repeated like a skipping record. The simplistic choreography and manic gyrations gave new meaning to the phrase "physical comedy." Reiner's feet moved so fast that they became a blur, and Morris kicked his legs out at angles that would have put a contortionist to shame. Sid's Haircut professed a blasé attitude toward their success. "We just made this record last night and it's already sold five million copies," he announced.

There were several reincarnations of the Haircuts, particularly in later network specials that reunited Caesar, Coca, Reiner and Morris. In the sixties they resembled the Beatles, with appropriate shaggy-dog wigs. In the seventies they returned as acid rockers with waist-length hair, striped bell-bottoms and triple-necked guitars. Their names had also changed with the times. Carl was Kabuki Goldberg, Howie played Lady John Edith Evans and Sid came on as Councilman Joseph Z. Zucker—"Vote for Me, You'll Get Hair!" One can only imagine how they would appear as today's punk rockers.

Another endearing character of Caesar's was Cool Seas. Sporting long black hair that stood straight up, he looked as though his finger had been in an electric socket for several years, and his mind seemed suitably frazzled as well. He wore two-inch-thick, rimless glasses, the most enormous shoulder pads known to men's fashion since the invention of football, and a perpetually spaced-out demeanor. The ultimate hipster, he held some extraordinary views:

> REINER: Have you been around the world?
> SEAS: No, I stand a foot off the ground and let the world pass under me....
> REINER: Mr. Seas, I wonder if you would play one of your new recordings for us?
> SEAS: I would be most admiredly so, [sic] sir. Here we are, this

is my latest release, on the "Prescription" label, sir. (Puts
the record on, seems oblivious to the fact that there is
no sound.) There we go, do you like it sir?

REINER: I can't hear it.

SEAS: Nobody can *hear* it! I just asked if you *liked* it, that's all.

REINER: Tell me, is that some special sort of hi-fi?

SEAS: Man, this is the hi-est they ever fi-ed! If they fi any
higher than this, they gonna *foo!* And I wanna be there
when they *do!*

Later during the run of "Caesar's Hour" Cool Seas was changed
to Progress Hornsby. Mail had been coming in from viewers com-
plaining that Cool's thick lenses seemed to be making fun of the
vision impaired. This had never been Caesar's intention, so the
glasses were removed and Progress Hornsby was born. In most other
respects the characters were the same, including the saxophone
number that Sid always did to finish the sketch. This was a charming
way for him to show his musical proficiency while remaining in
character.

Satire continued to be a major theme on "Caesar's Hour," as it
had been on "Your Show of Shows." "Bullets Over Broadway"
parodied *The Roaring 20's* and other gangster films. Sid played
Moose, the gangland leader with acute hearing ("What ears! What
ears!"). Nanette played a cigarette girl in Moose's nightclub, who also
happened to sell ammunition ("Cigars, cigarettes, bullets! Do you
want .38's or .45's, sir?"). A "good" girl from the Midwest, she had a
lot of moxie; so much, in fact, that her name was Moxie Hart. Moxie
tells Moose that she could never love him because he is so uncouth,
so Moose and "de boys" go for couth lessons with Professor Bernard
Cyranosa (Reiner). Ultimately the heroine and the professor fall in
love and Moose dies in a shoot-out with his arch rival, "Duke" Well-
ington. Yet even after his death he hears Moxie and the professor
talking about what a fine man he had been, and a smile creeps over
his lifeless face ("What ears! What ears!").

Caesar wielded such an adept hand in satire because he never
allowed the spoof to become overly magnified. He was always low-
key in his parodies; they never descended into farce or burlesque. By
staying close to the original concept of the subject being satirized, he
was able to capture its flavors and nuances without losing any of its
own identity. Caesar *became* the person he was satirizing; he let the
script be funny rather than create an absurd characterization.

"Dragnyet," a takeoff on the popular detective series, featured Sid at Sergeant Joe Borscht of the Moscow Police Department. Opening with the intro "Dos is dat city—Moskva," he and his assistant Frank Shashlik (Reiner) go after the famous vodka smuggler "Bullets" Tomachevsky (Morris), whose moll (Nanette) is busy devouring chocolates and reading cheap "Mickey Spillansky" novels. Even the sponsor of Dragnyet was purportedly Russian—"Tolstoy's Frozen Caviar," which also served well as a shoe polish and a ladies' skin cream.

In the fall of 1956 Janet Blair replaced Nanette Fabray (who had asked for more money than Sid was willing to pay) on "Caesar's Hour," and though she was pleasant as a Caesar screen wife, she was nowhere near the comedienne that Nanette had been. The show's ratings began to suffer, also due to the competition on ABC, "The Lawrence Welk Show." The handwriting seemed to be on the wall, and after eight years on weekly television Sid was cancelled, on May 25, 1957.

But fans and coworkers remained staunchly loyal. A group calling itself "Committee for Caesar Longevity" was formed, with "Don't Bury Caesar" and "Do We Get Sid Caesar or Do We Throw Away Our TV Sets?" as their mottoes. Howard Morris and Carl Reiner both refused to accept other offers for work until Caesar "set them free." Reiner went on to create "The Dick Van Dyke Show," on which he played Alan Brady, a talented, tyrannical television comedian. Morris went on to create the role of Ernest T. Bass, the troublesome hillbilly on the "Andy Griffith Show," and to enjoy a lucrative career doing voice-overs for cartoons.

Although Caesar was to return several times to the medium to which he had contributed so much, the magic was never the same. He had enjoyed continuous success since "Tars and Spars" 12 years earlier and had never had to struggle; his tremendous talent insured easy achievements. When the rug was pulled out from under him, he was psychologically unable to cope. It only exacerbated his already serious dependence on alcohol and sedatives, which in turn seriously affected his once-perfect sense of timing. Audiences who saw him during the sixties were aghast at his considerable loss of weight and haggard appearance. He once stated that timing in comedy was "like handball, as fast as the wall sends the ball back is how fast you have to react to hit it back to the wall again."[6] It seemed that drink and drugs had ruined his handball game.

Having regained his physical and mental health, Caesar is once again a vibrant performer.

After the demise of "Caesar's Hour," he did a number of short-lived television shows, including series for the BBC and ABC with Imogene Coca, and a number of specials on NBC with Art Carney, Audrey Meadows, and Shirley Maclaine. They were not critical successes, though there were flashes of the old Caesar. In addition, he returned to Broadway to play seven different roles in Neil Simon's musical comedy "Little Me," and played a number of small roles in such films as *It's a Mad, Mad, Mad, Mad World, Silent Movie, Grease I & II,* and *History of the World, Part I.*

In 1966 the Caesars sold their house on Long Island and moved to Beverly Hills. Sid entered into what he later referred to as his "Dark Period" and isolated himself from family and friends. Not until 1978 did he begin the long and arduous climb back to physical and mental health, which he accomplished with an unusual method of self-healing that involved talking to himself on a tape recorder. This technique is only recently gaining acceptance from mental health therapists.

Sid Caesar has run the gamut of success and failure, from being the boy wonder of Broadway and television while still in his twenties, to withdrawing from the world in a miasma of depression. But it is the genius who made us laugh to tears that America will remember, a genius who inspired so many others, writers and comedians, to strive to greater achievements in comedy; who showed by example that it was far better to avoid the easy laugh and go for something more meaningful: elevating comedy to a high art. Sid Caesar had an innate quality that honed in on the subtleties, the small moments in life that can translate themselves into a joyful kind of humor. He has always looked for the little curlicue.

During "Your Show of Shows" it was not uncommon for Caesar to walk into the writers' room and announce: "Let's hear the brilliance." Millions have been fortunate enough to witness that brilliance, and Sid Caesar was its shining light.

Imogene Coca

Imogene Coca, the gamine with the mischievous grin, was a pioneer on early television. Before Lucille Ball or Carol Burnett, it was Coca who proved that a woman could be a clown, make it on television, and hold her own against male co-stars. With her large, baleful eyes, elastic mouth and woebegone, vulnerable expression she elicited laughter and sympathy and admiration from her devoted fans. An established Broadway personality by the time she first appeared on television, she was to enjoy some of her greatest successes on that new medium, beguiling the public with her winsome smile and pixyish demeanor.

Baby Imogene was born into the midst of a show-business family. Her mother, Sarah Cecilia Brady Coca, known as Sadie, had been an actress and as assistant to Thurston the Magician, a well-known vaudeville act of the time. Her father, Joseph, was a musician and for many years the conductor of the Chestnut Street Opera House, a vaudeville theater in their native Philadelphia. His family, of Spanish, Cuban and Mexican descent, had originally carried the lofty name of Fernandez y Coca, but it was shortened to Coca by Joseph's grandfather who had fled Spain during the Spanish Rebellion.

Though Imogene generally gives her date of birth as 1492, her birth certificate states that she came into the world as Emogeane Coca at 6:00 A.M. on November 18, 1908, at 3009 North 11th Street in Philadelphia.

Young Coca was an only child, yet she never lacked for companionship among all the show folk around her. In addition to her parents' being in the business, Sadie's four sisters were all married to actors, and Joe's father played the bass fiddle in his son's orchestra. Despite the preponderance of performers in the Coca/Brady clan, Imogene's paternal grandmother literally fainted when Sadie announced that she was sending her ten-year-old daughter to dancing school. At the end of the term the school held a talent contest that Imogene entered with an act that she says was "a combination of Jerry Lewis and Martha Raye. I was supposed to sing and obviously I went into a panic. I must have gone berserk on stage because people laughed a lot."[1] She was such an oddity that, with her father's connections, she was booked to tour on the renowned Keith vaudeville circuit.

The following year the three Cocas moved to nearby Atlantic City, where Joe had secured a job with a local orchestra and where Sadie was happy to no longer be living with her in-laws (she also hoped that the move would cut down on Joe's gambling expenses). Imogene benefited by attending a better dance school which featured more ballet, with a strong accent on pantomime in the dance. This early exposure to mime was the seed of a talent that would blossom later in her career.

At the age of 15 Imogene and her mother came to New York— Imogene to try to make it as a dancer and Sadie to be a chaperone and stage mother. Photographs of Imogene during this period show a girl who was lovely and willowy, with a shy expression and a face that was reminiscent of a painting by Modigliani. In 1925 she was hired as a chorus girl in the ill-fated, short-lived Broadway musical "When You Smile." She was again hired for the chorus line (her small 5'3" stature did not seem to deter producers) by Jimmy Durante for his nightclub, the Silver Slipper (known to those who worked there as the Upholstered Sewer), a notorious hangout for gangsters and racketeers. In 1928 Coca appeared in "Queen High" at the Mayfair Theater in Brooklyn. In this musical comedy she apparently looked androgynous enough to play Jimmy—the Office Assistant. Imogene was now on her own in the big city, for Sadie had suffered a small stroke and gone back to Philadelphia, leaving her daughter in the care of the Sturgeses, family friends.

After the close of "Queen High" Imogene returned to working in nightclubs and for a while teamed up with a young, handsome dancer named Leonard Sillman to form a double act. Sillman later proved to be instrumental in launching her career as a Broadway artist.

In 1930 Coca got a break when she was hired as a featured performer for the last of a series of Broadway shows known as "The Garrick Gaieties," which opened on June 4 and starred Sterling Holloway and Philip Loeb. Some of the show's music was composed,

The high-stepping Coca sought a career in show business while still in her teens.

coincidentally, by Vernon Duke, who would later inspire Coca's future television partner, Sid Caesar, to enter show business. "The Garrick Gaieties" spoofed other Broadway shows, happenings around New York, and celebrities around town, such as columnist Walter Winchell and his unique style of reporting. Although not as popular as previous "Gaieties," the show did run through the summer and then went on tour. Imogene was gaining valuable experience being a Broadway "gypsy," one of the dancers who goes from show to show in order to earn a living.

In 1931 she joined the cast of "Shoot the Works," a revue written by newspaper columnist Heywood Broun to provide work for more than 100 of his unemployed actor friends during the Depression era. Somewhat like the 1975 musical "A Chorus Line," the show began with a bare stage and the chorus being selected. Contributions to the show's book and music were made by Broun, Dorothy Parker, Nunnally Johnson, Ira Gershwin and Irving Berlin. But even this impressive list of credits could not save a show that opened in the stifling New York summer in the days before air conditioning, and Imogene once again found herself "making the rounds" of the offices of casting directors, producers and agents.

Times being hard, Coca accepted the job of Patsy Kelly's understudy in a revue produced by Max Gordon called "Flying Colors," which opened on September 15, 1932. Due to the dire economic situation, the show's best seats had to be reduced from $4.40 to $2.20 for lack of an audience, but even this drastic measure could not save the show, which closed after 188 performances.

After briefly returning to vaudeville, Imogene was provided with a first-class opportunity to showcase her talents by her old dance-partner-turned-producer, Leonard Sillman, in his revue "New Faces of 1934." Sillman himself was a bit of a wunderkind, having moved to New York from Detroit at the age of 14, determined to forge a career as a dancer. At 16 he replaced Fred Astaire in the road company of "Lady Be Good." Radio wit Fred Allen once remarked on Sillman's talents as a dancer: "He was the loudest dancer in history—he sounded like a log jam in a dry river." Sillman produced his first revue at the age of 23, a production entitled "Low and Behold" at the Pasadena Playhouse in California, which starred the (then) unknown Tyrone Power and Eve Arden. In 1934 he renamed the show "New Faces" and brought it to Broadway, where he recast it with Imogene Coca and an unknown actor with penetrating good looks, Henry Fonda. Coca's salary was $40 a week and it is interesting to note that she was still being hired as a dancer, not a comedienne. It was not until her confrontation with an oversized man's coat that she went from being a gypsy to a clown. As Coca tells it:

> Everything I do is by accident. In "New Faces" I was wearing Chuck Walters' coat backstage to keep warm, and began imitating a funny little step the dancers were doing. It was Henry Fonda's idea to add Sally Rand's fan. There was no preview but it was a celebrity-packed opening night. We all walked on stage single file, and walked off again, all wearing coats.[2]

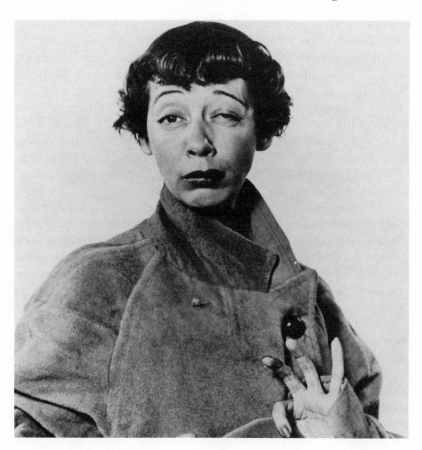

A clown is born—Coca in the oversized coat that turned her from a dancer into a comedienne.

The show was an immediate success, with the critics hailing Coca as a combination of Fanny Brice and Beatrice Lillie. A clown was born.

Leonard Sillman was one of two men who were mentor to Coca—the other was Max Liebman—giving her the time and encouragement she needed in rehearsal to develop new characters and comic ideas. Unlike many performers, Imogene has always been shy and self-effacing, never able to forcefully assert herself in the dog-eat-dog world of show business. It took a special type of producer with the patience to nurture her talent and the foresight to believe in it. Besides Coca, Fonda, Arden and Power, Sillman went on to discover and launch many budding performers—Nancy Walker, Rags Ragland, Van Johnson, Lotte Goslar and many more.

Imogene was obviously a favorite of Sillman's, and he brought her back to Broadway six more times after "New Faces of 1934," for "Fools Rush In" (1935); "New Faces of 1936" (Coca played a Cinderella who begged her fairy godmother to let her be a stripper); "New Faces of 1937" (with Sonny Tufts and Rags Ragland); "Who's Who" (Coca did a spoof on Billy Rose's extravaganzas done in the austere style of "Our Town," 1938); "Calling All Men" (1939); and "All in Fun" (with Bill Robinson. The show had a rather short run—it opened on December 27, 1941, and closed the next day).

Leonard Sillman also figured in Imogene's meeting her first husband, Robert Burton. An actor, singer and pianist whose family, like Coca's, were show people, Burton lived with his parents in New York. A big, beefy man, he had worked (like Coca's future television husband, Sid Caesar) as a doorman at the Capitol Theater. They met at a party thrown by Sillman, and again when they both appeared in "Fools Rush In" in 1935.

They fell madly in love, yet had a hard time cementing their relationship for lack of funds. Forty-eight hours after "Fools Rush In" closed, they borrowed two dollars for a marriage license and headed for Harrison, New York, where they were married at midnight with a three-piece tweed suit serving as Coca's bridal gown. Unable to afford an apartment, they kept their marriage a secret for a year while Bob continued to live with his family uptown and Imogene stayed with friends downtown. After disclosing their secret to family and friends the following year, they still could not afford a home of their own, and lived a hand-to-mouth existence in boardinghouses, cheap hotels and with any friends who could put them up. The worst humiliation came when, having been evicted from their hotel, yet again, for nonpayment of rent, they were forced to sleep for two nights on the benches at Grand Central Station, moving every hour so that the police would not pick them up for vagrancy.

One day in 1938 the young couple was walking down Seventh Avenue, out of work as usual (though Coca appeared in many shows during the thirties, more often than not they closed after a few days or weeks. Bob had less luck finding employment), when they ran into a friend who told them about Max Liebman. Liebman was looking for performers for Tamiment, the resort in the Poconos where he was director of entertainment. The friend gave Max their number and he called them that night. Liebman had already seen Imogene in a number of Sillman's revues and thought he could use her. She and Bob visited the Austrian-born impresario at his Greenwich Village apartment, and he invited them to visit the resort. As Coca recalls: "I went reluctantly. The conditions were very rough for the actors there—cots, army blankets. We met Jules Munshin who was already working there. Bob and I and Jules and Max ended up talking, drinking, and laughing late into the night. Bob and I ended up going back to Tamiment for five summers. There was a lot of Yiddish used in the sketches there (which I don't speak) so I had to use a lot of my own sketches."[3]

The writers of the weekly Saturday night show at Tamiment included Mel Tolkin and Lucille Kallen, who went on to write for "Your Show of Shows," and Sylvia Fine, an accomplished lyricist who later married Coca's fellow cast member Danny Kaye. The shows they produced week after week were so successful that Max managed to bring an assortment of sketches to Broadway in "The Straw Hat Revue," which opened at the Ambassador Theater on September 29, 1939. Brought to New York for a mere $8,000, the show was a breath of Pennsylvania's fresh air transported to jaded Times Square. The show featured Coca, Kaye, Alfred Drake and a young dancer/choreographer, Jerome Robbins. Imogene appeared in eight of the show's 25 sketches, including a Carmen Miranda spoof called "Soused American Way" that had been successful in her nightclub appearances. The show lasted ten weeks and helped make Coca a household name among Broadway cognoscenti.

Imogene had made her cinematic debut a few years earlier with a short film for Education Pictures (a cheapo film studio in New York that specialized in casting young actors on their way up and faded stars on their way down) about a bad ballet dancer. The *New York Times* described her as: "a tiny fragile girl, suggesting a slightly undernourished squab, with even larger and sadder eyes than usual, Miss Coca seemed to be trying to get a perspective on the incomprehensible world of the films." She also appeared in a short film with Danny Kaye called "A Dime a Dance" in which she played a Plain Jane who works in a dance hall and who, with the help of a judo manual, gets a shy soldier (Kaye) to propose marriage.

In 1940 Coca went to Boston to appear in a revue called "A Night at the Folies Bergère." She remained out of town to appear in "Tonight at 8:30," a Noel Coward play that had originated on

Broadway with Coward and Gertrude Lawrence. She then returned to New York and did her act in a variety of nightclubs, including the chic nitery La Martinique, where her satirical impersonations of Carmen Miranda, ballerina Vera Zorina (Coca's creation was called "Vera Farina"), Fanny Brice, Lillian Gish, Pola Negri, Clara Bow and Jane Withers made her a popular attraction. She never enjoyed working in nightclubs, however. She said, "The drunks threw things at me — salt cellars sometimes. Sometimes money. This is a terrible way to get money. Worse than being without."[4]

In 1942 Bob Burton entered the army for four years. Coca, never an aggressive, independent personality, was desperately lonely without him, and for a while returned to Philadelphia to stay with her family. She had more or less given up on a career in show business; despite her frequent periods of employment in the theater and in nightclubs, there were too many days of deprivation. In 1943 she was asked to audition for a new musical called "Oklahoma!" but did not get the part. Instead, she returned to doing her club act at such fashionable nightspots as Le Ruban Bleu. On September 26, 1944, the New York *Sun* reviewed her act: "Miss Coca has the light lunatic touch which she uses to satirize fur fashion shows and torch singers in general. Her properties include everything from a voluminous evening wrap, probably made by Worth about 1910, to jack-in-the-box toys. 'Drunk with Love,' which relates her adventures in a quaint little cocktail lounge is hilarious." Despite her dislike and fear of the clubs, she continued performing in them, satirizing everything from Phil Spitalny's all-girl orchestra to the changing vogue of Hollywood's femmes fatales.

In the summer of 1948, although loath to step into the shoes of the great actress Helen Hayes, Coca agreed to take over for her in the role of the timid librarian who lives a night of liberated, uninhibited joy in Anita Loos' play "Happy Birthday."

In late 1948 Max Liebman was putting together the television show that would premiere as "The Admiral Broadway Revue." Because he had wanted to work with Coca again after "The Straw Hat Revue," she was one of the first he asked to join his new venture. For the show's debut on January 28, 1949, she reprised a number she had originated at Tamiment and done again in "Concert Varieties," a takeoff on Vaslav Nijinsky's powerful, erotic dance, "L'Aprés Midi d'un Faun." Jerome Robbins had recreated the original Nijinsky choreography, with minor changes to make room for Coca's talents for farce. William Archibald (who later became a playwright and screenwriter) danced the role of the satyr with proper solemnity. Coca alone contributed to the piece's hilarity by a subtle mocking of the choreography and use of her prodigious talent of facial expression. In it, she tries to entice the Faun with winks, nods and beckonings to no avail, until she finally realizes that it is the scarves that adorn her waist that he desires, not herself. Coca's "L'Aprés Midi d'un Faun" was a tour de force of dance satire and understated mockery, due almost entirely to her elfin spirit.

During the first weeks of the "Admiral Broadway Revue" Coca and Sid Caesar appeared together in a few group sketches, but otherwise had no duet pieces written for them. In fact, they usually saw one another only while passing in the hallways. There was certainly no thought of combining them into a comedy team; for the most part the show's writers wrote for Sid and Imogene was left to do material she had done earlier on Broadway or in clubs. But that material could not last forever, and she began to run dry. As Coca tells it, she approached Max Liebman with an idea:

> Bob Burton [her husband] and I had a pantomime that we had done together and we showed it to Max. He liked it but wanted me to do it with Sid, and I was too shy to object. Sid looked at me suspiciously at rehearsal (after all it was *my* material). It was about a boy and a girl sitting on a doorstep, they go to the movies, a woman behind them bothers them.... Also, Rags Ragland had given me his version of "Slowly I Turn," the old burlesque routine, which I had done in "New Faces." I didn't want to do it on TV, it was too corny, but it worked [Coca's version featured her as a young girl from "a little town outside of Chicago — San Francisco" who attempts to kill herself by jumping off of a roof, and Caesar as the good Samaritan who tries to stop her, only to nearly end up going over the edge himself]. After that Sid told the writers to write for both of us. And we've never had an argument in all the years we've worked together.

It would seem an unlikely pairing: the 5'3", 110-pound Coca with the strapping 6'1", 200-pound-plus Caesar, but some magic took place that no one was ever able to explain. Each seemed to know instinctively what the other's next move was going to be. Coca's diminutive impishness was a perfect complement to Caesar's towering strength, something that was not achieved by any of Caesar's other television "wives," no matter how deft they were at comedy.

Imogene and Sid enjoy a moment backstage at "Your Show of Shows." Many who saw them appear in husband-and-wife scenes every week believed they were married to each other in real life as well.

After the "Admiral Broadway Revue" segued into "Your Show of Shows," the partnership continued to flourish. Many Americans were under the impression, seeing Sid and Imogene enact husband-and-wife scenes week after week, that they were married to each other in real life as well. Coca referred to herself as "the only socially acceptable bigamist in the United States." Although they spent hours together in rehearsal and on stage, they did not see each other a great deal after work. Caesar usually ate and socialized with Carl Reiner and the other writers; Coca felt more at ease with her fellow gypsies, the show's dancers.

Besides Coca and Caesar, the other great partnership on the show was Coca and choreographer/dancer James Starbuck, and they collaborated on some of the finest dance satires ever done on television. As she had done with "L'Aprés Midi," Imogene leaped and arabesqued her way through parodies of "Giselle"; "Swan Lake"

James Starbuck and Imogene Coca rehearse one of their dance sequences for "Your Show of Shows." The two collaborated on some of the finest dance satires ever done on television.

(in which she used her swan wings as Sally Rand used her fans); "Sleeping Beauty" (where the princess prefers to go back to sleep rather than stay with the handsome prince); and "Les Sylphides," where two dancers discuss everyday matters while going through the motions of the ballet:

COCA:	I went to Nora's party last night.
STARBUCK:	How was it? Who was there?
COCA:	Nobody who was anybody. . . . Nora introduced me to a man. A toothpick manufacturer. . . . Five minutes after we were introduced, he asked me up to his place to listen to symphony records. I told *him!*
STARBUCK:	What did he say?
COCA:	I said: "Listen Mr. Ludlow, don't go getting any ideas just because I'm in the ballet."
STARBUCK:	So what did he say?

COCA:	He said: "I only want to show you my collection of records."
STARBUCK:	So what did you say?
COCA:	I said: "Listen, if you were Ezio Pinza and you wanted to give me a *private concert,* I wouldn't go after only knowing you for five minutes!"
STARBUCK:	So what did he say?
COCA:	He said: "All right, don't go. See if I care."
STARBUCK:	So what happened?
COCA:	He has a very nice collection of records.[6]

The Coca/Starbuck ballet send-ups were eminently successful because they remained faithful to their source. The ballets were done as realistically as possible, with credible corps de ballet, costumes, scenery and choreography. Only in the execution of the dance steps was the audience shown the satiric side of the presentation and then it was not done with gross caricature or buffoonery, but with small motions of ineptness and missteps as well as Coca's marvelous facility to convey confusion, impishness or wantonness with her pliable face. "We did not burlesque them," Coca states firmly. "We satirized them."

Like Caesar, Coca had a tramp character who appeared regularly. Unlike the German Professor, however, Coca's tramp delighted audiences through the use of song and motion, not dialogue. Imogene had seen tramp characters for years in vaudeville and had admired the antics of tramp/clown Joe Jackson. Reminiscent of Chaplin's "Little Fellow," Coca's tramp danced her way through a variety of situations that invariably tugged at the audience's heartstrings. She was ably abetted in these numbers by Jimmy Starbuck's portraying a number of foils: a scarecrow, a store window dummy, a janitor.

In the final episode of "Your Show of Shows" Coca reprised a favorite number with her tramp done to the tune "Wrap Your Troubles in Dreams." In this simple vignette the homeless, ragamuffin tramp meets up with the snobby doorman of an expensive apartment building (Starbuck), and they engage in a charming waltz until he regains his composure and she is wheeled off in the cart of a street cleaner. The scene was so touchingly poignant that a New York *Herald-Tribune* critic reported:

> She hadn't much to work with. She was dressed as a tramp and was singing the song to a rather stuffy doorman. She has that rare facility of singing a song as if she not only understood the words but

meant every word of it. The number ended with a little dance which was just great; no smaller word would apply. Then the door-man blew his whistle; a street cleaner came up with his little cart and Miss Coca made a perfectly wonderful exit perched on the cart.

It was a very sweet, heart-warming number with just an over-tone of mockery to keep it from getting too sticky. And it was the sort of thing that sticks to your ribs, a number that you may recall with pleasure long after it's over. How many song-and-dance numbers can you recall ten minutes after they're finished?

Opera was another target for Coca's uncanny sense of satire. She was able to send up the imperious nature of the opera diva with the raising of an eyebrow. Even as a child she had astonished and delighted her parents with her version of a one-eyed opera singer, dropping her left lid like a theater curtain and belting out her impression of a soprano's wobbly coloratura.

On "Your Show of Shows" she poked fun at grand opera with a rendition of the well-known aria "Du Bist Mein Herzen's Leibe in the Sheida of the Old Apple Tree." She was also hilarious as the singer attempting to escape the noxious fumes of the garlic-eating tenor's breath in a comic version of "Lucia di Lammermoor." In "Rigoletto" she played a last-minute replacement for the soprano for a touring opera company in Idaho who attempts to impress the handsome tenor, played by Bill Hayes. In the opera satires, as in the ballet sequences, there was no overt burlesque, just wonderfully subtle comic devices.

Having been trained in pantomime since her childhood ballet lessons, she was able to take part in the silent sketches with Caesar like an actor takes to applause. Whether they were two people fight-ing over the same subway seat, a jealous married couple at a cocktail party, or an indecisive customer and a shoe salesman, they were able to convey to the audience—without the whiteface or stylized gestures of the traditional mime—the difficulties of their absurd situations. Not since Laurel and Hardy were two actors so attuned to each other, and the audience, on a seemingly extrasensorial level. Coca did not do as many solo pieces as Caesar, but seemed to be at her best as a comic foil and complement to his character.

In the many spoofs of silent films done on "Your Show of Shows," Coca could be counted on to give an outstanding performance as the vamp, rolling her eyes in the most leeringly seductive fashion since

Coca—an unlikely vamp, but a charming clown.

Mae West: an incongruous gesture considering Imogene's decidedly unsexy figure. But she was always delightful as the decadent siren who is the cause of Caesar's downfall, dripping with jewels (gifts from him) while she wrecks his family and career with lustful enticements. When his money is depleted she hard-heartedly shows him the door ("I have a quarter left," his screen title reads. "Can I hold your hand?"), leaving him a ruined man.

In the domestic comedy series "The Hickenloopers," Coca was the social-climbing Doris to Caesar's lumbering Charles. Doris was always searching to improve their situation in life; Charles just wanted to work, have dinner, watch television and go to bed. In her quest for an improved life-style, Doris drags her husband to a French restaurant, a concert, or to the theater. She tries to bring the refined and exotic into their mundane Staten Island existence, only to be brought back to reality by Charles and his unromantic demands.

When Doris manages to get Charles to attend the symphony for an evening of classical music, he grouses the whole time:

> COCA: Oh, look! In the second half of the program they're play-ing Tchaikovsky's Pathetic Symphony. Tchaikovsky had a very pathetic life, you know. When you hear his music, you actually feel all the pain and agony and torture and misery.
>
> CAESAR: I got my own aggravation. I don't have to come here and listen to his torture.
>
> COCA: You'll enjoy this. Look ... the musicians are taking their places.
>
> CAESAR: [Listens] He must've had a miserable life.
>
> COCA: They're just tuning up.

Doris and Charles would always manage to find fault with one another. He would call her a lousy cook ("Who boils bread?" he would shout); she would nag him about his cigar smoking. On one oc-casion he complains about her stubbornness, and as usual she has the last word.

> CAESAR: You and your stubbornness! Stubborn, stubborn, stub-born! Why don't you apologize?
>
> COCA: You apologize!
>
> CAESAR: I should apologize? For what? What?
>
> COCA: You know.
>
> CAESAR: I'll never apologize for that!
>
> COCA: I think it's absolutely ridiculous for two grown-up peo-ple to act like children. Let's talk it over, discuss the whole thing from your point of view, look at the situ-ation like adult people, and then we'll find out that I've been right all the time![8]

Of the three actresses who would become Caesar "wives" over the years (Coca, Nanette Fabray and Janet Blair), only Imogene presented such a formidable adversary to her husband's bullying. Ironically, in real life Coca was probably the biggest shrinking violet of the three; she was painfully shy, overwhelmingly modest ("Somebody once told me that paying me a compliment was like taking a cold shower," she says. "Sometimes I think maybe he might have been right!"), and swamped with phobias. She has always been terrified of airplanes, cars (especially taxis), elevators, boats and just about anything else that moves. She was never able to stand up for herself in her professional life, leaving Caesar to take charge of the writers and the show's weekly material. All of the writers except Lucille Kallen were men, and it was not until many years after the show's demise that Coca came to the conclusion that she and Kallen may have been given short shrift by the atmosphere of male clubbiness and macho that pervaded the show's sanctum sanctorum, the writers' room.

Even at the expiration of "Your Show of Shows" in 1954, Coca was not treated with the respect and courtesy she merited:

> I had heard rumors that the show was going to close, so I finally managed to sit Max and Sid down to talk about it, but they wouldn't say anything. The next day I was in rehearsal and the Public Relations man came to get me (I knew it had to be important for them to interrupt a rehearsal) and took me to a small room full of cameras and people with flashbulbs going off. I was asked "How do you feel about the show's closing?" That was the first I knew about it and I started crying.[10]

In addition to the end of "Your Show of Shows," Imogene had to deal with troubles at home. After his release from the army in 1946 Bob Burton had not returned to being a performer, but entered a number of professions, none of which seemed to succeed. He tried his hand at leading a band, being a record company executive, and managing his wife's career, but as much as Imogene's star was in its ascendancy, Bob's was going nowhere. More and more he took to alcohol to ease his frustrations. He was always supportive of Coca and her success but was unable to find his own.

After the Caesar/Coca/Liebman triumvirate split up, Imogene was given her own show in October 1954 by NBC with a one million dollar contract, payable over the next ten years. The show was broadcast on Saturday evenings from 9:00 to 9:30, taking over part of the spot vacated by "Your Show of Shows." Unlike Sid Caesar, Coca had little interest in taking charge of the production details of the show; she had enough on her hands at home with her mother and husband being ill. "The Imogene Coca Show" was a mistake from the beginning. Done in a situation-comedy format, it lacked any of the vitality and spontaneity of either "The Admiral Broadway Revue" or "Your Show of Shows," and, of course, everyone was making comparisons. Hal March, a good-looking, leading-man type who had gained the public's attention as the moderator of "The $64,000 Question," was brought in, at Coca's suggestion, to play what could only be construed as the Sid Caesar role. But neither he nor anyone else could save this endeavor, and the show folded after one season. Like Caesar, Coca gave up the remaining monies ($900,000) owed on her contract, which would have prevented her from appearing on any other network.

The year 1955 was a bad one for the hapless Imogene. In addition to the closing of her show, she was burdened by the illnesses and deaths of the two people closest to her: Bob Burton died on June 17, 1955, at age 46, within a few weeks of the death of Imogene's indomitable mother, Sadie Brady Coca. As she tried to cope with their attendant medical bills, the IRS came after her. Under tremendous strain, she had dreamed of being able to escape the pressures of the world and take a vacation in Cape Cod, but it was not to be; she had to go back to work. In April 1956 she entered a hospital for 36 hours. The newspapers reported that she had attempted suicide by taking an overdose of sleeping pills, which she denied, saying only that she had slipped while polishing the floor in her home. Later in the season she was back at work, replacing Claudette Colbert in the play "Janus" on Broadway.

In the summer of 1958 Coca and Caesar had their first professional reunion when they went to London to tape 13 half-hour episodes for the BBC. "Caesar's Hour" had been shown in England, so the British public was aware of Sid's talents, but no one knew who his tiny partner was. She was reviewed separately from Sid and given excellent notices (his were less than enthusiastic). Coca enjoyed herself immensely in London and wanted to stay on; however, she had already contracted with Broadway producer Alfred de Liagre to return to the stage in "The Girls in 509," and as usual she was too shy to ask to be relieved of her promise.

It is just as well that she did return to do that show, for she fell in love with a fellow cast member, veteran actor King Donovan. They went on tour with the show and were married, after he obtained his divorce, on October 17, 1960.

Earlier she had been invited to join Caesar, Howard Morris and

Carl Reiner in the first of several reunions of the stars of "Your Show of Shows," in a half-hour production on ABC called "Sid Caesar Invites You." It is indicative of Caesar's ego problems at the time (complicated by his addictions to alcohol and drugs) that his was the only name in the title. Like most attempts to recapture the magic of an earlier era, this one failed. According to Coca, Caesar was rarely at rehearsals (he used a stand-in until taping), and he seemed so manic all the time that she feared he was going crazy.

After her marriage to King Donovan, she moved to California for six years to help raise his three children. She and her new husband were (and remained until his death in 1987) very popular on the regional and summer stock theater circuit, generally acting together. Coca's many phobias had never left her, and unfortunately by moving to California she added earthquakes to her list of dreaded fears. In 1966 Imogene and King were appearing at a dinner theater in Dallas when she decided that it would be more prudent to remain in Texas rather than go back to the San Andreas fault, and she and her understanding spouse relocated to the Lone Star State for five years. (Unfortunately, on the night they moved into their new home a tornado struck, giving the frightened Coca more fodder for her fears.)

During the sixties, in addition to guest-starring on a number of television programs, Coca starred in two situation comedies, neither of which was very successful. In "Grindl," Coca played a maid sent out on temporary jobs by the Foster Employment Agency, the stories depicting her attempts to complete her assigned duties. The show ran for 32 half-hour episodes on NBC beginning in September 1963.

"It's About Time" had an unlikely plot about a family of cavemen in modern day America. Coca co-starred with Joe E. Ross in this loser that ran for 26 half-hour episodes on CBS beginning in September 1966.

On New Year's Eve in 1973 Coca and her husband were driving near Tampa, Florida, when Donovan inadvertently ran a red light, resulting in a crash which caused extensive injuries to the comedienne. As she tells it: "I was sleeping in the front seat with my seat belt on. I'm deathly afraid of riding in a car, incidentally. When the crash occurred, the side of my head hit the rear view mirror mounted on the dashboard. Maybe nothing would have happened to me if I had the shoulder strap on, but I've never learned how to put the darned thing on."[11] Donovan had her flown to New York in order to put her in the care of the best specialists. She underwent extensive facial surgery, but they were not able to prevent the loss of sight in her right eye. It seemed that one of the timid Coca's many phobias was finally justified.

Recuperation took some time, but in 1978 Coca returned to Broadway as the eccentric, religious fanatic Letitia Primrose in the musical comedy "On the Twentieth Century" with co-stars John Cullum and Madeline Kahn. Although the role was not a large one, she was considered by most to have stolen the show.

Always a "gypsy" at heart, Coca and Donovan continued doing tours around the country of various plays, most notably D.L. Coburn's two-character work "The Gin Game," about the loneliness of an old-age home. In addition, she joined Sid Caesar in a rather lame production for HBO called *A Touch of Burlesque,* and she was the only redeeming feature in the banal *National Lampoon's Vacation,* with Chevy Chase.

Well into her seventies, Coca remains as spry as ever, still enthusiastic about work in films or theater, still flashing the same goofy grin and elfin expression with which she began in vaudeville more than 60 years ago. Between tours she lives in New York with an assortment of dogs. She has no thought of retiring; her love of the stage and her zest for entertaining are too great. Still modest to a fault, willing to give an interested listener the benefit of her many years in show business, she has disproved the old axiom that nice guys finish last. No matter that it may have happened unintentionally, Coca was a trailblazer for comediennes on television, a gentle soul who delighted her loyal fans. Having come to terms long ago with the fact that she was not a classic beauty, she made full use of the rainbow of expressions her vulnerable and elastic face could convey. From the day she donned an oversized man's coat in the backstage area of a chilly Broadway theater, Imogene Coca has searched for and developed the clown within herself, and has lovingly shared it with the world.

Tim Conway

Tim Conway is one of those extraordinary talents whom television has produced, but television has been unable to sustain him in his own series. A phenomenally funny man, he seems to have shone to best advantage as a supporting player to other comedians, while often stealing their spotlight. His sense of character and comic pacing are extremely accurate, and his physical expression harkens back to the films of Harold Lloyd or Harry Langdon. In off-camera interviews he reveals himself to possess a caustic, tongue-in-cheek wit, while remaining very much the modest, self-effacing Midwesterner.

Born Thomas Daniel Conway, he later changed Tom to Tim because there was already a mustachioed actor named Tom Conway, the brother of actor George Sanders. Tim was born on December 15, 1933, in Willoughby, Ohio. His father, Dan, was a horse trainer-turned-tinsmith of Irish extraction; his mother, Sophie, was from a Romanian family. Conway grew up in Chagrin Falls, a suburb of Cleveland with a population of 3,000. Conway describes it as "a Tom Sawyer kind of place."

Conway's childhood was uneventful in this quiet hamlet, but it was obvious even then that he had a swift sense of humor. As he told an interviewer from *TV Guide:* "Somebody would ask, 'Who was the fourth President of the United States?' and I'd say, 'Not *my* dad.' People laughed. Nobody noticed I had no idea who the fourth President was. Acting helps overcome personal embarrassment—you are embarrassed by your looks, or your intelligence, or your background, or whatever."

After graduating from Chagrin Falls High School, Tim went on to become a radio-television major at Ohio State University at Bowling Green. After college he spent two years in the army, during which time he behaved much as the bumbling character he later portrayed in "McHale's Navy," Ensign Charles Parker. He recalls that "I was stationed in Seattle in a section that was responsible for sending out troops as replacements to bases in the Far East. I was a private at the time but I had to keep the books on all of the shipments. In one month I lost 7,500 men, but that was my worst month. In the average month I lost only about 1,500. Of course, I had other troubles, too. There was the time when a unit in Korea needed two cooks. Somehow, they received 350 of them."

After his ineffectual stay in the U.S. Army, and following an unsuccessful stint as nightclub comic with a partner in Seattle, Tim returned to Ohio and landed a job with a local television station. He soon became the producer-director of "Ernie's Place," starring Ernie Anderson. Their limited budget forced Tim to join in as a performer: "We didn't have enough guests to appear on the show every day, so I'd turn on the camera and jump into the scene with Ernie." The show was apparently not very popular with the local notables it was supposed to be interviewing. "The show was so bad the celebrities we were supposed to interview wouldn't show up. We'd say the Mayor was going on the show. The Mayor'd call up and say, 'Are you out of your skull? I wouldn't be on that show for money.' We'd say, 'The Mayor just called and is on his way.' He'd call back and say, 'Mention my name one more time and I'll have you arrested.' We'd say, 'The Mayor just walked in but he's late. We won't have time to interview you today, Mayor. Too bad. See you tomorrow.' The audience soon got on to us."

While he was up to these shenanigans on "Ernie's Place" he was spotted by Rose Marie, the comedienne who would later star as Sally Rogers on "The Dick Van Dyke Show." She recommended the chubby Conway (at this time his 5'8" frame was carrying 200 pounds; in later years his weight would fluctuate between 160 and 180 pounds) to Steve Allen. Soon Tim was invited out to Los Angeles to perform on "The New Steve Allen Show," where in 1961 he became a regular on the show, along with Louis Nye, Pat Harrington, Bill Dana, and the Smothers Brothers. One of Tim's most enduring characters on the show was as Doug Hereford, who might one week be "The World's Fastest Draw" and another "The World's Greatest Detective," or "The World's Greatest Racing Driver."

The year 1961 brought another big step in Tim Conway's life: He married his godmother. Actually, the circumstances for such an unusual event were explainable. Three years earlier, mostly at the urging of a girl he was dating, Tim decided to convert to Catholicism.

When the priest asked him who would be his godmother, Tim suggested the girlfriend. The priest demurred; in case Tim should ever marry the girl, he did not want Conway to be marrying his own godmother. Instead the priest suggested a friend of theirs who had come along to witness the ceremony. She turned out to be Mary Anne Dalton, whom Tim married on May 27, 1961.

From September 11, 1962, to September 7, 1965, Tim portrayed Ensign Charles Parker in the naval sit-com "McHale's Navy." Co-starring Ernest Borgnine as Lieutenant Commander Quinton McHale and Joe Flynn as Captain Wallace B. Binghampton ("Old Lead Bottom"), the show owed much to the Phil Silvers "You'll Never Get Rich" armed forces comedy format. Conway often stole the show as the feckless, bumbling Parker (Conway was nominated for an Emmy as Best Supporting Actor for the 1962–63 season), and Parker became the standard for the type of character Conway would portray in situation comedies and films for the next 25 years. "McHale's Navy" gave rise to two films in which Conway co-starred, the first also entitled *McHale's Navy,* (Universal, 1964) and *McHale's Navy Joins the Air Force* (Universal, 1965).

Conway once again played a dim-witted, awkward character in "Rango," a western comedy which struggled along as a midseason replacement from January to June 1967. In it, as the title character, Conway played a useless Texas Ranger struggling to do his job with the help of Pink Cloud, his corrupt Indian assistant, played by Guy Marks. The reviews and the show's ratings were equally dismal.

On February 5, 1969, Tim Conway was part of television history when he hosted "Turn On," produced by "Laugh-In's" George Schlatter. The show was promoted as "a visual, comedic, sensory assault involving . . . animation, video tape, stop-action film, electronic distortion, computer graphics, even people." The show's regulars were to include Chuck McCann and Hamilton Camp, but apparently the sketches contained so many double entendres that it was considered tasteless and objectionable. The opening sketch, for instance, featured a beautiful woman standing before a firing squad. Instead of asking her if she has any last requests, the squad leader says, "I know this may seem a little unusual, miss, but in this case the firing squad has one last request." The inference certainly seems tame by today's standards, but at the time it caused such a furor that the sponsor, Bristol-Myers, withdrew its support, as did many of ABC's affiliates, and the network cancelled after the first show.

Conway embarked upon the first of several endeavors entitled "The Tim Conway Show" on January 30, 1970, a 30-minute situation-comedy on CBS. Once again Tim traded on his talents as a hapless inadequate, this time as Timothy "Spud" Barrett, the pilot of "Lucky Linda," a decrepit plane owned by the irascible Herbert Kenwith, played by former "McHale's Navy" co-star Joe Flynn. The story line, created by Gail Parent and Kenny Solms, dealt with the small charter company's struggle to survive, but the reviews were not good and the mid-season replacement was cancelled on June 19, 1970.

Conway was back, however, the following season, on another "Tim Conway Show," this time a 60-minute variety show that debuted on September 20, 1970, at 10:00 P.M. The premiere was presented as a Christmas show. "I've never had a show that lasted till the holiday season," he explained, and "This time I'm taking no chances." Conway was only half joking. He'd been cancelled so many times that he got special license plates for his car that read, "13 WKS." "The way I understand it," he announced, "They're going to make me do it til I get it right."

This time the reviews were considerably better. Jack Gould of the *New York Times* reported on September 21, 1970:

> [Conway] started very well, presiding over an hour of offbeat variety that, given sufficient discipline, could be a click of the season. He is basically low-key in demeanor and savors under-stated wackiness, which the experienced director, Bill Hobin, capitalized upon with a deft touch.
>
> Mr. Conway, always looking slightly pained and uncertain . . . tried to convince prospective Kamikaze pilots of the delights of los-ing their lives by dive bombing and did a wonderful slapstick take-off on a midday gourmet who could never achieve a gallop in the kitchen.

The show's regulars included MacLean Stevenson, Sally Struthers and Art Metrano, but in spite of the energetic perfor-mances of the cast the show was cancelled, after 13 weeks, on December 28, 1970. At least it made it to Christmas.

Conway's many attempts to succeed at his own show are in-teresting to note, but he will probably always be best known for his regular guesting on "The Carol Burnett Show." Starting in 1975 he became a member of the troupe, including Harvey Korman, Vicki Lawrence and Lyle Waggoner, who made up the supporting group

Conway is one of the funniest men on television, but he is unable to have his own show last more than 13 weeks.

Top: The dynamic duo—Harvey Korman and Tim Conway on "The Carol Burnett Show." Conway's excellent work on the show earned him three Emmys (in 1973, 1977 and 1978) as Best Supporting Actor in a Comedy. Bottom: Tim Conway as the little old man who moves only slightly slower than a snail.

of players on Burnett's show. Korman, in particular, was a perfect foil for the craziness Conway was likely to get into. Tim was known for improvising during the scene, or at least not revealing all of his intentions during rehearsals. It became one of the show's trademarks for Korman to lose control at least once during his interplays with Conway, cracking up before millions of viewers. Conway was so outstanding on the Burnett show that he won Emmys in 1973, 1977 and 1978 (beating out the immensely popular Dan Aykroyd and John Belushi) as Best Supporting Actor in a Comedy. He was also nominated for the years 1974, 1975 and 1976.

Conway had several characters that he repeated over the years on the Burnett show. The best known was probably Mr. Tudball, a woeful Swedish businessman with a slipping toupee, who tries to teach his moronic secretary, Mrs. Wiggins (played by Burnett) the basics of doing her job. Operating the intercom was beyond her capabilities, much to Mr. Tudball's frustration, and her shorthand never seemed to progress beyond "Dear Sir."

Conway's other well-developed character on the show was the little old man who moved along at a snail's pace. Shuffling his feet an inch at a time, this diminutive, ancient fellow was seen in a variety of jobs from fireman to butcher to orchestra conductor. No matter what occupation he was engaged in, his lack of pace invariably infuriated Harvey Korman as the straight man.

Conway's home life continued in a serene manner until 1978. By then he and Mary Anne had five children: Kelly Anne (b. 7/30/62), Timothy Dalton (b. 10/13/63), Patrick (b. 12/5/64), Jaimie (b. 9/22/66), Corey (b. 11/11/68), and Seann (b. 8/8/69). Their home in Encino was comfortable without being ostentatious. In November of 1978 he and Mary Anne were separated, however, with Tim moving to bachelor quarters nearby.

Over the years Conway made a number of movies, almost all of which pointed to how wasted his talents were in these second-rate endeavors. Several films co-starred another Steve Allen alumnus, Don Knotts, including those made for Disney Studios. His films included *The World's Greatest Athlete* (1973), *The Apple Dumpling Gang* (1975), *Gus* (1976), *The Billion Dollar Hobo, They Went That-A-Way and That-A-Way* (both 1978) and *The Apple Dumpling Gang Rides Again* (1979). He also wrote the screenplay of *The Longshot* (1986) about four small-time horse bettors, starring Jack Weston, Harvey Korman, Ted Wass and himself.

In March 1980 Conway attempted one more "Tim Conway Show," a 60-minute show produced by Carol Burnett's husband, Joe Hamilton, and scripted by Burnett writers. Not surprisingly, many of the reviews called it "the Carol Burnett Show without Carol Burnett." In March 1983 Conway switched gears and appeared in a sitcom, "Ace Crawford, Private Eye," in which he played an American-style Clouseau. The show got terrible reviews and was cancelled.

In many ways, it is a mystery why this supremely funny man, a fine physical clown and a comedian's comedian, cannot survive in a variety or sit-com format. Some say it is because he is more suited to being the perennial second banana; that he cannot mastermind a show in which he is the focus. But he has done too much good work, even on shows which have ultimately failed, to prove this point. More likely than not the networks simply do not allow him enough time (that is, beyond 13 weeks) to develop his routines and build up an audience. This gentle, balding, cross-eyed, pudgy man is one of the gifted funnymen of the airwaves, and television would be richer if it could accommodate his talents.

Jackie Gleason

In the 1950s Jackie Gleason was the personification of the American dream come true. From the lowly origins of the streets of Brooklyn to the zenith of conspicuous consumption, he tantalized the average American with the fanciful possibility of what could be. His most obvious feature, his girth, was a symbol of prosperity and the good life. With a glass of Scotch in one hand and a beautiful show-girl in the other, he was the epitome of the hail-fellow-well-met, a good time Charlie always ready to buy a round of drinks, crack a few jokes, and greet every stranger as "pal."

Yet behind the facade of the public Gleason lay a more private personality. Occasionally brooding, fiercely intellectual, and sometimes confused, he was dubbed "The Great One" by those who knew and respected him. Gleason the king held court on our television screens for more than 21 years, an amazing time span considering the burnout nature of the medium, and dispensed his talents in regal proportions.

Herbert John Gleason was born on February 26, 1916, the second son of Herbert and Mae Kelly Gleason. His brother Clemence had been born nearly 11 years earlier. The family lived in a tenement on Herkimer Street, in the Bushwick section of Brooklyn. Gleason's father worked in the Death Claims department of the Mutual Life Insurance Company in downtown Manhattan, his salary so meager that he sold candy bars to the other employees to supplement his income.

Jackie's mother was a pretty, gay colleen of only 15 when she married, and Jackie inherited her good looks and bright blue eyes. Mae had high hopes for her family and yearned desperately to escape the sordid existence of life in the slums.

Tragedy struck the struggling Gleason family when Clemence, always a sickly child, died at age 14, when Jackie was three. From that

"The Great One," circa 1950.

time on Mae placed all of her hopes and adoration on her remaining child. His father also cared for him and on occasion took little Jackie to the Halsey Theater in Brooklyn to see touring vaudeville shows and movies. Gleason remembers that these early visits to the theater with his father may have engendered his later love of performing. "I thought it was sensational. When the lights went on for intermission I got up, turned around and faced the audience. That was even greater than watching the guy on stage."[1]

Despite an outward tranquility, all was not well within the Gleason family. It was not uncommon for Jackie's father to go on periodic binges with the bottle. On occasion he would disappear on Friday afternoon with his week's wages and drink until Sunday night, consuming the impoverished family's sole source of funds. Mae got into the habit of taking Jackie into Manhattan to wait outside her husband's office building, hoping to head him off before his serious drinking could begin. One can only speculate on the traumatic effect this experience had on the young boy.

In time his father's behavior became more and more erratic. He fraudulently secured a $150 loan by forging his wife's signature. One day he brought home the family photographs that he kept on his office desk and flushed them down the toilet. He then went through the family photo album and destoyed all of the pictures of himself. The next day, December 15, 1925, Herbert Gleason left his office as usual at lunchtime and disappeared, never to be seen again. The sole clue that he was still alive surfaced some years later when his only brother died and a wreath was sent to his wake signed "From Your Loving Brother." His disappearance was never solved. It is possible that Jackie's father became one of the nameless, faceless men who populate skid rows and transient hotels, always trying to scrape together the last few pennies to purchase a bottle of liquor. If Jackie's national fame later was known to Herbert, if indeed he was still alive to see his son on television, we will never know, for he never came forward.

Mae Gleason carried a heavy burden in her life: one son dead, a husband who had deserted her, eight-year-old Jackie to care for — and no money. She took a job as a subway cashier for the Brooklyn Manhattan Transit Line (the BMT). The pay was low and the long hours were lonely, but for a woman who had never had to support herself this was the best she could do. Gleason often recalls the day he saw his mother wrapping his old leggings on her legs against the bitter winter cold. He vowed to be better behaved for her sake.

Not that young Jackie was a bad boy, but he did hang around with groups of buddies on the streets and in playgrounds. It was more fun to be down with "the guys" than to concentrate on schoolwork. In the classroom at P.S. 73 he was known to fight with his teachers. "I was irritating. Why, I don't know. I know what I did but I'm puzzled as to why I did it. I would sit back until Miss Pappen or Miss Caulfield or Miss Miller would make a point to the class, then I would get on my feet and argue with them. I would tell them that, by coincidence, I had just been reading up on that subject and that the authorities did not agree with them. They would try to shut me up and I would tell them that they were losing their tempers because they were wrong."² This absolute need to be in the right was something that would be the bane of his comedy writers and production staff in the years to come.

After graduating from P.S. 73 he attended high school for all of two weeks before dropping out. To his mother's dismay, Jackie had decided to become an actor. To fill his days he hung out with friends at the local pool hall, where he quickly became proficient at the game and often earned a tidy profit by playing for money.

Due to their diminished circumstances, Gleason and his mother moved several times, always searching for a cheaper apartment. They finally settled down on Chauncey Street in an apartment within what was known as "Dennehy's flats" where Tom Dennehy (pronounced DUNN-a-hee) and his wife Anna were the building's superintendents. The Dennehys and their children, particularly their daughter Julie, who became Jackie's first girlfriend, were to remain lifelong friends of Gleason and his mother, often lending the deserted wife enough money to tide her over until payday. Millions of Americans were to become acquainted with the Dennehy name in later years while watching the "Joe the Bartender" soliloquies, when Mr. Dennehy became the silent listener, the camera.

As a teenager Jackie began appearing in the amateur night talent shows held at the same Halsey Theater where his father had taken him as a small child. He was very popular with the crowd (it was, of course, to his advantage that his schoolyard buddies were in the audience) and was soon promoted to emceeing the amateur acts as well. For this he earned several dollars and the admiration of the audience, with the exception of his mother. Mae Kelly Gleason never felt that show business was a worthwhile profession for her son, especially since she did not find him particularly funny.

At age 19, yet another tragedy struck Jackie. His mother died of erysipelas, an infectious disease caused by streptococcus bacteria that result in inflammation and fever. She was one day short of her fiftieth birthday. This was a staggering loss to Gleason, leaving him virtually orphaned with no job, no prospects, and no money. The BMT contributed $250 to pay for the funeral, for there was no insurance. Friends and neighbors came forth with food and flowers. Yet when it was all over, Jackie was left truly alone in the world. To make matters worse, on the day his mother was buried Jackie had to go on stage and be funny in his new job as emcee at the Foley Theater.

What kind of young man is it who can endure such tragedy and deprivation in a short lifetime and yet pull himself up by the proverbial bootstraps to forge a career in comedy? Jackie Gleason proved himself to be such a fellow, and it was the same grit and determination he showed on the night of his mother's funeral that sustained him through hard times and prosperous times and ultimately kept him at the top of his profession for many years. Gleason may not have been, laugh for laugh, the funniest man on television, nor the most inventive or clever, but through sheer guts (both literally and figuratively) he thrust himself into the popular culture.

In 1935 Jackie made his break into professional comedy (as opposed to the amateur shows he had been working in until then) as master of ceremonies at a dive called the Club Miami in Newark, New Jersey. Newark is and always has been a tough waterfront town, playing host to merchant seamen and petty gangsters. Gleason had a tough audience to please, so he became tough right back at them. He developed an insult patter that played off the audience, always improvising and ad-libbing to get a laugh. Years before Don Rickles turned the insult joke into a high art, Gleason was learning that it was the only way to survive in front of a group of cannibals, and they loved him. On one occasion Jackie began trading insults with a heckler in the crowd. One thing led to another and soon the entertainer and the spectator agreed to meet in the back alley to settle the affair with their fists. What Gleason did not find out until too late was that his opponent was the prizefighter "Two-Ton" Tony Galento, who quickly scored a knockout on Jackie's tender chin.

Although Jackie was still a comparatively thin young man, his famous appetite was beginning to show itself. According to Gleason's biographer Jim Bishop, after Jackie's show at the Club Miami,

> Gleason and Tony [Amico, Jackie's close friend, roommate, and future valet] went down the street to a cafeteria at 4:30 A.M. and ordered a pot of beef stew. Sometimes Jackie asked the waitress to drop a ball of ice cream into it. There was another place, called the Ideal Restaurant, which was a hang-out for vegetarians. The M.C. did not patronize the place until he saw a sign outside: "All you can eat for fifty-five cents." He and Tony went inside and ate triple portions of every vegetable on the counter (Gleason alone finished two packets of seed rolls). When they walked out, the sign came down.[3]

Food and comedy were not the only things that preoccupied Gleason. He became infatuated with Genevieve Halford, a sweet, blonde, Catholic girl who worked as a nightclub dancer. They were married on September 20, 1936. The bride was 19, the bridegroom 20. The wedding party was held at the Club Miami, with Jackie doing much of the entertaining. For a honeymoon Genevieve moved into Jackie's room at the boardinghouse where he lived.

Jackie and Gen shared a devotion to the Catholic faith. The problems that were to divide them later on stemmed from her belief in the dogma of the church that did not leave room for tolerance for his more private devotion to God. Although Gleason had always been amenable to performing at Catholic charity benefits and was a close personal friend of Bishop Fulton Sheen, he also maintained an interest in things outside the church's teachings: parapsychology and psychic phenomena, for example. Gleason would eventually own one of the largest private collections of books on these and related subjects. But in the thirties and forties his growing interest in these topics seemed to Genevieve to be heresy and blasphemy against the church.

Soon after they were married, it became obvious that Jackie had outgrown the Club Miami. For a while he performed in a number of New Jersey nightspots, including one in Hoboken where a subsequent entertainer was a young unknown, a skinny Italian singer named Sinatra. The life of a nightclub performer encouraged Jackie's already overly generous nature, and he was always signing tabs to buy others drinks, having a good time until all hours of the night and spending money he did not have.

With the birth of their first daughter, Geraldine, on July 31, 1939, Genevieve tried to impose a normal family existence. She wanted her husband to leave show business with all its insecurities and settle down at a real job to support his family. Having to stay alone with a baby every evening until her husband, usually having had a good deal to drink, came home during the wee hours of the morning did not provide for a harmonious relationship.

Jackie got a big break when he was hired to appear at the Club 18 at 18 West 52nd Street in Manhattan, a street known for its nightclubs and jazz joints. No more playing in the suburbs; this was the big time! There he was up against the pros, playing to the more sophisticated downtown audiences. Club 18 was known as a celebrity hangout, and the famous were not immune to Gleason's verbal barbs.

One night Sonja Henie, the Olympic ice skater and movie star, was out front. Without a second thought Gleason plucked an ice cube from his drink and, handing it to Henie, snarled, "All right, honey, do something."

Two significant events befell Gleason in 1941. His daughter Linda was born on September 16 and Jack Warner, the Hollywood movie mogul who had caught Jackie's act at Club 18, hired Jackie and gave him a $250-a-week contract. This was a lot of money, as well as a first-class opportunity for the boy from Brooklyn, so he headed west, leaving Gen and the two girls behind.

Unfortunately what transpired was not the success and adulation that Jackie expected, but a series of unremarkable roles in unremarkable films: a sailor in *Navy Blues*, a gangster in *All Through the Night*, Betty Grable's manager in *Springtime in the Rockies* and a bass player in *Orchestra Wives*. He was not catapulted to stardom. However, one of the advantages to being in Hollywood was the chance to meet other actors and comedians. In *Navy Blues* Jackie worked with Jack Oakie, who became an inspiration to the young comic/actor, and whom Jackie later referred to as "my personal Knute Rockne." The two shared certain similarities of size and mannerisms, and some of Gleason's critics have insinuated that Gleason stole a number of Oakie's shticks. It is quite possible that as a Hollywood newcomer, young Gleason would adopt some of his hero's characteristics in order to emulate him. It would certainly not be the first time, nor the last, that one comic would take what he could from another.

Part of Jackie's problem in Hollywood was convincing producers and directors that he was a *comedian*. His parts were never big enough to show off his comic talents. Gleason began doing his act at a nitery called Slapsie Maxie's, named after pugilist Max Rosenbloom who appeared there nightly. Jackie was very well received by the audiences, which often included the same producers he was trying to get better acting jobs from during the day. His appearance at the nightclub encouraged his boozing and womanizing until the early morning, but he always managed to be at the studio by 8:00 A.M. if he was on call for a picture. As was his habit in New York, Jackie continued to pick up the tab for all his drinking buddies, and often Gen and the girls were lucky if they saw anything from either one of his paychecks, from Warner Bros. or Slapsie Maxie's.

Even with working days at the studio and nights at the club,

Gleason's career seemed to be on hold. California did not appear to offer much promise for the young comedian, so Jackie returned to New York and his family. Although to some people absence does indeed make the heart grow fonder, in this case it promoted only more animosity between Jackie and Gen. There were bitter recriminations for his continued high living while his family waited in vain for support. If he had been a big success in Hollywood Jackie might have been able to withstand the arguments. However, he was crestfallen over his failure to take the movie world by storm, and it all became too much for him. He and Genevieve separated for the first time, and Jackie moved into a hotel room.

Meanwhile, he scoured New York for work. He appeared in several Broadway musicals (not his Broadway debut; a few years earlier he had been in a musical revue with Jimmy Durante) in supporting roles in "Along Fifth Avenue" and "Artists and Models," neither of which was a long-running hit. In 1945 Gleason's luck changed and "Follow the Girls" was a smash, although it was more of a musical burlesque than a true musical comedy. Gertrude Neisen played burlesque queen Bubbles La Marr, who goes to work in a servicemen's canteen as part of the war effort. Her hapless suitor, Goofy Gale, played by Jackie Gleason, was forced to sneak into the canteen in the drag outfit of a WAVE, due to his 4-F status. The show's slightly racy songs and leggy chorus line guaranteed its popularity with visiting soldiers and sailors, and the show ran for two years.

His steady paycheck of $600 a week enabled Gleason to indulge his carousing and barhopping. Toots Shor's soon became the comedian's favorite hangout. Toots himself was not exactly svelte and over the years Gleason and he would engage in insult-flinging matches over who carried more avoirdupois, who could run farther, who could drink the most. On more than one occasion Shor carried Gleason's tab when the portly comic had overspent himself. As Jim Bishop relates:

> When Gleason's bill began to creep above $800, Jackie told Shor that he wouldn't sign any more checks.
>
> "Who's asking you for money, you creep" said Shor with manly affection. "If you're tired of signing your own name, sign mine."
>
> "Okay" said Jackie, and immediately invited some friends for dinner. When it was over, he studied the check and marked down a ten dollar tip for the waiter. "I'd have made it more, my boy" he said to the waiter, "but you know how cheap Toots is."[4]

After the close of "Follow the Girls" Gleason returned to being a nightclub comic, playing some of the most prestigious clubs in New York: the Ritz, the Palace, and frequent returns to his old haunt, Club 18. As a stand-up comic he was at the top of his profession. If he was not as well-known as the very popular Milton Berle, he did at least have a certain following and was able to command up to $1000 a week for his talent. His reputation was growing, yet he found it difficult to take the next step to big-name stardom. As can happen in show business, Gleason was sometimes unemployed for weeks, but he would always manage to live the good life of booze, restaurants and chauffeured limousines. More often than not he would have a large outstanding tab at these establishments, especially at Toots Shor's.

In an attempt to keep working, Gleason went back to California and Slapsie Maxie's. But in 1948, as in 1941, Hollywood did not sit up and take notice of Jackie Gleason. He gained a not undeserved reputation as a hell-raiser and a two-fisted drinker. His weight was down to 178 pounds, which made him handsomer and healthier, but Jackie always found it harder to be funny when he was thin. His girth became the embodiment of his persona. As a circus clown relies on his make-up or Harold Lloyd needed his glasses to become his character, Gleason used his outsized stomach like a mask. When he was thin he no longer had it to hide behind, and the joke was lost. The best thing that happened to Jackie in Hollywood on this second trip was that he gained George "Bullets" Durgom and Jack Philbin (later to produce Jackie's television shows) as his managers. They helped Gleason make his debut in the new medium that everyone was talking about (but few people owned), television.

"The Life of Riley" premiered on October 4, 1949, on NBC. Unlike most early television it was not done live but on film. Also starring Rosemary DeCamp, it featured Jackie as Chester A. Riley, a sweet, lovable boob who had to deal with family and friends. The show, with a classical situation comedy format, had been successful for some time on radio with William Bendix. Originally the producers had sought Bendix for the television version as well, but as a movie actor he had a contract that forbade him any work on television. Not until 1953 was Bendix able to work out his contractual difficulties and assume the role of Riley.

Bendix's unavailability worked to Gleason's advantage. He did 26 episodes of "The Life of Riley" and although he was somewhat miscast as the good-natured but dumb Chester, it was at least an opportunity to be seen by more than nightclub audiences. As personalities, Chester and Jackie were diametrical opposites; Jackie was the womanizing, boozing smart aleck who used a great deal of blue material in his act; Riley was the innocent, straitlaced, hardworking family man. Gleason was well liked in the role, but not enough to continue in the series.

Once again Jackie returned to Hollywood and Slapsie Maxie's. He had not been back long when he was asked to appear as the temporary emcee and comic on Dumont's hour-long variety show, "Cavalcade of Stars." Previously Jack Carter, Jerry Lester and Larry Storch had been hosts of the program, but the producers were looking for someone more lively and engaging. An emissary was sent to California to look Gleason over and offer him the job for a period of two weeks at $750 weekly. Though wary of television after only moderate success on "The Life of Riley," he agreed to return to New York and do the show (on the condition that he be hired for four weeks), fully expecting to be back at Slapsie Maxie's in a month.

One of Jackie's first contributions to the show was to bring in June Taylor, a talented young choreographer he had met some time before. She hired six long-legged female dancers to act as a mini–chorus line (the show's budget and stage size did not permit more than six girls in the troupe), and they were used in the show's exuberant opening. Gleason had learned his lesson well when he was in "Follow the Girls" on Broadway; a bunch of scantily clad beauties can keep even a mediocre show going strong, and he kept the dancers on all of his shows in the years to come.

The show's writers were comprised of two teams: Arnie Rosen and Coleman Jacoby, and Joe Bigelow and Harry Crane. The producer was Milton Douglas (the sponsor was Whelan Drug Stores and the rumor was that one was paid off in toothpaste); the director, Frank Bunetta.

Jackie Gleason premiered on the hour-long "Cavalcade of Stars" on WABD (the station's call letters stood for its founder, Allen B. Dumont) at 10:00 P.M. on July 8, 1950. He was 34 years old. After all the struggling since his mother's death 15 years earlier—years of boardinghouses, owing money, holding onto the fringe of success by his very fingernails—Jackie Gleason was about to become a household name. His earlier experience with television had been anticlimactic: As Riley he had played a role; on "Cavalcade," however, he was himself, The Great One, in all his glory. In addition, Gleason had always been at his best when appearing in front of an audience, as he had been doing in nightclubs, rather than on film, as he had been in his few cinematic attempts and on "Riley," and "Cavalcade" had a live studio audience. Gleason was a resounding success when he opened on "Cavalcade"; he was so funny even the writers laughed, a rare occurrence.

For the second show an actor was needed who could act as Gleason's foil. Someone recalled that there was a funny guy appearing on Morey Amsterdam's show as Newton the waiter, a skinny fellow named Art Carney. Carney came aboard the Gleason bandwagon for what was to be many fruitful and often hilarious years. Art had a sweet, self-effacing type of personality, in contrast to The Great One's gregarious, take-charge attitude, and the two hit it off beautifully. Unlike his overweight friend, Carney had no desire to be on the writing or producing end of things; he was content to receive his script, rehearse his scenes, and be as funny as possible.

The second show was as big a hit as the first one, particularly one sketch with Jackie as that inimitable drunken playboy, Reginald Van Gleason III, and Carney as a photographer hired to shoot him for a whiskey advertisement as "The Man of Distinction." By the end of the sketch, of course, both photographer and subject are too drunk to accomplish anything, having tested the product far too liberally. The show's sponsors, reassured that Gleason's triumph on the first show was not a fluke, offered him a two-year contract at $1,500 a week. Ironically, Gleason was earning the same as his rival and role model for many years—Milton Berle was earning $1,500 a week at CBS on "Texaco Star Theater," and both Gleason and Berle were making payments to estranged wives and children out of their salaries, as well as paying managers, agents and taxes.

"Cavalcade of Stars" gave rise to many of the sketches and characters that would become Gleason regulars, perhaps the most enduring of which was "The Honeymooners." Starting out as a short sketch, the idea was to portray the lives of an average working class stiff and his shrewish wife. Ralph Kramden in his bus driver's uniform and his wife Alice in her worn apron were like many people Gleason had known in Brooklyn, barely able to make ends meet on a meager salary. Their apartment on Chauncey Street was almost identical to the one that Jackie had shared with his mother on the street of the same name. Alice had no more modern convenience than the out-

Gleason as Ralph Kramden. The New York bus driver was both a bully and a loudmouth but had a heart of gold.

dated icebox with the drip pan underneath, few furnishings and no luxuries. Ralph relies on shooting pool, going bowling and belonging to his men's fraternal organization (the Raccoon Lodge) for amusements. By the end of a long day, when Ralph comes home from driving a bus up Madison Avenue all day and Alice is tired from the tedium of keeping house in her drab environment, they are cranky and irritable and cannot help bickering with each other. Yet love and tenderness and selflessness sustain them.

Much has been written about Ralph Kramden as Everyman, and "The Honeymooners" has become a cult favorite and trivia buff's delight.[5] But from 1950 to 1952 Jackie, Pert Kelton (an actress from

Montana who originated the role of Alice Kramden but because of a heart condition was forced to retire and relinquish the role to the inimitable Audrey Meadows), Art Carney (as Ralph's good buddy and neighbor, sewer worker Ed Norton), Joyce Randolph (in the role of Trixie, Ed's wife, originated by Elaine Stritch) and the show's writers could not have known that they were beginning a ritualistic portrayal of American life. The Kramdens had obviously been left behind during the economic upswing of the Eisenhower years, when moving to the suburbs and owning a home were not only hoped for, but expected. The opportunities of the American dream were not within the grasp of the Kramdens or the Nortons or many other families like them, so they remained firmly entrenched at the bottom of the economic ladder.

All of this is not to say that Ralph did not try to climb that ladder. Often he came up with schemes that were surefire, no miss, get-rich-quick: the Handy Housewife Helper (a do-it-all kitchen gadget); lo-cal pizza; glow-in-the-dark wallpaper and many other brainstorms were dreams that went up in smoke for the hapless Kramden, leaving him in the same boat as when he started, if not worse off. Fortunately Alice was patient and loyal and forgiving of Ralph's overzealousness and obstinacy. Norton usually went along for the ride on these endeavors, willing to leave the details and responsibilities to Ralph, but when all was said and done Ralph returned to driving his bus and Ed went back down to the sewer.

Gleason was known to drive the production staff to distraction over his refusal to rehearse—he felt it made him stale. As he had a photographic memory, he was able to riffle through his script a few times and have it down cold for performance. This habit was particularly frustrating to his co-actors, who were used to rehearsing a scene, but since everyone knew who was the star of the show, he was indulged in his unusual practice. In any case he was quite right; by not overrehearsing the cast was able to bring a fresh, spontaneous air to the show, often improvising and ad-libbing their way over the rough spots. On live television, this represented a risky gamble, not unlike walking a razor's edge. On "The Honeymooners," for example, the cast made it a practice to return to the kitchen table if they forgot

Opposite: The immortal cast of "The Honeymooners": Jackie Gleason as Ralph Kramden, Audrey Meadows as Alice Kramden, Art Carney as Ed Norton and Joyce Randolph as Trixie Norton.

their lines or lost the thread of the plot. The table became a safe harbor for those in trouble on the rocky seas of live television.

In addition to Ralph Kramden and the Honeymooners, Gleason and his writing staff created several characters with which Jackie would delight his audiences. He cleverly reckoned that television viewers would become bored watching the same comedian over and over again from week to week, no matter how funny that person was. The characters allowed Jackie to escape his own larger-than-life persona and form an amalgam of Gleason the man and performer.

Reginald Van Gleason III was the ultimate profligate—a drunken, spoiled, effete son of wealthy parents. Gleason played him with a flowing black cape, eyes at half-mast and a Chester Conklin moustache. Reginald is suave and debonair; he definitely has class. He is not above buying a new car because the old one points in the wrong direction. He is the kind of booze-swilling dandy, a bachelor who chases pretty girls, that Gleason must have dreamed of becoming in the days when "all-you-can-eat" vegetarian restaurants represented a good deal. Reggie is a wastrel, a roué and a hedonist who intends to enjoy as much of life's pleasures as he can—not unlike Gleason himself, who was not happy about recognizing the similarities between himself and his creation. "He's the drunk," said Jackie. "You'll notice he always combs his hair flat, because he hasn't got the time to fool around. He has no regard for his parents because he's only interested in what they'll provide him to continue his drinking. And he has no appreciation for anyone's dignity but his own. He's always wearing formal clothes because he associates them with his most enjoyable moments."[6]

The Pour Soul was the most sensitive and touching of Gleason's portrayals. This nameless, silent, baby-faced bumbler owed much stylistically to the great film comedians, particularly Harry Langdon. Both Langdon and the Pour Soul were wide-eyed, innocent babies trapped in the bodies of grown men. Jackie held a soft spot for his silent clown. "The Poor Soul is the most saint-like of my characters. He accepts the harshness of life without complaint, and never fights back. You'll observe he wears a sweater and a lot of buttoms. These give him a sense of security. His many buttons suggest he can lock himself in, womblike."[7] Not much is known about the Pour Soul except that he has no family or worldly possessions, that although he means well he usually manages to exasperate those with whom he comes in contact, and that over and over again he must deal with a cruel, uncaring world where small pleasures are to be savored. As Gleason's only pantomime character, the Pour Soul had to be acted using body language, gesture and facial expression. Infantlike, he clenches and unclenches his fingers as though trying to grasp onto the air for support. His bug-eyes stare with exaggerated awe at the world around him; his awkward gait propels him from one pathetic situation to the next. The Poor Soul was the saddest of Jackie's creations, and even when the improbable dilemmas in which he found himself made us laugh, it was with a bittersweet feeling. The Pour Soul was able to move us perhaps more than any other comic television character because he was so psychologically attuned to Jackie's own nature. It has been said that Reginald Van Gleason III represented Jackie when he was happy/drunk, and the Poor Soul when he was sad/drunk, but it is more likely that Reginald symbolized the cynical side of Gleason and the Poor Soul the innocent side. In 1961 Gleason reprised a Poor Soul kind of character in *Gigot,* a film written and scored by himself and directed by Gene Kelly. The movie was filmed in Paris and centered on Gigot's love for a little girl, a waif in the streets of the French capitol. The film, maudlin and sentimental, had moments of real warmth and emotion, as well as some fine acting by Gleason, but the critics were not kind.

Joe the Bartender was the most realistic Gleason character. Based upon the father of a boyhood friend, this friendly publican presented Gleason at his most relaxed. He had spent many hours in bars such as Joe's and knew well the easygoing male camaraderie and bravado that existed there. Joe addressed the unseen Mr. Dennehy (the camera) as an audience for his monologues. Joe was the typical neighborhood philosopher: ready to give advice on any number of problems, bemoan the ills of the world, recount a memory. Like Jackie he was gregarious, occasionally short-tempered, generally easygoing—a real man's man. Joe's stories were his raison d'être, often recalling the adventure of his neighborhood cronies: Crazy Guggenheim, who loved to crash wakes (in the years to come Frank Fontaine was known to millions as the mug-faced, slightly imbecilic Guggenheim who surprised folks with his rich baritone voice), or "Bookshelf" Robinson, whose nose was so big he rolled over in his sleep one night and got it caught in his ear—when he sneezed he nearly blew his brains out (the real Thomas "Bookshelf" Robinson was one of Jackie's schoolyard buddies, so-called for his devotion to his studies. Mr. Robinson later became vice-president of Pace College).

Gleason (as Charlie Bratton) pesters Carney (as Clem Finch) at the lunch counter.

Jackie played Joe with his hair parted down the middle, slicked down, with spit curls on his forehead, giving him a gay nineties look. The apron was worn high, right under the armpits, possibly in an attempt to hide his ample girth in a show of vanity. Although Joe's watering hole in Brooklyn was a far cry from the elegance of Toot Shor's authentic establishment in Manhattan, and although Toots certainly did not stand behind the bar as did Joe, nevertheless the two shared the same comfortable atmosphere for heavy drinking, raucous laughter and male companionship that Gleason so enjoyed.

Gleason had other characters that he did less frequently and who eventually disappeared from his repertoire. Charlie Bratton was the archetypal loudmouth, a know-it-all who had to be in the right. He was inspired by a relative of Jackie's called Uncle Fat, who used to drop by and flash a wad of bills to his young nephew. Charlie delighted in any opportunity to torment his friend Clem Finch, a fussy Felix Unger type played to perfection by Art Carney. It was not unusual for Charlie and Clem to meet at a lunch counter and for

Gleason as Fenwick Babbitt, during the two-year run of "Cavalcade of Stars" on the Dumont network.

Bratton to destroy his friend's appetite with "What's that slop you're eating?" as a greeting. Charlie wore a straw hat, chewed a cigar, and often scowled.

In temperament, Fenwick Babbitt was a cousin to the Poor Soul. A harassed clerk, he was a bumbler and loser and had a natural naivete of which people took advantage. Stanley R. Sogg was the late night television pitchman for assorted merchandise such as Mother Fletcher's Pastafazool, Homely products ("For you girls with heavy thighs, a cowbell"), or the booklet *How to Slide Downhill on Your Little Brother.*

By the time Jackie's contract with Dumont had expired in 1952 he was a huge success, rivaling such established comedians as Milton Berle and Red Skelton. It had become obvious that he had outgrown the facilities and financial capabilities of the small station and was ready to join a larger network. In 1952 Gleason signed a three-year contract with the Columbia Broadcasting System to bring "The Jackie Gleason Show" to the public every Saturday night from 8:00 to 9:00 for 36 weeks a year, effectively avoiding any conflict with the popular "Your Show of Shows" on NBC at 9:30. Unlike Jackie's employee status at Dumont, he was now head of "jackie gleason enterprises" (always printed in lower case), which put the show together as a package and sold it to the network. Now Gleason was not only responsible for being entertaining, but he assumed the administrative duties of hiring and firing, financial budgeting, technical requirements—in short, all aspects of production. A lesser man might have been daunted at the prospect of doing all this without even having attended high school, but not Jackie. He succeeded through sheer energy, a great deal of native intelligence, and the wisdom to surround himself with first-rate advisors, technicians, writers and assistants.

The costs of the show were $50,000 a week for the production, $70,000 for the airtime, and $7,500 for the star. This larger budget allowed for such luxuries as a large office and apartment complex in the Park Sheraton Hotel at 56th Street and 7th Avenue, increasing June Taylor's chorus line to 16 girls (How do you get so many legs to fit into the camera's viewfinder? Easy, you shoot them from above, and the result is kaleidoscopic), and engaging a full orchestra and music arranger. Professionally Gleason's life was taking off.

The same could not be said for his private life. Despite the attempts Jackie and Genevieve made, at the urging of the Catholic clergy, to repair their rocky marriage, it simply could not be done. Her nagging depressed him, and his womanizing and boozing infuriated her. Try as they might to preserve their marriage for the sake of their daughters and their religion, and despite a two-year reconciliation from 1949 to 1951, their efforts were in vain, and in 1952 they obtained a legal separation.

Their problems were complicated by the fact that Jackie had fallen for one of the statuesque dancers on his show, June Taylor's younger sister Marilyn. A sweet-faced blonde, she remained patient in view of Jackie's refusal to seek a divorce because of his Catholicism. The situation came to a head on January 30, 1954, when Gleason was in the hospital with a broken ankle incurred on the show. Marilyn was at his side administering tender loving care when Genevieve arrived unannounced—the scene was not pleasant. Marilyn was unwillingly cast into the role of the other woman, Gen was the indignant, outraged wife, and Gleason waffled his way through the situation with as much aplomb as Ralph Kramden's "Hmena, hmena, hmena." The press soon heard about the confrontation and splashed it across the front pages. Shortly thereafter Jackie and Marilyn split up; there seemed to be no future for her as Mrs. G so long as he resisted getting divorced.

In addition to his marital difficulties, Gleason continued to gain weight at an alarming rate. He got into the habit of maintaining three wardrobes for his 5'11½" frame—for weighing in at 185, 240 or 280 pounds. The first group of clothing was rarely worn. He was known to devour an entire lasagna before breakfast, and dinner could be 12 oysters, spaghetti with meat sauce, two pounds of roast beef with mashed potatoes and gravy, vegetables, and dessert, with a mountain of food in between. Radio wit Fred Allen once remarked that if Gleason had been a cannibal, "he'd eat up the whole neighborhood." Periodically Jackie would check himself into Doctors Hospital for a near-starvation diet, drop a few pounds, and then return to his normal eating habits, with the predictable result of gaining back all the weight he had lost and then some. Coupled with his nonstop cigarette habit, which could reach four or five packs a day, and his prodigious consumption of alcohol, it is amazing that Jackie remained as relatively healthy as he did.

Gleason himself seemed perplexed by his gargantuan appetite. "Why am I overweight?" he wondered. "It might be that I'm troubled. Everyone who's overweight—with the exception of some glandular cases—has some insecurities. It doesn't have to be anything of depth. It can be a small insecurity . . . the scenery didn't arrive, the jokes didn't turn out well, or the barber cut your hair wrong. Or that bum over there [Khrushchev] might drop the bomb. And then you hop into the icebox and pick up a cream puff. And Khrushchev disappears."[8]

In exasperation Gleason's doctors recommended that he see a psychiatrist to deal with his overeating. His reply, as he later recalled it, was "If you think I'm going to walk into his office and have everybody saying there goes Gleason to be analyzed, you're nuts. Have him come see me. This is against a psychiatrist's better judgement, to see the patient. But he did come. And he weighed 285 pounds. The first time he was there I tried to find out what was wrong with him. He came back a second week and hadn't lost a pound. So I let him go." It would have been a case of "the fat leading the fat," he said.

Food was not the only comestible that contributed to Gleason's size. His drinking continued to amaze even his barroom cronies. He was frank about his drinking: "I've said it before and I'll say it again. I never take booze to stimulate my appetite. Or to quiet my nerves. Or to get some sleep. I take booze only for the ancient and honorable purpose of getting bagged!" Alcohol did serve its purpose, though: "Drinking can remove warts, wrinkles, pimples and blemishes. Not on yourself—on other people."

While wowing audiences on CBS Jackie indulged his love of music by composing and conducting more than 30 albums on the theme of love and romance, with such seductive titles as "Music for Lovers Only," "Music, Martinis and Memories," "Aphrodisia," and "Music to Make Her Change Her Mind." These records sold in the millions on the Capitol label, in spite of the fact that Jackie was not a musician and could not read or write music. His method of composition was to hum a melody of his invention into the ear of an expert arranger, who would write it out. Gleason had a musical vocabulary all his own—if he had a glissando in mind for a musical passage he would say, "Gimme some pussycats." He used the same method of composition for the theme of his television show, the "Melancholy Serenade."

By the mid-fifties Jackie Gleason's image, mannerisms and idioms were American passwords. "You're a dan-dan-dandy bunch!" "How sweet it is!" and "And away we go!" with his trademark "traveling walk" could evoke The Great One as surely as his picture on the screen. In 1954 Buick deserted Milton Berle as sponsor and joined the Gleason camp, with an $11 million contract for three years. In 1955 Gleason taped 39 half-hour episodes of "The Honeymooners" on the Dumont Electronicam System, unaware that they would continue to be shown through all the years to come on local stations across the country. He certainly could not have known that "The Honeymooners" reruns would inspire nearly fanatical, cultish devotion from large segments of the public, until no small piece of trivia connected with the show would escape the eyes and memories of its admirers. He declined to continue doing the show beyond the first year because he felt the situation was getting stale and could only become more contrived. In 1956 he returned to his usual format of a live 60-minute show in which "The Honeymooners" was one segment, and continued to feature Art Carney, Audrey Meadows and Joyce Randolph.

Despite a hiatus on the small screen from June 1957 to October 1958, Gleason continued his relationship with CBS when he returned in a half-hour version of "The Jackie Gleason Show." By this time, however, Art Carney had left the show to seek other opportunities and was replaced by Buddy Hackett. In addition to shortening the length of the show, the network changed its air time from the usual Saturday night to Friday evening. The loss of Carney, 30 minutes, and his normal time slot was more than the show could take. It lasted only one season, but Gleason received a 15-year $100,000 contract that tied him exclusively to CBS, whether he worked or not.

On October 22, 1959, Gleason opened at Broadway's Shubert Theater in "Take Me Along," a musical version of Eugene O'Neill's "Ah! Wilderness," composed by Bob Merrill with a libretto by Joseph Stein and Robert Russell. Also in the cast were Walter Pidgeon and Robert Morse. Jackie played a drunken bachelor who vows to give up the bottle if his beloved will marry him. The role fit Gleason like a glove, the show was very well received, and it ran for more than a year.

In early 1961 Jackie joined a venture that turned out to be a small catastrophe. He became the moderator for a game show called "You're in the Picture." The first show, broadcast on January 20, was so bad that on the following week Gleason set a television precedent by giving a 30-minute apology to his audience. Revamped, the show limped along until March 1961.

Until 1959 Jackie had been living in the duplex/office complex

at the Park Sheraton. In that year he had a white elephant of a struc-
ture built in Peekskill, New York, about an hour and a half from the
city. The Peekskill house was certainly an architectural oddity—it
resembled a flying saucer complete with a bubble dome, sliding glass
walls, a marble dance floor, waterfalls, two bars, pool tables, juke-
boxes and a hi-fi with 35 speakers. And one bedroom. As Jackie was
a man who loved to party, additional accommodations were built on
the grounds for overnight guests. The house cost more than $650,000
to build, but Jackie found he was lonely there; it was too far away
from the center of things, there were no nightclubs to go hopping off
to in the middle of the night, and so he decided to sell. Because there
were no buyers, Jackie virtually blackmailed Jim Aubrey, then head
of CBS, into having the network buy the house for $350,000 in order
to get him to renew his contract.

In 1961 and 1962 Gleason made two films that firmly established
him as a fine dramatic actor. In *The Hustler* with Paul Newman,
Gleason gave a riveting performance as the pool shark Minnesota
Fats and was nominated for an Academy Award for Best Supporting
Actor. In *Requiem for a Heavyweight* he co-starred with Anthony
Quinn, Mickey Rooney and Julie Harris in a tough, realistic drama
of a prizefighter in the twilight of his career.

In September 1962 Jackie returned to television with his
"American Scene Magazine," a 60-minute variety show on Saturday
nights. The "American Scene Magazine" called upon weekly topics
drawn from newspapers and magazines to form the basis for comedy
sketches. The new ensemble of supporting players included Sue
Anne Langdon, Frank Fontaine and Alice Ghostley. It also introduced the Glea Girls—beautiful, statuesque models who presented
each skit. Gleason continued to maintain strict control of all aspects
of production, from writing to choreography.

During the sixties Gleason's girlfriend was a tall, lovely woman
named Honey Merrill. They were together for so long that most of
his friends and associates (including Earl Wilson in his column)
predicted they would marry, in spite of the fact that Jackie was not
yet divorced from Genevieve. But they came to a parting of the ways
and Honey married singer Tony Roma. After a long, drawn-out battle
in the courts, Gleason received his divorce in 1970. In a decision that
set a legal precedent, Jackie was able to cite his separation from Gen
(since 1954) as grounds for divorce, the minimum period having been
set at two years. She received 12.5 percent of his income as alimony,

plus 1 percent for each daughter for child support. Jackie had finally allowed his own conscience, not his religion or public pressure, to dictate his private needs.

In 1964 Gleason decided that he had had enough of New York's cold and wet weather. By then he had become an enthusiastic golfer, and when the public relations man for Miami Beach tantalized him with the prospect of teeing off 365 days a year, Gleason's response was, "Pal, it's beautiful. Let's do it." Thus the fate was sealed for the show's writers, technicians, musicians, dancers and all the other staff and their families to pack up and go south. In August 1964 the "Gleason Express," a private, 12-car train filled to the rafters with Gleason's friends, cronies and staff held a continuous party during their migration towards their new home. The city of Miami Beach was thrilled to welcome Gleason, with the hopes that he would bolster their sagging tourism and economy. They refitted the old Miami Beach Auditorium into a television studio (including dipping into the emergency hurricane fund to provide the proper type of television cameras) as well as renamed a portion of Collins Avenue "Jackie Gleason Boulevard." The Great One had found a new home.

Jackie indulged himself in a golfer's dream. His house in Lauderhill looked directly onto the beautiful Inverarry golf course. He immediately ordered a customized fire engine–red golf cart for his special needs, complete with siren, telephone, AM-FM stereo, and, of course, a bar. His new home also contained all the toys necessary to entertain its sybaritic owner: several bars, pool table, craps table, etc. The bar stools were reputed to have seat belts.

In 1971 Gleason married Beverly Hunseman McKittrick, a divorcée from Easton, Maryland, who was 17 years his junior. This was not a match made in heaven. They were divorced in 1974, and Beverly received a total of $150,000 in alimony.

It seems, however, that true love was finally to find Jackie Gleason. In a twist of fate worthy of a romance novel Gleason was reunited with his love of 20 years earlier, Marilyn Taylor, whom he had not seen since 1956. She had been married, had a son and was widowed by the time she saw Jackie again in 1974. By coincidence she too was living in Florida. In December 1975 Jackie married the woman he had had to renounce two decades before. "This script took 27 years to write," said the happy bridegroom, "but it was worth the wait."

Gleason continued to broadcast his show from Miami Beach

until 1970, including several seasons with Art Carney, who had returned to play Ed Norton in a rebirth of "The Honeymooners" sketches (later episodes featured many musical production numbers written by Jerry Bresler and Lyn Duddy), with Sheila MacRae as Alice and Jane Kean as Trixie. The 1966–67 season featured the Kramdens and Nortons winning a trip to Europe in a contest held by Flakey-Wakey breakfast cereal, and their adventures abroad.

In 1970 "The Jackie Gleason Show" was cancelled, and the time slot given to "Mission: Impossible." In 1976 and 1977 he switched networks and went over to ABC for a series of "Honeymooners" reunions with Art Carney and Audrey Meadows. But Jackie was getting older, and his years of overeating, overdrinking and oversmoking were affecting him. In 1978 he was admitted to the hospital with angina pains. He underwent a six-hour triple bypass operation that took veins from his leg to replace clogged veins and arteries near his heart.

In the previous year Gleason had made his debut as the ornery, relentless, foul-mouthed lawman Sheriff Buford T. Justice in the film *Smokey and the Bandit* and continued that role in the *Smokey II* and *III* versions. He also starred in the 1982 film *The Toy*, with Richard Pryor as a millionaire attempting to buy his son's affections, and in a movie for cable television with Sir Laurence Olivier.

On June 25, 1987, Jackie Gleason died of adenocarcinoma, a form of cancer, which spread from his colon to his liver. He was 71.

The Great One had left us a remarkable legacy: a silent clown, an accomplished creator of comic characters, a charming master of ceremonies, a fearless stand-up comic, a surprisingly deft dramatic actor. Gleason the performer is the sum of these parts. To many he will live forever as the stubborn, woebegone Ralph Kramden, desperately trying to be the king of his Brooklyn castle. John O'Hara once wrote that if Dickens were alive in the fifties, he would have been writing something similar to "The Honeymooners." Dickens and Gleason both maintained a love for the struggling underdog, who made up for his lack of material possessions with a nobility of spirit. From the streets of Brooklyn to the sunshine of a Florida golf course, Jackie never strayed from the path of providing laughter for his grateful public. Through personal adversity and soul-rending searches he emerged victorious as one of the grand old men of modern entertainment, and when the memories of other lesser clowns have faded from the annals of television history, Jackie Gleason will be there for all to remember and smile upon. How sweet it was.

Danny Kaye

Of all the entertainers known to the public through film, stage and television in the last 40 years, none was more beloved than Danny Kaye. A true jester both to Western and Third World countries, he captured the hearts of millions of adults and children to whom he will always be the singing clown with the shaggy red hair and whimsical, generous nature. His span on television was short but rewarding and brought him into the homes of millions who had already loved and admired him on stage and film. His seemingly quicksilver tongue could rattle off the lyrics to the most nonsensical songs, and his easy pace and gentle demeanor onstage made audiences feel as if this former boy from Brooklyn were their oldest friend.

But soon his reputation changed, and his public heard disquieting reports from friends and co-workers that he was moody and temperamental. He turned away from the show business he had worked in for many years to seek out other interests, anything to take the place of going before an audience. Danny Kaye rose to heights he never could have imagined in his youth, but the happiness that he gave so many millions often eluded its giver.

David Daniel Kaminsky was born in Brooklyn, New York, on January 18, 1913. His parents, Jacob Kaminsky and the former Clara Nemerovsky, had emigrated two years earlier with their two sons, Larry and Mac, from Ekaterinoslav, in the Ukraine. Jacob had eked out a meager living as a horse trader, but like thousands of other Jews, he sought to come to the United States. Young David (affectionately called Duvidl, meaning "little David" in Yiddish), their only American-born son, represented a new beginning in the land of liberty. They sought to improve their lot from a tenement in the Brownsville section of Brooklyn known as East New York, and from Jacob's place of work as a tailor in the garment district of Seventh Avenue.

141

Young David was an average student at the local elementary school, P.S. 149, and it was there that he had his first taste of show business. His class play was a minstrel show entitled "The Watermelon Fantasy," with the future star of stage, screen and television portraying a watermelon seed in blackface. There are no surviving newspaper reviews of this historic occasion.

From P.S. 149 he went on to study at East New York Junior High and Thomas Jefferson High School, but soon after he entered his teens tragedy struck. His mother, the gentle and hard-working Clara, whom Duvidl adored and who always encouraged his impromptu living-room clowning and impersonations, died. This was a severe blow to the struggling family and especially to the sensitive and insecure youngest Kaminsky. Not long after, David left school to run off to Florida with his best friend, Louis Eisen; they earned a little money singing, with Louis playing the guitar. David eventually returned to New York, but not to high school. His father, with a benign attitude and faith in his son's innate abilities, did not press the troubled youngster to return to school or to find work. He knew that his youngest son first had to find himself.

David took a number of jobs to help make ends meet, including working as a soda jerk and as an errand boy for a dentist, Dr. Samuel Fine. In future years Dr. Fine's clever daughter Sylvia was to become as integral to Danny's career as his own talent. He was fired from the dentist's office, however, for using the dental drill for carving wood.

Young Kaminsky also worked briefly as an auto appraiser for an insurance company. That is, until he inadvertently sent a client a check for $40,000 instead of $4,000. Needless to say, the company's executives were not too pleased. The excuse that this forerunner of Walter Mitty was simply not very good at math did not sit well with them. Soon David was once again seeking employment.

Kaye always maintained that he had wanted to be a doctor, especially a surgeon, when young. Watching Danny Kaye's mesmerizing hand gestures while he performs, one can see that those hands may well have been proficient in the operating room. But the Depression arrived and there was no way that Jacob Kaminsky could afford the fees to send his young son to medical school.

Since a medical education was out of the question, David got back together with his old hitchhiking buddy, Louis Eisen. Their act was called "Red and Blackie" (guess who was Red) and they were soon hired as "toomlers" at the Jewish resorts in the Catskills. "Toomler" derives its origin from "tumult," in other words, those who create a noisy commotion, and in this case, particularly on rainy days when the guests could not go outdoors to laze by the pool. If it was not exactly the fast lane to stardom, it was, at least, working in show business, sort of. At this time the unwieldy and ethnic Kaminsky was shortened to the more generic Kaye and David became Danny.

It was also in the Catskills that Danny met up with his future dance partners, Dave Harvey and Kathleen Young. The three formed an act called "The Three Terpsicoreans," regardless of the fact that Danny could not dance any more than he could become a doctor. Nevertheless, the three budding performers managed to get themselves booked into third-rate vaudeville houses. Their biggest break came when they were hired by producer A.B. Marcus to join one of his extravaganza/revues, "La Vie Paris." In the show, which was filled with beautiful girls, singers and dancers, Danny had four numbers. The program lists him as taking part in "a lyric fantasy founded on the celebrated poem of 'Trees'" (number seven spot on the bill), as well as appearing in the sketch "On Riverside Drive—More Triangles" (number 10), a song and dance number called "Yeah Man" (last number before the intermission) and finally dancing a "Specialty" with Harvey and Young before the final curtain. Quite a lot of work for $40 a week.

While the revue was playing Detroit the flamboyant Marcus (legend had it that he entered show business because he was a clothes cleaner in New England and got stuck with a lot of stage costumes when a traveling unit could not pay its bills. He supposedly decided that the only thing he could do was go out and get the costumes filled, and thus he became a producer) came backstage and asked his talented employee, "How would you like to go to China?" and the boy from Brooklyn jumped at the chance. On February 8, 1934, the troupe boarded a ship in San Francisco and set sail for the Far East. For six months the 75 actors played the Orient: Tokyo, Hong Kong, Shanghai, Singapore, Osaka and other spots on the eastern circuit.

It was in Osaka that the world nearly lost the future talents of Danny Kaye. In his hotel room during a hurricane he was nearly killed when a piece of the building's cornice came flying into his room. That same hurricane continued to wreak havoc at the evening's performance by causing a blackout, whereupon Kaye took it upon himself to keep the Japanese audience amused (and un-panicked by the storm) by holding a flashlight to his face and singing all the songs he could think of at the top of his voice. He also learned the value of pantomime for non–English-speaking audiences on his tour of Japan.

Returning to the United States, he quit the show and was out of work. Being a big hit in Singapore or Shanghai did not assure him of a job in New York. The theatrical agents he visited were baffled by how to categorize him. He could sing, but he was not a singer, could dance a bit but was not a dancer, and though he was a fine comedian, he did not tell jokes. What exactly did the young redhead do?

Except for a brief engagement as an assistant to famous fan-toting ecdysiast Sally Rand, he remained mostly unemployed until he was hired to act as the stooge for Nick Long, Jr. Long, who came from a vaudeville family and whose father was an Italian dialect comic, was a good-looking, dark-haired dancer who later became known for jumping headfirst over the backs of ten showgirls into a net held off-stage by six stagehands. His career was cut short when he was killed in an auto accident on August 31, 1949, at the age of 43.

Long and Kaye played Billy Rose's New York nightclub, the Casa Manana, and Danny even got to sing a few numbers in the act — including one he appropriated from Cab Calloway, "Minnie the Moocher." From there they were hired to play at the posh Dorchester Hotel in London for eight weeks. But England in 1938 was a country on the brink of war, and the tension, combined with Kaye's rather unsophisticated style of the time, kept him from being a success with the cafe crowd. In fact, he was a total bomb. It was to be ten years before Kaye would return to the English city to capture the heart of its audiences.

Back in New York he auditioned for a revue called "Saturday Night Varieties" being put together by the energetic showman Max Liebman at the Keynote Theater on 52nd Street. The pianist for the auditions was a dark-haired girl from his past, Sylvia Fine, whose dentist father Danny had worked for back in Brooklyn. After majoring in music at Brooklyn College, Sylvia was giving piano lessons until the day that she could make a career as a composer and lyricist. Professionally they seemed to be a perfect match: He needed songs written for him that could show the range of his talents; she was quick-witted with a facility for words and rhythms. Offstage, it was love.

After the close of the show both Fine and Kaye were persuaded by Liebman to join him for the summer season at Tamiment, the resort in the Poconos where he was in charge of entertainment. Kaye joined with Imogene Coca, her husband, Bob Burton, and others in the weekly shenanigans that became the Saturday night show. Their efforts at Tamiment were so amusing that the show came to Broadway as "The Straw Hat Revue," opening at the Ambassador Theater on September 29, 1939. Although Coca was the star of the show, Danny got his fair share of favorable notices:

> Another standout in the company [besides Coca] is Danny Kaye, a young funster who should click in big time company. Kaye's humor is not always subtle but it is surefire. He's got what it takes. — Robert Coleman, New York *Daily Mirror*

> Mr. Kaye, for all his youthfulness has the brash professional air of an experienced funny fellow and makes his points sharply, if a little insistently. With surer material he should be more genially laughable. — John Anderson, New York *Journal-American*

> Danny Kaye ... knows how to drop irony into burlesque without overdoing it. . . . — Brooks Atkinson, *New York Times*

> Next to Miss Coca, the most active member of the cast is Danny Kaye, who seems to be what I hope it will not sound too patronizing to call a comedian of promise. . . . — Richard Watts, New York *Herald-Tribune*

> Danny Kaye, out of vaudeville and night clubs, is a tall young man with a comic way, and he makes a lot out of a skit in which he is Anatole of Paris (late of Bellevue), maker of hats for women. He shows off some hats, but they aren't as funny as Mr. Kaye, or as the contrivers of the revue innocently expected. — Richard Lockridge, New York *Sun*

Upon the closing of "The Straw Hat Revue" after only ten weeks, Danny took off for a Florida vacation and Sylvia soon joined him. They were married in Fort Lauderdale on January 3, 1940, with their friend and mentor Max Liebman as the witness. To mollify their families for not being present at the wedding, they were remarried in Brooklyn on February 22, 1940, and soon moved into an apartment at 414 East 52nd Street.

When they returned to New York, Danny was hired by the swank nightclub La Martinique to do his act for $250 a week.

Considering that the newlyweds were broke, this was pretty good pay. Sylvia was hired as his accompanist, which was a wise choice; few pianists could keep up with the improvisatory nature of Danny's talent, but Sylvia was with him all the way. One evening, for lack of having a prepared encore, Danny began a Conga line that included the club's waiters and clientele. The number was so popular that it became a regular part of the act. He sang the songs Sylvia wrote for him, including the famous "Anatole of Paris" number from "The Straw Hat Revue," as well as a piece called "Rhythm" in which he recited a sort of double-talk gibberish which seemed to make sense but didn't. There was a satire of the Stanislavsky-Moscow Art Theater as well as a takeoff on a Carnegie Hall recital. He also sang his version of a song called "Dinah" (he pronounced it Dee-na) which would become a signature piece for him in the years to come.

Variety reviewed his act in its own inimitable fashion:

> Danny Kaye is out of the "Straw Hat Revue" by way of the borscht circuit, with quickie stopoffs in London and Australia, before returning to America for the stage musical. . . . On his own now, Kaye is a big, breezy and refreshing personality with a unique style of general kidding that should carry him along in good style, depending upon his material. Considering that Sylvia Fine, his pianist-author . . . becomes Mrs. Kaye some time this month, he's assured of an author. . . .
>
> Comic is a self-assured worder on the floor and his general alfresco style commends him for class or mass appeal.

His act at La Martinique was very successful and became a favorite among New York's chic nighttime crowd. One night Broadway playwright and director Moss Hart caught Danny's show. "If I ever do a show," he told Kaye (he had already done several, including "As Thousands Cheer" with Irving Berlin); "it will be just so you can be in it." Kaye did not think much of this rather unsubstantial offer and was surprised and pleased to be cast in Hart's next endeavor, "Lady in the Dark."

A literate, imaginative show, "Lady in the Dark" starred the riveting Gertrude Lawrence as a successful magazine editor who is troubled by dreams about the men in her life, which she relates to her psychoanalyst, and which are acted out in a series of dream sequences. Kurt Weill's haunting score, Ira Gershwin's clever lyrics and Moss Hart's fine book combined to make for theatrical success

Kaye and his wife, talented lyricist/composer Sylvia Fine, circa 1981, reminisce about his show-stopping performance in the original Broadway production of Moss Hart's "Lady in the Dark." The show, and Kaye, received much critical acclaim after its opening in January 1941.

when the show opened on Broadway's Alvin Theater on January 23, 1941.

Danny played the role of Randall Paxton, the magazine's rather fey photographer. His shining moment came with the song "Tschaikowsky," with which he nearly stole the show. Although not terribly relevant to the show's plot, the song was a perfect showcase for the 28-year-old Kaye, for in it he named 57 Russian composers in 40 seconds (a time he was to beat on many occasions in future years):

There's Malichevsky, Rubinstein, Arensky and Tchaikowsky,
Sapelnikoff, Dimitrieff, Tscherepnin, Kryjanowsky,
Godowsky, Arteiboucheff, Moniuszko, Akimenko,
Solovieff, Prokofieff, Tiomkin, Korestchenko.
There's Glinka, Winkler, Bortniansky, Rebikoff, Ilyinsky;
There's Medtner, Balakireff, Zolotareff and Kvoschinsky;
And Sokoloff and Kopyloff, Dukelsky and Klenofsky;
And Shostokovitsch, Borodine, Gliere and Nowakofski.
There's Liadoff and Karganoff, Markievitch, Pantschenko;
And Dargomyszki, Stcherbatcheff, Scriabine, Vassilenko;
Stravinsky, Rimskykorsakoff, Mussorgsky and Gretchaninoff;
And Glazounoff and Caesar Cui, Kalinikoff, Rachmaninoff,
Stravinsky and Gretchnaninoff,
Rumshinsky and Rachmaninoff
I really have to stop, the subject has been dwelt upon enough!
Stravinsky, Gretchnaninoff, Kvoschinsky, Rachmaninoff!
I really have to stop because you all have undergone enough!

The critics were unanimous in their praise for the new "discovery":

Next to Miss Lawrence the honors of the evening went to Danny Kaye, who is extremely adept in his comedy role and who practically stopped the show with his own rapid-fire song, Tschaikovsky, an interpolated number that has absolutely nothing to do with the play but which provides its most exciting diversion. This is Mr. Kaye's first appearance here in a legitimate play, although he was seen briefly two years ago in The Straw Hat Revue. He is something of a discovery. — Sidney Whipple, New York *World Telegram*

Danny Kaye caused the first nighters to put callouses on their palms with his version of a sprightly patter song. — Robert Coleman, New York *Daily Mirror*

Mr. Kaye was excellent as the unburlesqued effeminate photographer who becomes Eliza's more forceful chauffeur in the dream sequence. — George Freedly, New York *Morning Telegraph*

As a comic fashion photographer, Danny Kaye, who was cutting up in "The Straw Hat Revue" last year, is infectiously exuberant. — Brooks Atkinson, *New York Times*

In her [Gertrude Lawrence's] support she has the newly-risen comedian, Danny Kaye, who steps forth confidently to justify his admirers in the belief that he is started on a fine career. — Burns Mantle, New York *Daily News*

Danny left the run of "Lady in the Dark" before it was over in order to become the star of another Broadway musical called "Let's Face It," Herbert and Dorothy Fields' adaptation of a 1925 hit, "The Cradle Snatchers," with music by Cole Porter. Special musical material for Danny was provided by Sylvia (a tribute to her abilities to write songs tailored for her husband, for Porter rarely allowed anything to be interpolated into his shows).

In the story, three wives get back at their philandering husbands by taking up with three soldiers. Kaye stopped the show with his rendition of one of Sylvia's songs, "Melody in Four F," in which with song, dance and double-talk he raced through the hilarious career of the reluctant draftee. The cast also included Eve Arden and Vivian Vance (later of "I Love Lucy" fame) and was successful enough with wartime audiences to run 547 performances. The day after the show's opening on October 29, 1941, the press was once again ecstatic over the young, blue-eyed actor:

> Last year Mr. Kaye disclosed an uncanny skill in racing through the names of Russian composers without stumbling over the vowels, and here he is in high fettle again. It is amazing. . . . Mr. Kaye conquered every ermine in the house last evening. — Brooks Atkinson, *New York Times*

> Danny Kaye is brilliantly funny. . . . There can be little doubt that Mr. Kaye has in the last two seasons become one of the important comics of the American stage, and he is in a happy vein in "Let's Face It!" — Richard Watts, Jr., New York *Herald-Tribune*

> (A Danny Kaye-O!) Mr. Kaye (short for kayelossal) is even funnier and more loveable than he was in "Lady in the Dark" . . . he is simply wonderful. — Walter Winchell, New York *Daily Mirror*

Having been the hit of two consecutive Broadway shows made Kaye a likely prospect for Hollywood. Movie mogul Sam Goldwyn had seen him in "Lady in the Dark" and according to Arthur Marx in his biography, *Goldwyn*, the famed destroyer of the English language came backstage:

> "You're a very funny man," said Sam. "But if I sign you, you're going to have to have your nose fixed. It's too long."
> "No," said Kaye.
> "He's doing all right with it the way it is," said his wife.
> "It's not photogenic," said Sam.
> "I'll make a deal with you," said Kaye with a smile. "I'll have mine fixed if you'll have yours fixed."[1]

Many years later Goldwyn, who was responsible for bringing Kaye to Hollywood, lived up to his reputation for absentmindedness when he sent flowers to Sylvia's hospital room addressed to "Mrs. Sammy Kaye."

As usual, Sylvia was watching out for her husband's career. She was Svengali to his Trilby. As she told an interviewer in 1941:

> Danny is the worst judge of material I've ever known. He's always one hundred percent wrong. We have to argue him into using scripts that later prove tremendous hits at the club. . . . He's never right. He leaves my scripts around for weeks, refusing to study them. Then, a few days before he's scheduled to open, he gets desperate and memorizes them in a few hours. After he finds out that people actually like them, he comes around to me and admits that he was wrong. But the next time, he acts the same way all over again. He's just stubborn.[2]

Danny was heard to remark more than once, "Sylvia has a fine head on my shoulders."

So to Hollywood they went. Danny was not totally unfamiliar with the routine of movie-making; in 1937 and 1938 he had made three short films for Educational Pictures at their Astoria, New York, studios: *Getting an Eyeful*, *Cupid Takes a Holiday*, and *Dime a Dance* with Imogene Coca. But comparing these minor efforts with the full-length productions of Sam Goldwyn was like comparing grapes to watermelons. Goldwyn put both Danny and Sylvia under contract (he may have lost the argument about the nose job but he did get his way about having Danny's hair dyed to a lighter shade) and put them to work on their first feature film, *Up in Arms*, a wartime comedy with Dinah Shore and Dana Andrews. The film included a typically Danny Kaye-type number by Sylvia and Max Liebman, "The Lobby Number," about the frustrations of moviegoers and the lines they were forced to endure.

Danny made three films in the next three years for Goldwyn, including *Wonder Man* (1945), *The Kid from Brooklyn* (a remake of the Harold Lloyd film *The Milky Way*, 1946), and *The Secret Life of Walter Mitty* (1947). The films had several things in common: They all starred Danny as a well-meaning but innocent sort of schnook, not unlike the Harold Lloyd character; they all had plots that were less important to the film than the opportunities they provided to showcase Kaye's prolific, and unusual, talent; they all had

specialty numbers by Sylvia; and they all co-starred Virginia Mayo.
On December 17, 1946, Danny and Sylvia became the proud
parents of a baby girl whom they named Dena, after Danny's unorthodox pronunciation in his song about Dinah. The man who was
to become the most adored entertainer of children around the globe
positively doted on this new addition to his family.

In 1948 Danny went to London to appear at the famed Palladium Theater, where he became a national craze. The English
equivalent of bobby-soxers adopted him as their idol and were known
to queue up days in advance to buy tickets, which quickly became
rare commodities on which scalpers made tidy profits. At his Royal
Command performance he became a favorite of the British princes-
ses, Elizabeth and Margaret. He was to return to the Palladium so
many times that other comedians joked that he owned the dressing
room. Danny's eccentric act and his abundant enthusiasm fit perfectly into the great tradition of the British music hall, and the British
people took him into their hearts.

Back in California, Kaye returned to the business of making
movies, but no longer for Goldwyn. He went over to RKO to make
A Song Is Born (with jazz greats Benny Goodman, Louis Armstrong,
Lionel Hampton and Tommy Dorsey) in 1948 and *The Inspector
General* (based on an 1836 play by Russian playwright Nikolai Gogol)
in 1949. In 1951 he made *On the Riviera* for 20th Century–Fox and
in 1952 he returned to the Goldwyn studios for the charming
children's fantasy film *Hans Christian Andersen.*

In 1953 Danny and Sylvia formed their own production company, called Dena after their daughter. They hired two comedy
writers who had worked for the Goldwyn studios, Norman Panama
and Melvin Frank, to act as writers, directors and producers. The col-
laboration seemed to hit the jackpot, for the films they produced
were probably the finest of Danny's career, including *Knock on Wood*
(Danny as a ventriloquist who gets mixed up with a spy ring, 1954);
The Court Jester (in which he portrayed Giacomo—King of the
Jesters and Jester of Kings and in which there is the famous line "The
pellet with the poison's in the vessel with the pestle; the chalice from
the palace has the brew that is true!" 1956). He also appeared with
Bing Crosby in the Irving Berlin musical film *White Christmas*
(1954).

Less successful but quite charming was *Merry Andrew* (1958),
about a schoolteacher who joins the circus. *Me and the Colonel* (also

1958) was a change of style for Kaye; in it he played a meek Jew flee-
ing from the Nazis who ends up traveling with an anti-Semitic German officer (played by Curt Jurgens). *The Five Pennies* (1959) was a
biographical film based on the life of jazz musician Red Nichols, co-
starred Louis Armstrong, and was written and directed by Mel
Shavelson.

Shavelson also wrote and directed *On the Double* (1961), which
was a return to a more typically Kaye-esque type of comedy, with
Danny as a private impersonating a British officer whose life had
been threatened.

The Man from the Diner's Club (1963) was a simple slapstick
comedy directed by Frank Tashlin, who directed many of the films
of Jerry Lewis in the same genre, and it probably would have suited
Lewis better than it did Kaye.

Danny's last starring role in a feature film was in the idiosyn-
cratic *The Madwoman of Chaillot* (1969), with him playing the Rag-
picker to Katharine Hepburn's Madwoman.

In 1960 Danny finally succumbed to the temptation to enter the
world of television, and his entry was full of trepidation. For years he
had felt in no hurry to enter the medium. "Television will be here a
long time. I'm in no hurry. When the time is right for me, I'll go into
television," he would often state. The time seemed to be right for him
on October 30, 1960, when he did the first of three annual specials
sponsored by General Motors for CBS. Simply called "An Hour with
Danny Kaye," the show was produced by Sylvia and directed by Norman Jewison. Reviews for the show were only fair.

By the third special, broadcast on November 11, 1962, the show's
quality was higher. Lucille Ball guest-starred, and together she and
Danny indulged in some fine clowning. The best sketch of the evening was a trilogy of the couple visiting restaurants. The first one, done
in pantomime, portrayed the pair's difficulties when trying to eat in
a Japanese restaurant. Lucy's skirt is too tight for her to be able to
sit on the floor, so she slides under the table. Neither of them can
figure out the correct way to use chopsticks, so their noodles end up
all over the table. Finally, in desperation, Danny uses his chopstick
as a pool cue and shoots a kumquat into Lucy's waiting mouth.

The second restaurant is a high-class French establishment,
with Danny and Lucy playing a couple of middle-class Brooklynites
who are obviously out of their element. They get so drunk on the
liberal dosing of sherry in the salad dressing that they start slurping

Dancing Pagodas. Kaye teams up with guest stars Don Knotts and Carol Lawrence on "The Danny Kaye Show," a weekly variety show that enjoyed a four-year run on CBS in the mid-sixties.

it up with their spoons, prompting Danny to command the waiter: "I'd like some more of that salad, but don't put any of that green stuff in it."

The third restaurant, the Tahitian Typhoon, takes its theme rather realistically. The maitre d' has a bone through his nose; the cigarette girl is in a gorilla costume. Danny and Lucy are given guns, machetes and safari hats and told to head to their table, due west, through thick jungle. On their way she gets stuck in quicksand. "Don't move, you'll only sink faster. I learned that in the Amazon," he tells her. "You were in the Amazon?" she asks. "Yes," he says, "it's a restaurant near Cleveland." By the time they finally locate their table a tropical thunderstorm is pelting down on them, and as they get up to leave, their waiter/witch doctor shrinks them into dwarves.

On September 25, 1963, "The Danny Kaye Show" began its four-year run on CBS. Taped on Saturday, it was broadcast "live on tape" (no retakes) every Wednesday night from 10:00 to 11:00 P.M. Sylvia was no longer involved with the production, but some of television's best writers were hired to create material for Danny's unique talents: Herbert Baker, Sheldon Keller, Saul Ilson, Ernest Chambers, Larry Tucker, Gary Belkin, Mel Tolkin and future film director Paul Mazursky. His comic sidekick on the new series was funnyman Harvey Korman.

The sketches on that first show included variations on "Take Me Out to the Ball Game" as it might be done in "My Fair Lady," "West Side Story," and "The Music Man." In the "My Fair Lady" segment, Kaye appeared as Professor Higgins explaining that "the aim of the game is mainly to complain." He also appeared as a Caspar Milque-toast–type taking his first airplane ride and in a routine about a three-piece orchestra required to make quick costume changes in order to masquerade as a South American combo.

The reviews of Kaye's emergence as a regular television performer were generally enthusiastic. Jack Gould reported in the *New York Times:*

> With lilt to his step and charm to his manner Danny Kaye appeared on television last night and it was the brightest and freshest hour since the first Fred Astaire program. To call it a TV show might be misleading; at heart it was a small Broadway revue tastefully turned in all particulars. . . . The true Kaye, both the performer and the personality, at long last found himself on the home screen.

Brooks Atkinson reported on February 2, 1964, in the same paper:

> His program is the finest weekly variety show that television emits. . . . There are several entertaining weekly shows. But none

of them equals "The Danny Kaye Show" in grace, lightness, taste and good humor. Talent outranks material. From week to week the material varies. The talent always remains unimpaired.

As always, much of Danny's show was devoted to his singing, but as time went by he did less of the double-talk and specialty numbers that he had become known for, and more often sang simple tunes in his ever-pleasing baritone voice.

Children were still a large part of his focus, and very often at the close of the show he would bring on a little boy or girl and just talk or sing to his tiny guest in an unrehearsed, unartificial manner.

The show had its followers. Although it did not place within the top 20 in the Nielsen ratings, it did win an Emmy for "Outstanding Program Achievement in the Field of Variety" in 1964 for its first season, and Danny also won for "Outstanding Performance in a Variety or Musical Program or Series," beating out Judy Garland and Barbra Streisand.

By 1967 material was running thin and the format was getting stale. Danny Kaye was one of the last major entertainers to have a weekly variety show, and his last show was aired June 7, 1967.

The indefatigable Kaye had other interests he wished to pursue. Danny was known for turning his hobbies into full-fledged passions. At one time he was the ping-pong champion of Hollywood. His devotion to the sport of baseball, and particularly the former Brooklyn "bums," the Dodgers, bordered on the religious, and he eventually became part-owner of the Seattle Mariners. An interest in flying impelled him not only to get his pilot's license, but to get his instrumental, commercial and jet ratings as well. A fondness for Chinese food that began with his first trip to the Orient as a young man led him to become a true master chef of that cuisine, and he installed a professional Chinese restaurant–style kitchen in his home.

For charity Kaye also devoted much time to guest-conducting many of the great orchestras of the world, though he could not read a note of music. His histrionics as he led the orchestra through a rendition of "Flight of the Bumble Bee" with a flyswatter in lieu of a baton caused many musicians to break up with laughter, as well as the audiences. At the podium of the New York Philharmonic he once pretended to scrape something off the bottom of his foot, asking "Does Lenny [Bernstein] chew gum?"

From the time of his teenage years, when medical school was an

Kaye and some of his most adoring fans, children. Through the years he dedicated himself to bettering the condition of children worldwide.

unattainable dream, Kaye's fascination with the world of medicine did not abate. He observed so many operations that he was elected an honorary member of the American College of Surgeons. Once while flying his plane over the Midwest, he diagnosed the pain he was experiencing as appendicitis and made an unplanned landing at the Mayo Clinic, where his diagnosis was confirmed.

The most public and enduring of Danny's devotions were to the cause of children around the world. As Ambassador-at-Large for UNICEF he crisscrossed the globe dozens of times trying to call attention to the sick, hungry and needy children in underdeveloped

Star of stage, film, and finally television, Kaye was certainly the world's most beloved entertainer, and perhaps the most unique.

countries. He entertained in orphanages, hospitals, and schools from Kenya to Hong Kong, using pantomime and song to overcome language barriers, bringing love and laughter and hope for a better life for future generations.

Kaye's eclectic interests and causes kept him from the public eye (as a performer) for some time. In 1971 he returned to Broadway as Noah in Richard Rodgers and Martin Charnin's musical, "Two by Two." Shortly after the show opened he tore a ligament in his leg, but soon returned in a wheelchair and then on crutches. The show's creators were less than thrilled with his performance, for most people agreed that he turned the Biblical story into "The Danny Kaye

Show." But audiences did not seem to mind, and the show ran for nearly a year.

In 1976 Kaye made two specials for television when he starred as Geppetto in "Pinocchio" and as the evil Captain Hook in "Peter Pan." In 1981 he took on the serious role of Max Feldman, a survivor of the Nazi holocaust, in *Skokie*. His intensity and fervor as the law-abiding businessman who confronts a group of neo–Nazis showed him to be a fine dramatic actor.

On February 18, 1983, Danny Kaye underwent quadruple by-pass surgery at Cedars-Sinai Medical Center in Los Angeles. No doubt he would have wanted to watch the operation if he could have. His health regained, the irrepressible Kaye continued to turn up sporadically on our television screens, including a guest appearance as a friendly dentist on "The Cosby Show."

Danny Kaye seems to have expended his not inconsiderable talents on several media: Broadway, nightclubs, films and television, just long enough to master each one. A restless soul, he continued to hone his craft and refine his artistry with each new endeavor. With the help of his gifted wife, he brought a new dimension to comedy, one that could not easily be pigeonholed. Quick-witted and intense, he was not always easy to work for. His mood swings were famous and at times he seemed to suffer from some internal demon, but when it came to his audiences his generosity and zeal were un-paralleled. On March 3, 1987, Danny Kaye succumbed to heart disease complicated by hepatitis. He was not just an American in-stitution, but an international figure who tried to make the world a better place through laughter, and he succeeded. Danny Kaye may well have been the most unique entertainer of the twentieth century.

Ernie Kovacs

The comedy of Ernie Kovacs was eccentric, surrealistic, outré, and occasionally silly. There were no jokes, there was no glitz, there was no breathless striving for a punch line. But there was a talent for the unexpected.

Kovacs was a genius, and like all geniuses was ahead of his time. That may sound like a cliché, but clichés are born from truth, and Ernie gave birth to a vision of life and laughs that was uniquely his own.

Ernie Kovacs was to television what Georges Méliès had been to silent films; he was the first to create television comedy using visual trickery. Manipulating the camera and other technical equipment, he created special effects that had never before been seen on television. In its very early days, television programming tended to be banal, much of it a rehash of what had been done on radio. As it aged, the programming grew less, not more inventive. But in the staid world of television, Kovacs was a true jester who dared to be innovative, take risks, and make magic.

Ernie Kovacs' creativity was like a violent force of nature, a virtual tornado of ideas. In his busy television career from 1950 to 1962 he wrote and performed more than 90 percent of his own material. He normally got less than four hours' sleep each night, feverishly setting down thousands of ideas and scripts while the rest of the world slept. Kovacs' approach to life could be summarized by the anti–Socratic motto, "Nothing in Moderation." Tragically, that motto became his epitaph far too soon.

Kovacs and television were made for each other. He was one of the few television performers who did not have a background in vaudeville, nightclubs or film. He did have some experience as an actor in summer stock, wrote a newspaper column, and had a local radio show in Trenton, New Jersey. Later in his life he starred in

159

several movies, but it was always in the unparalleled intimacy of television where he did his best work.

Born on January 19, 1919, in Trenton, New Jersey, Ernie had one older brother, Tom. His father, Andrew, had emigrated from Hungary at the age of 13, and at various times had been a policeman, a bootlegger, and a restaurateur. Being a bootlegger during Prohibition was by far the most lucrative, and he was able to move his family into a 20-room mansion in the upper-class part of town.

Ernie's interest in the theater began at Trenton High School, where he made his debut as the Pirate King in the "Pirates of Penzance." He was a poor student; he failed history, Latin, algebra, and chemistry, and did not graduate with his class. In 1937, however, with the help of his high school drama teacher he received a scholarship to study acting at the American Academy of Dramatic Arts in New York City.

The end of Prohibition also meant the end of the Kovacs family fortunes, and they returned to living among the lower middle class. In New York, Ernie lived in what can kindly be called squalor, in a fifth-floor walkup above a brothel on West 74th Street. His usual form of entertainment was going to second-rate films for a dime. These grade–B movies later provided the inspiration for his parodies of those flawed epics. On the November 21, 1953, broadcast of "The Ernie Kovacs Show," a series of printed cards, reminiscent of silent film credits, announced:

SILENT MOVIE

IVBIN TROO DE MILL PRESENTS
   A TALE OF ESPIONAGE
      UNDERCOVER GOINGS ON IN A RESTAURANT
      COLD CUTS OF STEEL IN HOTBEDS OF SPIES
        RANSACKED RADAR
        HIJACKED HYDROGEN
        PILFERED PEROXIDE

BOY!

      SEE SNEAKY SPIES AT WORK
      SEE UNCLE SAM STRIKE BACK
      SEE THE CHARGE OF WILD BULL ELEPHANTS

   SWOLLEN RIVERS
   THE DYNAMITING OF HOOVER DAM (NARTB)

WITH A CAST OF A FEW!

SEE HEADLESS HEROINES
ON THE STRETCHOMATIC SCREEN!
WITH SCHIZOPHRENIC SOUND!
IN GLORIOUS GRAYS AND BLACKS!

AS TOLD TO IVBIN TROO DE MILL BY A
FORMER IRISH SPY!

WE ARE INDEBTED TO THE FBI FOR THE
LOAN OF
THEIR TYPEWRITER WITHOUT WHICH THIS SCRIPT
WOULD NOT HAVE BEEN POSSIBLE

THE CAST IN ODOR OF THEIR AP-
PEARANCE

ARCHDUKE O'TOOLE...MANNY SHEVITZ
CAROUSEL TICKET COLLECTOR...BUSHMASTER
KREEL
LADY PAMELA MAINWARING...BESSIE LOU
COSNOWSKI
THE HOODED STRANGER...LISTERINE GOLD
FARB
USED GONDOLA SALESMAN...CORDELIA
PFUNF
ELDERLY MAN..."WHITEY" GROOTZ
THE CHINESE COOK...SIR BRADFORD
SHULTZ
AND INTRODUCING

MOISCH!

In 1939, while working in summer stock in Vermont, Kovacs was stricken with pleurisy and pneumonia. He spent the next 18 months in several hospitals, often near death. There were plenty of reasons for his illness: the five-floor walkup, the lack of nourishing food, the many all-night poker games (an obsession that lasted the rest of his life), not to mention his heavy cigar smoking, a habit he had been cultivating since the age of 16.

While far from a perfect patient, he was an amusing one. According to David G. Walley in his unusual biography of Kovacs, before going for a fluoroscope examination one day he wrote "Out to Lunch" on his chest in aluminum paint.[1] Although seriously ill, he entertained staff and patients alike with his burgeoning off-the-wall sense of humor. He also organized endless poker games. The doctors were surprised when Ernie did not die, but they had not counted on his enormous energy, insuppressible vitality and infectious joie de vivre.

During this convalescence Kovacs' lifelong love of classical music began. Someone gave him a radio to keep him company in the hospital and he spent hours listening to WQXR, New York's classical radio station. Later he would often write comic pieces set to the music of the composers he called "Ricky" Strauss, "Hank" Haydn, and "Bubbles" Bartok, among others. He began his 1959 special "Kovacs on Music" by explaining: "I have never really understood classical music, so I would like to take this evening to explain it to others." Ernie was being modest, for he had an uncanny, instinctual sense of the rhythms and shadings of classical music. He exalted and demystified the works of the great composers for his television audience.

After he was released from the hospital, Ernie held several menial jobs, none of which lasted very long. For a while he worked as a clerk in a drugstore, and later fondly reminisced that "it was the only place I could get my cigars for nothing." He lived with his mother, Mary, in two rooms over a candy store in Trenton (his parents had separated by this time). Fortunately his clerking days did not last. He auditioned and was hired for a staff announcer's job at WTTM, a local radio station.

Starting in 1941 with a 15-minute show, over the next nine years Ernie worked himself up to the position of Director of Special Events, a catchall title of his own invention that gave him free rein to do what he wanted, including pulling some crazy stunts. On February 2, with a remote unit, he waited by a groundhog hole to see if the creature would show (it did not; he lay down on railroad tracks to see what it would be like to be run over by a train (happily he lost his nerve, bolting up from the tracks at the last minute, and all that the audience heard was the sound of the microphone being crushed); and he took flying lessons, broadcasting from the plane's cockpit (until his first solo flight scared the hell out of him and subsequently he always preferred trains).

During this same period Ernie started writing a column for a weekly paper, *The Trentonian*. It was entitled "Kovacs Unlimited" (which would later serve as the name of his television show) and for which he was paid the grand sum of 25 cents a column inch.

Between his radio shows from midnight to 9:00 A.M. and from 1:00 to 1:30 P.M., his weekly tirades in *The Trentonian*, scores of personal appearances, and acting with the local theater company, Ernie was easily the most celebrated man in Trenton. A big fish in a small pond, but still a fish who might go places.

In addition to all his other activities, Ernie found time to court Bette Wilcox, a dancer, and on August 13, 1945, they were married. Now there were three people living in two rooms over the candy store, not an auspicious way to begin a marriage. Soon enough Ernie found himself mediating arguments between his mother and his bride.

Over the next three years Ernie and Bette had two daughters (Bette Lee on May 17, 1947, and Kippie on January 5, 1949), but having children could not cement what was obviously a foundering relationship. In 1949 the marriage fell apart and Bette left her husband and children. Kovacs' family life was fragmented, strenuous, and miserable, but then Ernie was hired for his first job in the magic medium of television.

He went to work for WPTZ, a small NBC affiliate in Philadelphia, hosting an afternoon cooking show called "Deadline for Dinner." Like much of the television of the time, it was done live.

The format of the show was fairly simple, if not simpleminded. Ernie was the host, while a different culinary luminary presented his or her recipe and incidentally served as straight man to Ernie's clowning. The chance to start cutting up (more than vegetables) was irresistible. The next two years were a series of cooking disasters. Ernie did everything he could to make the food turn out as badly as possible. Joe Behar, the show's director, recalled those days in an interview: "It was like what they do now when they do sketches about a cooking show and a guy gets loaded or gets funny or makes a mess. That's what Ernie would do with his [cook]. The guy would try to make a dish and Ernie would just screw it up completely."

With the unexpected success of "Deadline for Dinner" (or as Ernie called it, "Dead Lion for Breakfast"), the management of WPTZ added "Three to Get Ready" to his schedule in November 1950. TTRG was basically a wake-up show interspersed with the time, weather, and news reports. It was an hour and one-half long and began at 7:30 A.M., Monday through Friday. This made it impractical for Kovacs to continue commuting from Trenton, so he moved to Philadelphia, leaving his daughters in his mother's care.

Soon, the crazy Kovacs shenanigans were attracting an audience of up to 60,000—not bad for 7:30 in the morning and the dawn of television production as well.

Kovacs often worked without a script, improvising on whatever idea came into his head. Often the springboard for these ideas was various props that might have been sitting around the studio, or a prop that someone had brought in just because it looked silly. Ernie also delighted in improvising to music chosen from the studio's library with the aid of his lifelong music director, "Fast" Eddie Hatrak.

Neither was the show's cast and crew immune to being utilized as straight men, even involuntarily. The poor fellow who was the newscaster on the show often had to read the news while Ernie poured water on his head or pulled his trousers off, all from off camera, of course, as he struggled to keep a serious face.

It was during this period that Ernie started playing with sight gags and touches of pantomime, two talents that he would develop and use with great success for the rest of his career. Along with these sight gags he created an entirely new kind of technical prestidigitation that had not been seen on television before. He devised a method whereby it would appear that he was inside a bottle, perhaps one with a miniature ship in it, and the bottle would be filled with water. Or through the use of an inverter lens he appeared to be vacuuming the ceiling. These "tricks" may seem old hat to us now, particularly in our age of videotronics and computer animation, but in 1950 they were revolutionary.

The creation of such marvelously unique effects was all the more impressive considering that "Three to Get Ready" was shown at an hour that was hardly prime-time, and on a virtually nonexistent budget. All these technical innovations had to be accomplished with improvised materials. Lit Sterno cans were held beneath cameras to create a smoky effect for fade-outs. The inverter lens was made of a soup can and mirrors. What could be imagined could be invented.

In 1951 NBC gave Ernie a new show, his first on a major network, called "Ernie in Kovacsland." It ran as a summer replacement for the popular puppet show "Kukla, Fran and Ollie" at 7:30 P.M., Monday through Friday, live as always. For this show he hired a beautiful young blonde chanteuse, a former opera student at Juilliard, Eddythe Adams. This was the beginning of a long and fruitful relationship, professionally and privately. Earlier, Edie had been voted Miss U.S. Television, had done a walk-on on Milton Berle's "Texaco Star Theater" and had competed unsuccessfully on the "Arthur Godfrey Talent Scouts" show. Because she was extremely near-sighted, cue cards were of no use to Edie, so she memorized all of her songs before she went on, making them the only unad-libbed parts of the show. Recalling this period, she has said, "My job was supposed to be a singer but what I really did was give Ernie a chance to think of what to do next."

During the last months of "Three to Get Ready," the E.E.F.M.S. was formed. It stood for the Early Eyeball Fraternal and Marching Society, ostensibly honoring all watchers who were able to train their eyes on the television screen at 7:30 A.M. The society's password was "It's Been Real," which was how Ernie signed off the show every day. Everyone who wrote in with a request could receive a membership card signed by Ernie or Edie (depending on who was at the studio early enough to answer the mail in the morning).

In November of 1952 Kovacs was given yet another show by WPTZ, a half-hour production entitled "Kovacs on the Corner," which aired from 11:30 to noon. It was a loser from the start. Ernie let himself be talked into doing a saccharine show with real sets, scripts, writers, and actors. There was, as the name implies, a street corner set through which would pass characters like Pete the Cop, Alfred the Dog, Todelayo the Cat, guest artists, and Edie Adams singing a song or two. It also featured a rather bizarre episode called "Yoo-Hoo Time," in which a member of the studio audience, usually a housewife, was invited onstage to peek through a window on the set and yell "Yoo-Hoo!" presumably to the folks back home.

Ernie hated the show, so much so that on the last one he destroyed the set with a hammer. He sought bigger and better things, and the answer to that was New York. On April 21, 1952, "Kovacs Unlimited" began airing on CBS in the afternoon from 12:45 to 1:30 in the New York area.

Because Ernie was almost unknown in the New York region, the show had a hard time finding sponsors. In fact, the show *had no* sponsors at first. To fill the gap, Ernie created his own products:

- Herman Guggenflechers Quick Frozen Noodniks
- Fu Manchu's Soy Sauce
- Choco-Spin Chocolate Covered Spinach
- Foop
- Hippo-Skin Paper Napkins
- Pancho Paganini's Pounds Off Pellets

It was during this show that Kovacs began doing take-offs on other television shows. One of the most successful was his version of "What's My Line?" except that Ernie's was called "Where Do You

Worka John?" He enters dressed in a costume that makes it patently obvious as to what he does for a living, that is, surgeon, fireman, miner. The panel asks totally inane questions such as "Is your work esthetic?" "Could I feel your biceps?" "What are your favorite tunes?" Finally a panelist (usually Edie Adams) makes a guess, "I know—you play marimba for an all-girl band!" or "You prepare the chopped chicken livers at Reuben's!" and the answer was invariably pronounced *correct!*

Over the years, some of the other television parodies would include:

> Who Dat?
> What's a You Biz?
> I've Got a Hush Hush
> Welcome Transients [Travel Show]
> You Asked to See It
> Mr. Question Man
> Peddle That Tune
> Whom Done It? [Where a victim would be murdered on every show]
> Tough [The panelists were murdered when they did not guess correctly]
> Big Fat World
> Pick Your Expert
> Das Sechzin-Seben Tausend Marks Fragen
> Whip the Wrist Watch
> How It Happened [You Are There]
> What's On Your Mind?
> What's in a Line?
> The Big Payola
> Rancid Camera [Starring Short Bunt]
> The $250,000 Bonanza
> Mr. Science
> Knock Off the Tune, Zeke
> Lemonade Party

Absolutely nothing was sacred; Kovacs satirized both the meek and the powerful without mercy. In a jab at Tennessee Ernie Ford's folksy style he read this "letter from a listener":

> Dear County-Nental,
>
> Every evening, when I turn on the television, I sit on the old kitchen rocker with Averill. He's muh pet pig, in muh lap. . . .

Every time yoh open your dadblamed gums, I know your a talking' right smack at me and Averill. . . . When you start a speilin' in them bull bass tones of yourn, I get goosebumps up and down my back and Averill's tail uncurls and goes into the darnest shapes. This throws off the antennas, and I have to get up and adjust the set. . . . But shucks, Guernsey, I don't keer. . . . The last time you sung your theme song, a whole gallon of ice cream curdled. . . . And two quarts of granny's homemade piccilli bust wide open and some of the chopped pickles were found as fur away as Cousin Walp's green silo. . . . I put some of that Scotch Tape on the pickled watermelon before turning you on tonight. . . . Yeh had such a devilish gleam in your eye lest night, I knew tonight was goin to be a humdinger . . . and it sure is . . . dadbusted it . . . there goes another jar of granny's piccilli. . . . I'll hev to stop now and wipe it up cause paw gits mad when he knows I been watchin' yew. . . . If I can get the pigs fed early tomorrow night, I'm goin' to sachey over to the studio and shake yer big luvable paw. . . .

Yours till the corn crib busts into flames. . . .

Tondelaya Sutter

Although Kovacs was very much an urbane type, the point of the satire was not to make victims of country hicks, but rather the type of television show that would sentimentalize them. False art and bad television were his targets, not the people to whom they catered.

On May 12, 1952, he took on politicians with the following "campaign speech":

Hello constituents . . . cizzens . . . in the upcoming campaign, you will hear many candidates who will use slander, exaggeration and false promises to get your vote.

I make no false promises. . . . I do not slander. . . . I give you my campaign forthright and square . . . first . . . before beginning. . . . Just a peek behind the scenes of my opponent J. Walter Puppybreath. . . . I do not slander nor gossip but feel it my bounden duty to give you facts that may be of interest to you. . . .

First off, J. Walter and Mrs. Puppybreath do not get along. . . . The Puppybreaths live like cats and dogs. . . . I say this not unkindly, but he is cheap, stingy tight with a buck, crooked, lying, and has had to use chlorophyll in his past record. . . . My own past is above reproach. . . . I put in eight years at State Penn . . . er Penn State, preparing myself for the job ahead. . . . I was no idle, rich college student. . . . I earned my way through State Penn . . . Penn State playing five card stud, three card monte and spent a lot of dough getting enough on the teachers to blackmail my way through. . . . It was fight, fight, fight all the way. . . .

> My platform is a simple one.... I make no promises to the
> voters who vote for J. Walter Puppybreath.... But those saga-
> cious, far-sighted, intelligent cizzens who cast a vote for me, I will
> not forget . . . to every student who casts a vote for me, I will pro-
> vide a Cadillac Convertible . . . a faked report card for the entire
> year and my campaign forger will personally sign all hookey notes
> for the end of this term....
>
>   To the honest, good-government seeking voter, I will give a bar-
> rel of Old Grandad, two cases of imported hashish . . . and a sum-
> mer home at Belmar, New Jersey....
>
>   To those of you who cast more than three votes, I give you a
> skeleton key to the side entrance of Fort Knox, the answer sheet
> to "Who Said That" forty-eight hours in advance of the program,
> and the warm handclasp of friendship....
>
>   Thank you

Here we have a politician who is the epitome of the corrupt, back-
slapping, baby-kissing, Tammany Hall–type officer seeker. This fellow is so obvious about his underhanded, dishonest, and downright
sneaky methods of campaigning that he confirms our worst fears
about those who seek elected office. It's a shame Kovacs wasn't
around to catch a glimpse of the Agnew/Nixon/Watergate circus
more than 20 years after he wrote this piece; he would have been the
first to appreciate that sometimes life really does imitate art.

    In these two monologues one sees Ernie's mischievously child-
like sense of humor emerge. What kid does not dream of getting permission to play hookey; what adult would not mind the key to Fort
Knox? Whether on the farm or in the political arena Kovacs evokes
visions of anarchy; be it jars bursting or the blackmail of professors,
it is a vision of life gone awry. Not surprisingly, in the years to come
Kovacs would get to know some of his admirers who worked at *MAD*
magazine and would become a frequent contributor to that ir-
reverent publication.

    CBS, however, was somewhat less appreciative of Ernie's mad-
cap ways and cancelled the show in April of 1953. His troubles
became even more serious in July of that year when his ex-wife, Bette
Shotwell, abducted their two daughters and disappeared (Ernie had
earlier been awarded sole custody). For nearly three years thereafter, Kovacs searched for his daughters, spending more than
$50,000 in private detective fees. Naturally he was not feeling par-
ticularly funny, but needing funds to continue the search he managed
to return to television the following year, despite his considerable

Edie and Ernie with his two daughters. After his ex-wife abducted the girls in 1953, it took Ernie three years and cost him thousands of dollars to find and retrieve them.

anguish. Not until June 1955 were his daughters found living in Florida where Bette was a waitress. Ernie whisked them back to New York where a new stepmother awaited them.

Ernie Kovacs had married Edie Adams in Mexico City on September 12, 1954, after a somewhat frantic courtship. After working on Ernie's television shows, she had starred in "Wonderful Town" on Broadway, and Kovacs had traipsed all over the Eastern seaboard wooing her during the show's out-of-town tryouts. At one point Edie had decided that it was do-or-die as far as Ernie was concerned, and she got on a ship headed for Europe for six weeks, either to forget

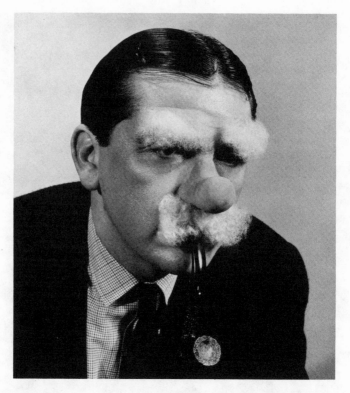

Kovacs as one of his many characters, Inspector Pummerie.

him or realize she simply could not live without him. Luckily for
Ernie, it turned out to be the latter, and after only a few days (and
many long distance phone calls) she cut her trip short and returned
to marry him.

After he found his children, Ernie moved his newly re-formed
family into a cavernous 17-room duplex at 300 Central Park West. In
this huge space, Ernie was finally able to fulfill some of his unconventional decorating ideas, such as his formidable collection of medieval
weaponry and armor. The bedroom boasted his-and-her television
sets at the foot of the bed, with earphones, in case man and wife did
not care to watch the same program. There were also several expensive humidors for the preservation of his beloved cigars. (Incidentally, he smoked an average of 18 a day, which at $2 a cigar came to
more than $13,000 a year.)

By 1954 Kovacs had returned to television, this time to the now-defunct Dumont network, station WABD, which broadcast in New York on Channel 5. This time the title was simply "The Ernie Kovacs Show" and was transmitted, live, every weekday from 11:15 A.M. to 12:15 P.M.

The show's budget was minuscule, but at least Dumont gave him total artistic control. As long as he stayed under budget, he could be as crazy as he wanted. The technical crews loved Ernie; when they worked for him there was never a dull moment. Though he would work them long hours and often ask the impossible, he was generous with gifts and dinners, and there was always a card game going on.

To this show Kovacs brought the stable of characters he had already developed on his past programs, and he added new ones. The many characters he portrayed reflected the multi-faceted, multi-talented, practically schizoid life Kovacs led. Kovacs the writer, Kovacs the performer, Kovacs the director, Kovacs the devoted husband and father, Kovacs the incessant cigar smoker, card player, and professional schnorrer. Over the years these characters would include:

Percy Dovetonsils — Poet
Pierre Ragout — French Storyteller
Miklos Molnar — The Melancholy Magyar
Cromwell Cranston — Semi-private Detective
Wolfgang Von Sauerbraten — German Disc Jockey
Matzoh Hepplewhite — Itinerant Magician
Charlie Clod — Chinese Detective
Inspector Pummerie — Sleuth
Rock Mississippi — Movie Star
Skodney Silksky — Gossip Columnist
Irving Wong — Chinese Song Writer
Luigi Prosciutto — Italian Movie Director
J. Burlington Gearshift — Inventor
Uncle Gruesome — Children's Storyteller
Leroy L. Leroy Leroy W. Bascomb McFinister — News Analyst
Wallie Streete — Stock Market Analyst
Lonely Luigi — Private Occhio
Arlington Pure — Boy Noodnik
Henri Souffle — Love Counselor
Bud Saturday Evening Post — Game Show Emcee

The international flavor of many of his personalities gave Ernie the opportunity to use his uncanny talent for foreign accents and ethnic details. Obviously he also relished inventing outrageous and descriptive names for each one. The sheer volume of characters he created testifies to his incredible prolificness. Most television comedy shows were on only once a week, had a staff of writers, and were still desperate for new material. Not "The Ernie Kovacs Show." Kovacs' staggeringly fertile imagination allowed him to exploit possibilities of television that were obstacles for other performers with roots in vaudeville or nightclubs, where one gag, sketch or character could provide them with years of repertoire as they toured the country. But television is the great devourer of material. It absorbs it, inhales it, chews it up and spits it back. A shtick a performer has been doing for 20 years on the stage is used up in five minutes before millions of people in their living rooms.

Kovacs was unique in these circumstances. He created more material than his producers knew how to use. Usually working late into the night, he would scribble, type and sketch new ideas. A few years later Ernie explained why he felt compelled to work so feverishly: "I hate to lose that little bit of life. I had a year and a half in the hospital which came from the same thing; I'd worked myself to death and got a physical relapse. I put in 18 months trying to patch up my body long enough to keep going. I got to appreciate living so much because I wasn't supposed to. When I left, they gave me three months to go, at the most. Every day's a bonus, you know." In retrospect, these words seem almost prophetic.

One of his most popular characters, and the one that stayed with him the longest was Percy Dovetonsils. The embodiment of the effete snob, this lisping, martini-swilling, limp-wristed poet wearing a smoking jacket and bottle-bottom glasses delighted audiences and was a favorite of the show's crew as well. Some examples of this bard's work follow.

Ode to a Cowboy

Oh cowboy so lean, oh cowboy so tall
You sit there straight as an arrow
But sidesaddle you ride, instead of astride
Are you a real gay ranchero?

To Lucy Schultz

Lucy, my dear, Lucy my love
You are to me, a tiny white dove
Your teeth are like pearls . . . although out of whack
They are round, and firm, and some are turning black. . . .

Your eyes are superb ... they really have class. ...
And one is inscribed ...
Pittsburgh Plate Glass
To say their color is superb ... I say,
Positive and Natch,
It's a bit of a shame that the colors don't match
Your hair is a dream, your hair I adore
If your head was a handle, I could mop up the floor. ...
Your laugh, though dear Lucy, is in its own special class
It reminds me of screwdrivers scratching on glass.

Ode to Mona Lisa

Mona Lisa, your quiet smile,
Like heather grown on a heath.
How come you never laugh out loud,
Do you perhaps have poor teeth?

Although Percy began as a Truman Capote–esque parody of pseudo-intellectualism, he was, in a sense, the most gentle and vulnerable of Ernie's cast of characters. As Kovacs himself said of his poet creation, "He's a beautiful soul who hasn't quite made it over the line into this rude, virile world."

During this period the famous Nairobi Trio evolved. These three apes became, to many, the most famous of Ernie's sketches and one that would be reincarnated several times over the years, with various people donning the simian masks. One writer, Frederic Morton, said that the Nairobi Trio

> restates the book of Job in terms of nihilistic opera. To the eerie tintinnabulation of a certain record tune [Solfeggio] three monkeys snap into unearthly motion; one at an upright, pushing down piano keys as though they were gearshifts, a second wielding a xylophone; and the baton of the third presiding over the whole madness with rigid precision. At a certain recurrent phrase Kovacs, the conductor monster, is clouted on the head by his ensemble's xylophonist. The manner, nuance and mood of the clout may vary with each performance, but it always produces a drool of consternation on the conductor's snout, it always dramatizes the unfathomability of fate and the treacherousness of life, and it always has the audience in stitches over seeing someone else betrayed.[2]

With the Nairobi Trio, as with much of Kovacs' humor, we are not always sure why the sketch is funny. The apes do not actually *do* very much. In fact they perform with a startling economy of movement. As when we watch Chaplin fall into an open manhole on the street, we laugh because we know what is going to happen, not because we are surprised. Charlie will fall down the hole (or not, occasionally fooling us); the conducting ape will be bonked on the head by his subordinate and do a "take" into the camera. It is the *anticipation of the expected* that has us on the edge of our seats; the laughter that follows is the catharsis of the realization of our expectations.

A regular feature on the show was the "Strangely Believe Its, familiarly known as Strangelies. It was a take-off on "Ripley's Believe It or Not," only Ernie's version made Ripley's phenomena look pedestrian. To the haunting question "Is It Coincidence or Is It Something More?" came responses like:

> No one has ever climbed Old Baldy. Old Baldy is a bartender in a saloon in Dallas.

> Hermione Costello was eight feel tall, and tried to find an eight foot husband for years. She finally married two four foot plumbers.

> A two-headed kitten was born in the home of Bettina H. Platitude, who accepted this singular incident quite calmly. However, the two-headed kitten surprised the dog who had been expecting puppies.

> Bicepular Q. Breaststroke, amateur sportsman, dove off a nine hundred foot ladder into a pail of water without injuring himself. Unfortunately, not being able to swim, he was drowned in the bucket.

The Strangelies' casual reporting of the bizarre seems to declare "Yes, life is odd, isn't it?" in the most offhanded way. They are presented as though they are the most normal events in the world, and like Alice down the rabbit hole, the audience is left with the subjective decision of what *is* normal?

Kovacs left Dumont when NBC offered him a substantial increase in salary to do "The Ernie Kovacs Show" mornings from 10:30 to 11:00. The show ran for six months, until poor ratings forced its cancellation in June 1956. Ernie brought along all of the old Dumont gang, including Edie Adams; Barbara Loden, a pretty girl who usually ended up with a pie in the face; Trig Lund, who filled in as straight man; Frank Yasah, who turned Ernie's fanciful imagination into reality with magical special effects, and Barry Shear, a meshuganah director for a meshuganah star.

For this show Ernie created Howard—the World's Strongest Ant, who quickly became a popular attraction. Soon audiences at home were sending in a multitude of props and toys for Howard: minuscule ski outfits, tiny fishing poles, ant-sized whiskey bottles. The show was soon receiving an average of 1,800 accoutrements a week for the tiny hero, and by the end there were more than 30,000. These accessories were an indication of how much audiences were ready and willing to be caught up in Kovacs' version of reality. He brought a sense of whimsy into their lives, where otherwise there may have been none.

In the summer of 1956 the Kovacs show was moved to an evening time slot as a half-hour replacement for Sid Caesar's popular "Your Show of Shows." Ernie knew that this was an opportunity to reach a new audience, one that did not watch morning television or was not already cultishly devoted to him. Therefore he brought to it some of his favorite bits, such as Skodney Silksky—Hollywood reporter:

(Sound of teletype)

This is Skodney Silksky with news, views and interviews of, from and about Hollywood, U.S. of A. Hollywood . . . where many an aging actress is on her last lap. First . . . to squelch an ugly rumor. There is nothing to the gossip, I repeat, there is nothing to the gossip that there is anything between Lassie and Rin Tin Tin. . . . Simply because they have been seen holding paws in a few night-clubs does not mean they are engaged. They just happen to be old fraternity brothers from the American Kennel Club.

• • •

The recent success of the exciting flicker, *The King and I*, has started a rash of sequels . . . perhaps the most outstanding will be Septic Studios release *Abbott and Costello Meet the King and I*. . . . Smith and Dale play Abbott and Costello, Mickey Rooney plays the King, and Elvis Presley plays "I" . . . In an exciting sequence, which takes place just eleven feet from Scotland Yard, Elvis sings: "Keep Your Cotton Pickin' Fingers Off'n My Lily White Throat," "You're Nothing But a Hound of the Baskervilles," "Blue Suede Handcuffs" and "Heartbreak Hilton."

These Skodney Silksky items (Sidney Solsky was a famous Hollywood reporter) were right on the mark. They not only parodied the whole idea of Hollywood gossips, but managed to poke gentle fun at the movie-making industry as well, with its sometimes ridiculous casting and exploitations of box office hits. As with all Kovacs' material, the satire was never meant to be vindictive or malicious. Years later when the formidable dowager of Hollywood gossip columnists, Louella Parsons, came to interview Ernie at his home, he was exceptionally nice to her and personally escorted her on a tour of the house.

In November 1956 Kovacs was made co-host of NBC's "Tonight Show." Ernie did the show on Mondays and Tuesdays, and Steve Allen did all the other nights. There was no love lost between the two funnymen, for Kovacs had accused Allen several times in the past of stealing material.

During this period, NBC offered Kovacs yet another show. Jerry Lewis was about to attempt his first solo after his act with Dean Martin had split up. The network had offered Lewis an hour and a half on Saturday nights, but he agreed to do only 60 minutes, leaving the network with half an hour to fill. Why the thought occurred to put another comedy show in that time slot is not known, but the network turned to Kovacs, who accepted on the condition that he have total control over content. NBC was desperate enough to agree, insuring Ernie of a larger budget and more rehearsal time than he had ever enjoyed before, and he took full advantage.

The show, which premiered on January 19, 1957, marked a point in Kovacs' career when he gradually turned further away from oral humor and increasingly towards visual comedy. Complicated visual gags and sound effects are more expensive to produce than funny scripts. Now that Ernie was in the prime-time big league, he was able to develop more sophisticated sight gags.

The show was called "Eugene," after Ernie's befuddled clown character. It soon became known as "The Silent Show," the first television comedy show to have no dialogue. Millions of Americans who might never have watched Kovacs' type of unconventional comedy kept their sets tuned to NBC after the Jerry Lewis show ended and saw him that night. The response was wildly enthusiastic.

In the show's opener the audience was introduced to Eugene, a simple soul who wanders around making squeaky noises when he walks, wears his pants three inches too short, sports a straw boater, and carries a lunch pail. As Eugene enters an art gallery he sees four Greek-style statues. When he passes the first, that of a nude man, he hears a sneeze. As he passes the second statue, lovers entwined in an embrace, he hears heavy breathing. As he passes the third, the famous "Thinker" by Rodin, he hears humming. The fourth statue, of a young girl playing a lyre, caresses him as he goes by, but when he turns to kiss her, the statue collapses.

Eugene then enters the library of a men's club (the pace and style of the piece were surreal enough that the audience did not feel it was strange for backgrounds to drift from one into the next; that Eugene is in an art gallery that becomes a men's club does not seem to matter at all) where he opens a tome on the life of Von Richthoven, and we hear the sound effects of an airplane propeller. He takes another book, *Camille*, opens it, and we hear a girl coughing. Eugene then opens *War and Peace* at the beginning, and we hear the sounds of battle, but when he skips to the end of the book, we hear birds singing and a live dove flies out from the pages. Last, he takes down *The Old Man and the Sea;* when he opens it water is spurted at him, and he quickly replaces it.

Eugene sits down at a large table to eat his lunch and takes several kinds of small round edibles from his lunch box. However, since the table has been built on a 15-degree angle (undetectable to the home viewer, as the camera is also on a 15-degree angle in the opposite direction), these round objects roll off the table and onto the lap of a dour-faced man trying to read a newspaper. As Eugene attempts to pour milk out of a thermos, gravity once again seems to go awry as he consistently misses the cup and the milk ends up in the lap of the man at the end of the table. Finally, our hero decides to rectify the situation by getting up, lifting one end of the table, and seemingly tilting it back in the opposite direction until it is on an even keel. This astonishing piece of business exemplifies Kovacs' genius in visual and technical wizardry, especially since he does not call attention to it as a technical exercise per se, but winningly incorporates it into comic effect.

Eugene is Ernie's Everyman, wandering—bemused and perplexed—in a complicated and cynical world. He is the perfect clown character, and he must deal with situations over which he has absolutely no control. Eugene does not know the social or cultural taboos, so he plunges ahead. And since he is always unfamiliar with his surroundings, his voyage of discovery will never end. In some ways Eugene brings to mind the Buster Keaton character, with his too-small hat and unsmiling countenance. But more than physical similarities, there is a likeness of passivity in the two roles. They share a certain fatalistic attitude, a trust in life that allows them to be buffeted about by the forces of nature and man. In both cases it is not so much what the character does that is funny, but what is done to, or befalls, him. Keaton spent his youth in vaudeville houses, being thrown about the stage by his father and billed as "The Human Mop." Kovacs, though not treated roughly, was also moved along by forces beyond his control: watching his family's financial conditions change radically, and spending 18 months in a hospital bed. Kovacs' fatalism manifests itself in Eugene's quiet acceptance of books that produce sound effects or douse him with water, of tables that reject objects being placed on them. Just as Keaton's heroine always seemed to be just beyond his reach, so does the beautiful statue that Eugene attempts to kiss crumble at his fingertips.

After the "Eugene" show, Ernie decided it was time to move to the West Coast. The move may have been precipitated by the publication of his novel, *Zoomar.* The book, written in 13 frenetic days and nights, was a thinly veiled account of life in television. Many of the less-than-flattering portraits drawn in the novel were of Ernie's colleagues and bosses, and perhaps he felt it would be a good idea to put some distance between New York and himself for a while. The fact that Columbia Pictures had offered him a role in the film *Operation Madball* for a considerable sum of money also may have had something to do with his move.

Hollywood and Ernie Kovacs seemed to fit together like two pieces in a jigsaw puzzle. In a sybaritic town of cigar-smoking, card-playing, lavishly extravagant hedonists, Ernie fit right in. He soon became friendly with the so-called "Rat Pack" of Frank Sinatra, Dean Martin, Sammy Davis Jr., and others, and all-night poker games were not unusual.

He moved Edie and the girls into a big house in Coldwater Canyon and quickly furnished it à la Kovacs. It was even more outlandishly appointed than the Central Park West apartment, complete with indoor waterfall and a steam bath, which Ernie used several times a day.

Though he no longer had a daily television show to do, Ernie was pretty busy in Los Angeles. He appeared on a number of talk shows and, sometimes with Edie, participated as a guest star on the shows of Polly Bergen, Dinah Shore, Perry Como and others. He also emceed a rather insipid game show called "Take a Good Look" for

The years 1957–1962 were the most prolific of Ernie's brief career. During that time he made nine movies (including *Our Man in Havana* and *Bell, Book and Candle*) and wrote, produced and starred in "Kovacs on Music" and a series of specials for Dutch Masters Cigars.

two seasons on ABC. In addition, he worked in nine movies from 1957 to 1962, usually cast as some sort of captain (naval, police, army). Eventually he resorted to taking out an ad in *Variety* imploring producers to give him other kinds of roles. His best films included Carol Reed's *Our Man in Havana* and *Bell, Book and Candle* with James Stewart and a man who would prove to be one of Ernie's closest friends, Jack Lemmon.

His best work took place in a series of television specials in which he wrote, produced and starred. The first one, entitled "Kovacs on Music," aired May 22, 1959, on NBC. Sketches included one with dancers jumping around on a giant piano keyboard, producing music as they pranced about; another was a concert of Tchaikovsky's "Romeo and Juliet" with comic musical emphases given by triangle, wood block and trombone; and one in which three jingle singers (including Edie and Louis Jourdan) are in a recording studio. Edie keeps singing the wrong note until the conductor, Maestro Kovacs, approaches and flicks a fly off her music sheet.

One of the best pieces of the evening was the gorilla ballet. Dressed in tutus, a corps de ballet of gorillas performs a simian "Swan Lake." During the curtain calls the Odette-Odile gorilla receives a large stalk of bananas in lieu of flowers and graciously hands one to her romantic lead, the Hunter gorilla. As Sid Caesar did in "Your Show of Shows," Ernie dared to use highbrow forms of culture: opera, ballet, Greek tragedy, as a basis for parody, and he made sure that the parody stood up on its own as comedy, even if the audience was unfamiliar with the original source.

After the success of "Kovacs on Music," Dutch Masters Cigars offered Kovacs the opportunity of doing a series of one-hour specials once a month. What better spokesman for a cigar company than 18-a-day Ernie? With the healthy budget he was given, Kovacs was able to turn out some impressive work. Much of what he did in the specials was silent and visual comedy—some of it old material, some re-worked, some new. In addition, Kovacs insisted upon writing and acting in nearly all of the cigar commercials, most of which were funny and imaginative and flowed right into the spirit of the show, rather than being the usual advertising banalities. These commercials proved so successful for Dutch Masters that the company later used them to sponsor other television shows as well.

In these specials Kovacs elevated the teaser (Kovacs' term for the short, visual gags that ended in blackouts) sight gag to a high art. Here are a few examples:

> A workman (Ernie) is on a scaffold, painting the nose of Abraham Lincoln at Mt. Rushmore. The nose sneezes and the man is blown away.

> A safecracker draws a safe on the wall, cuts through the "canvas," opens the safe and takes the money.

> A girl taking a bubble bath. A submarine periscope surfaces next to her.

> A man in a park bends down at a fountain to get a drink of water. Bubbles come out of the back of his head.

> Betsy Ross has just finished sewing the flag. She reads a newspaper

headline, "Alaska Admitted to Union." She does a straight "take" into the camera.

A man watching television. On the screen is a scene of a man serenading a woman in a canoe. The man watching the television becomes irritated, takes a drill and bores through the top of the set, sinking the canoe.

A large woman makes a grand entrance (a take-off on Loretta Young); she falls through the floor.

Several of the teasers were used over and over again as running gags, such as the woman in the bathtub or the woman who makes a grand entrance. Occurrences would befall these hapless women over which they had absolutely no control, from the merely astonishing to the sublimely ridiculous. Both situations were used to deflate an existing cliché. The woman in the bath was reminiscent of a fifties' sex symbol, titillation in a tub. That is, until dozens of people emerge from her bath. The woman who crashes through the floor (or gets a pie in the face) spoofs the grande dame about to bestow herself on a supposedly grateful audience. Like a Bach fugue, there were many variations on a single theme.

During this period, Ernie became fascinated by the oscilloscope and the patterns created on it by sound and music. Kurt Weill's "Mac the Knife" (sung in German) from "The Threepenny Opera" became a recurrent theme during the Dutch Masters specials, the oscilloscope lines playing an eerie accompaniment. Kovacs even had an oscilloscope installed in his home to facilitate choreographing the dancing lines created by the vibrating frequencies.

In later years Kovacs' comedy became objective and impersonal. That is not to say that he became cold to his audience; rather, increasingly it was not the character himself or his emotional state that was the focus, but the situations, actions, or objects that Kovacs manipulated to produce his visions. Eventually, human characters and emotions were dispensed with altogether. The oscilloscope was a machine, without feelings or sensibilities, yet Kovacs shaped its lines like a conductor leading an orchestra. Similarly, the Office Orchestra piece and the Street Scene study, neither of which was meant to be really funny, provided sensitive treatments of classical music and visual effects in almost balletic formats.

The Street Scene, done to the music of Kara Kareyev, was simply a sort of living still life. The people in it were larger-than-life stereotypes: the Irish cop, the Italian fruit-seller, a thug, a "loose" woman. There were no lines, no gags, no laughs, merely a soberly representational look at life on an American street as a means of interpreting the music to which it was performed. This tableau was a forerunner of today's avant-garde performance art, where the creation of an "event" or "happening" is more closely related as an art form to sculpture or painting than acting in theater or television.

The Office Orchestra was more whimsical. Done to a jazzy version of "Sentimental Journey," the cast was made up entirely of objects, except for one dismayed human who departs early on. The set is a rather mundane, grayish office. But when the music begins the office takes on an energized vitality. The drawers of the filing cabinet open and close as a trombone. The typewriter becomes a piano. The bubbles in the water fountain add their own percussion, and the clock ticks in tempo. Switchboard lights play an arpeggio; the wires become a dancing chorus line. Paper clips and desk drawers add harmonious movements. A leaky fountain pen, the telephone, a pencil sharpener and a radiator spewing steam join in the symphony. On paper all this may seem easy, but it took a full crew working around the clock (and fortunately Kovacs had some of the best special effects men working for him) to make this panorama come alive. Here we see the impersonal quality of Kovacs' later work; the inanimate objects take on a life all their own. Heretofore this sort of living tableau was seen only in animated cartoons; that is, the uncontrollable broomsticks in Disney's *Fantasia*. The objects in Kovacs' fantasy do not, however, take on any semblance of human form; no little eyes, noses or mouths appear. They are what they are—desks, telephones, wires, and so forth; they never pretend to be anything else. Although the scene may preclude human involvement and emotion, the scene is charged with a certain superrealism, as though we were watching through a telescope, with each item assuming crystal clarity—no romantically hazy camera lens, no diffused lighting. The scene's magical quality comes from the interrelationship between the seemingly innocuous office equipment and the music.

Kovacs left no potential for comedy undeveloped on his specials. Just as he had insisted on writing funny commercials, so could the shows' credits not be taken seriously. Interspersed with the names of cast and crew were such non sequiturs as:

Tristan and Isolde is okay, Bob, but I'm not giving up my banjo lesson for anything.

Give up taxidermy Thurmond, all these mounted squirrels.

Cell Meeting Tonight. It's Your Duty as an Agitator to Attend.

Very well, Bertram, you may kiss me, but first you'll have to remove your clarinet.

She had a funny kind of smile, Cheddar . . . three rows of gums.

The last of the specials Ernie Kovacs did for Dutch Masters was taped on December 2, 1961, and was aired on January 23, 1962. By then Ernie was dead.

On January 13, he had gone to a party at the home of director Billy Wilder in honor of the birth of Milton Berle's son. Edie was also at the party, but they had arrived in separate cars: Ernie in the white Rolls-Royce, Edie in the Corvair station wagon. He left the party at approximately 1:00 A.M., telling his wife that he would drive the station wagon home. It was raining lightly, and, apparently unused to the heavier, rear-engine car, he lost control, possibly while searching for the car's lighter. He began to skid and ran into a telephone pole. Less than one week before his forty-third birthday, Ernie Kovacs died of a hairline skull fracture incurred when his head hit the steering wheel. He was dead by the time help arrived a few moments later, a cigar between his fingers.

Ernie Kovacs' contributions to television comedy and technology are immeasurable. His humor was uniquely his own, and he dared present ideas because *he* felt they were funny, not to please sponsors, network vice presidents or Nielsen families. Choosing to ignore limitations on what could or could not be done on television, he plunged ahead to realize his mad fantasies by whatever means it took. His indefatigable creativity and courage in the quest for originality have never, and probably will never, be seen on our television screens again. We owe you a great debt, Mr. Kovacs; as you would say:

IT'S BEEN REAL.

Olsen and Johnson

John Siguard (Ole) Olsen and Harold Ogden (Chic) Johnson were two of the looniest characters ever to hit vaudeville, Broadway, and briefly, television. The unexpected was the norm with this rambunctious duo, and their anarchistic style earned them many fans over the years. Like Ed Wynn, however, they were unable to translate their appeal from stage to small screen.

Ole Olsen was born on March 5, 1895, in Peru, Indiana, the son of a boilermaker. His future partner Chic Johnson, a toolmaker's son,

Broadway stars Olsen and Johnson were unable to adjust their anarchistic style of oversized gags and broad farce to the subtler, more streamlined comedy of television.

was born on November 6, 1892, in Englewood, Illinois. In November of 1904 the two met in the office of a theatrical agent. Olsen played the violin; Johnson had played piano in a quartet that had recently broken up. The two young men decided to cast their fates together as a comedy act. They soon found work in vaudeville touring the famed Keith circuit, where they were known as "Likeable Lads Loaded with Laughs."

Olsen and Johnson enjoyed a fair amount of success on the vaudeville stage, but their greatest triumphs came on Broadway. With "Hellzapoppin'" (September 22, 1938) they were firmly ensconced as stars of a major magnitude. Called a "screamlined" revue in 2 acts and 25 scenes, the show featured broad comedy, slapstick, puns, firecrackers, sirens, guns and Hitler speaking with a Yiddish accent. Broadway had never seen anything quite like it. When "Hellzapoppin'" closed after 1,404 performances, it held the record for the longest-running musical on Broadway.

Subsequent revues starring Olsen and Johnson always had the same formula of irrepressible mayhem and outrageous stunts, including "Sons o' Fun" (1941), "Laffing Room Only" (1944), and "Pardon Our French" (1950). They also toured with such "Hellzapoppin'"-style revues as "Hellzasplashin'," "Jerks-Berserk," and "Crazy House."

In 1949 Ole and Chic tried to bring their spontaneous shenanigans to television, without much luck. The camera was too limiting for the kind of free-for-all comedy they were used to providing. For them, it was not so much the quality of the material they did, but how it was done. Unlike Milton Berle, who had a machine-gun fire of jokes to launch, Olsen and Johnson could not make the leap from oversized gags and broad farce to the subtler, more streamlined comedy needed for television.

On August 27, 1959, Chic Johnson told a reporter for the New York *Morning Telegraph:* "We have never made any pretense at being glib, satirical, stand-up comics. We manufacture gimmicks and gags that are about as basic as you can get. We are salesmen. We sell laughs. We have never tried to be subtle. Apparently people all over the world still like that sort of thing."

Chic Johnson died on February 25, 1962, at the age of 66. Ole Olsen, his partner for nearly 60 years, passed away on January 1, 1963, at age 71.

Martha Raye

In the world of female clowns Martha Raye has engraved an image of herself as actress, comedienne and singer. Her wide mouth was a natural for mugging, and she managed to carve a niche for herself against formidable male stars.

Raye began life as Margaret Theresa Yvonne Reed on August 27, 1916, in Butte, Montana. She was born backstage at the local vaudeville theater where her parents, Pete Reed and Mabelle Hooper, were performing a double act of song, dance and comedy. Brother Bud and sister Melodye soon rounded out the performing family.

As a teenager, after having always been on the road with her parents, Raye formed an act with her brother, billed as "Bud and Margie." Life was hard on the traveling family of troupers, and some weeks they were forced to sleep in their car.

At the age of 15, Maggie, as she was known, went solo. Lucky to have been born with a strong-belt voice, she got work as a singer with a variety of bands. Later she headlined at such well-known nightclubs as the Riviera and the Chez Paris in New York.

In 1936 Raye went out to Los Angeles, where she appeared at such nightspots as Louis Prima's Famous Door, the Casanova, and the chic Trocadero. It was while singing at the latter that she was spotted by Paramount studio chiefs Adolph Zukor and Darryl F. Zanuck. They signed her to a contract right away and cast her in *Rhythm on the Range* opposite Bing Crosby. From then on, her fortune was made. Generally cast as the female comic relief (never the romantic lead), Raye went on to appear in dozens of films, many of which were amusing and some, mediocre. Her credits included *The Big Broadcast of 1937* (1936), *Waikiki Wedding* and *Artists and Models* (both 1937), *College Swing* (1938), *$1,000 a Touchdown* (1939), *The Boys from Syracuse* (1940), *Hellzapoppin'* (1941), *Four Jills in a Jeep* (1944), *Monsieur Verdoux* (1947), and *Jumbo* (1962).

Through the years, wide-mouthed Martha has been a camera favorite and frequent foil for some of television's brightest male stars.

Raye tried a number of ways to become a regular on television. She was one of the rotating hosts on "All-Star Revue" in 1951–52. The "Martha Raye Show" ran once a month from December 26, 1953, through May 15, 1954. She did 13 weekly shows for the next season, from September 20, 1955, to June 29, 1956. Her second banana on the 60-minute NBC show was former boxer Rocky Graziano. Featuring song-and-dance production numbers as well as comedy sketches, the show was amiable without being wildly popular.

Many of Raye's best moments on television were as guest star. She was a frequent foil for such major talents as Milton Berle, Red Skelton, Bob Hope and Steve Allen. In the seventies, the six-times-married Raye made a reputation for herself as a Vietnam War "hawk" when she entertained the troops on several tours. Raye returned to television on a regular basis as Rock Hudson's housekeeper on "McMillan and Wife" and as the mother of diner-owner Mel in "Alice." She has also recently appeared on "The Golden Girls" as the Sicilian sister of Estelle Getty.

Soupy Sales

Baby boomers around the country grew up with the wonderful shenanigans of Soupy Sales. The funny man with elastic face entertained the postwar generation with pies, puppets and puns. Setting a precedent for his modern-day counterparts, Uncle Floyd and Pee Wee Herman among them, his was the first hip kiddie show. He kept children and many of their older siblings and parents glued to the set.

The future king of cream pies was born Milton Supman on January 8, 1926, in Franklinton, North Carolina. Soupy was the third son of Hungarian Jews, and his father owned a small clothing store in Huntington, West Virginia, where Sales was raised.

As a young man Soupy served in the Navy during World War II ("I found a way to beat the Army, I joined the Navy!") and was at the invasion of Okinawa while serving on the USS *Randall*, flagship of the Seventh Fleet. After the war he got a job writing for radio and then became a disc jockey. For show business, his name underwent several alterations. Milton Supman became Milton Hines, which later became Soupy Hines, and finally Soupy Sales.

It was in Detroit that Soupy found his true calling. In 1953 he was given his own children's television show, "Soupy's On," where he stayed until 1960. In 1955 he had been the ABC summer replacement for "Kukla, Fran, and Ollie." In 1960 "The Soupy Sales Show" moved to KABC in Los Angeles and, in 1964, to New York's WNEW and syndication.

He brought to his one-man show a cast of puppet characters. There were the two mongrels, White Fang ("the biggest and meanest dog in the United States") and Black Tooth ("the kindest dog in the country"), Pookie the Whistling Lion, Hippy the Silent Hippopotamus, Herman the Flea and Willie the Worm. Occasionally there were human characters too, but for the most part only their arms and hands were seen gesticulating by an open door.

Soupy, who would try any gag, sometimes himself became trying—to his employers. In 1965 the famed "wallet incident" brought him a two-week suspension from New York's WNEW.

Soupy Sales—the silliest clown around.

Celebrities dropped by, however, for it had become the "in" thing to get hit in the face with one of Soupy's cream pies (actually composed of crust and shaving cream). Soupy himself got pelted in the puss at least once during every show (he estimates that he has had tens of thousands of pies in the face in his career), and others, such as Frank Sinatra, Tony Curtis, Mickey Rooney, Burt Lancaster and Dean Martin showed up to join in the fun. It was estimated that approximately 65 percent of the audience of Soupy's "kids" show were adults. *New York Magazine* called him "a great clown in the tradition of the commedia dell'arte."

No gag was too low for the bow-tied comedian. "Show me a dead Communist and I'll show you a Red Skelton!" he declared. "How do you drive a baby buggy? Tickle his feet!" he exclaimed.

On January 1, 1965, he overdid it, at least as far as the station was concerned. That was the date of the famous (or infamous) "wallet incident," in which Soupy exhorted his young viewers to slip into the bedrooms of their still sleeping (and presumably hung over) parents and over to daddy's wallet to extract the funny green paper with pictures of George Washington and Ben Franklin and Lincoln and Jefferson and to put them in envelopes and send them to Soupy, in care of WNEW. Needless to say, it was just another corny gag to Sales, and of course no children did respond to his request, but the station became irate and suspended him from the air for two weeks. There was an uproar and college students picketed the suspension. Soupy's pride was hurt; he left the show at the end of the season. It was also the end of an era.

In 1966 Soupy made his Broadway debut in "Come Live with Me," which quickly bombed. Walter Kerr said of the effort in the *New York Times:* "'Come Live with Me' has no doubt been produced on Broadway in order to introduce us to Soupy Sales. Now that we've met, it might be nice to see him in a play."

Today Sales has returned to radio, where he has a talk show on New York's WNBC. At least there he is not bombarded with pies in the face, but he has kept the same silly humor and spontaneous sense of the sublimely ridiculous.

Red Skelton

Red Skelton is the quintessential clown. While others may arguably be called wits, comics, or comedians, Red is a clown first and last. With his rubber limbs and an equally elastic face, his only goal in life seems to have been to make the audience laugh. His humor is without guile or sophistication, and his style has not changed in the more than 50 years he has been in show business. But he is honest in his simplicity and remarkable in his staying power. Red's "shucks, ma'am" good 'ol boy demeanor breaks down the walls of resistance in the viewer; his insane giggle breaks all of the rules of comedy. His eccentricities are legend and his personal tragedies heartbreaking, but in the end we are left with a man who knows how to wrest a laugh or a tear from his public and whose bittersweet smile never forgets to bless and keep us.

Over the years Red has conquered stage, screen, radio and television. His most famous routines are actually few in number, and it is a tribute to his artistry that audiences still want to see them over and over again. Television was both a boon and a thorn in his side, eating up as it did the routines he had been performing in vaudeville and burlesque, and yet providing him with the necessary visual medium for entertaining countless numbers of viewers.

Richard Skelton was born on July 18, 1913, in Vincennes, Indiana, the fourth son of Ida and Joe Skelton. Ida was a cleaning lady and Joe was a circus clown and roustabout. Then, as now, clowns did not earn a great deal of money, and frequent travel was part of the job. Joe was also a heavy drinker, and in the end it was alcohol that killed him, just three months before Red's birth. Ida barely managed to scrape by and provide for Paul, Denny, Christopher and baby Red — so called for the bright carrot-colored hair with which he was born. They lived in what was basically a shack, with the barest amenities. "My mother was so poor," says Red, "that she used to get all her furniture from the Salvation Army, so if we had to move out fast without paying the rent, she didn't mind leaving it behind." His older brothers were apparently not thrilled with the latest addition to their family, and on several occasions they nearly killed young Red through thoughtlessness, carelessness or downright hostility. Even as an adult, Red was never close to his three older siblings.

The youngest Skelton was obviously meant for better things in life. Even as a small child he was a hustler, trying desperately to earn a few pennies to augment his mother's meager income. By the age of seven he was hawking newspapers on the streets of Vincennes. His future career in comedy may have been inspired by a chance encounter with the great comedian Ed Wynn, to whom he sold a newspaper one day and who in turn gave the young salesman a ticket to that night's vaudeville show where he was headlining. And as a child Red was acutely aware of the show-business profession of the father he idolized but had never known.

Red made his first break into show business, if it can be called that, with the Doc Lewis Medicine Show. This was the most rudimentary entertainment, providing a diversion in the form of amateurish singing and dancing for the people of small towns and farm communities, the aim being to sell them some magic elixir that would cure them of all ills, real or imagined. Ninety-nine percent of what was sold under the guise of medicine was, of course, pure quackery, though very often the potion would be made up of large quantities of alcohol or extract of cocaine, which would elevate the mood of the user and encourage him to become a repeat customer. Twelve-year-old Red Skelton apparently was lacking in talent, unable to amuse the folks with his singing or dancing, but he did have a fine knack of falling off the stage to the amusement of the assembled crowd, and Doc Lewis did a good business selling his brew. "That stuff was nothing but epsom salts, water, and brown sugar," said Red, "and the Doc was getting a buck a bottle for it. One bottle of that junk in your stomach and you either called in the undertaker or you had a constitution that could take arsenic."

Red was never much of a student and had been left behind several times, so it was no great heartache for him to drop out of school altogether by the time he was 14. Since he was tall for his age he was able to talk himself into a number of jobs, including entertaining on a Mississippi riverboat, from which he was eventually kicked off for trying to seduce the captain's daughter. Even in his early teenage years Red had had an eye for the ladies and a randy nature, neither of which abated as he matured.

After being unceremoniously chucked off the showboat, Red joined an acting troupe known as a "Tom Show," since its entire repertory was acting out *Uncle Tom's Cabin* in one-night stands throughout the South and Midwest. He then enjoyed an opportunity to work for the same outfit his father had clowned for, the Hagenbeck-Wallace Circus. He was hired as a walk-around clown, a position inferior to the senior clowns', who performed tricks, sketches and musical numbers.

As much as Red was in awe of working for his father's former employer, life in the big top was not for him. He went back on the road and worked for various stock companies, riverboats or minstrel shows. It was a time of third-rate boardinghouses, unscrupulous managers and greasy spoons—a particularly dreary existence for a 17-year-old boy hoping for upward mobility in a country in the grips of the Great Depression. Yet Red did not waste those years on the road; he learned as much as possible from his fellow performers, gradually building up a small collection of bits, songs, dances and pratfalls that he used to make up what could loosely be called his act. Through the sheer luck of being in the right place at the right time, he was able to make his break into burlesque at the Gaiety Theater in Kansas City. It was there that he met the person most responsible for honing his talents, expanding his repertoire and ultimately making him a star.

The daughter of an undertaker, Edna Marie Stillwell was a blonde, 15-year-old usher at the Gaiety, with pert good looks and a flashing smile that made her the all–American girl. But Edna was not just a pretty face. Aggressive and efficient, she attracted Red's attention right away. She saw in him a brash, handsome, friendly fellow with a hokey act and no inhibitions, and from the time they were married in 1931—the bride was 16, the bridegroom had not yet turned 18—until she stopped editing and writing his material in 1951, long after their divorce, it was always Edna who maintained unswerving confidence in her teenaged lover.

At the time of their marriage no one could have been more broke than these two adolescents. Red was "between engagements" and had to borrow the two dollars for the marriage license from Edna's mother. Soon afterward, however, he began to make a mark in show business—as a Walkathon clown.

The Walkathon, also known as the Dance Marathon, was that particularly gruesome form of Depression entertainment in which contestants shuffled around the dance floor for as long as they could endure it, with ten-minute breaks for food, toilets, or what rest they could grab in those few moments. But to persevere in the Dance Marathon one quickly learned to sleep on one's feet. These torture sessions masquerading as amusements sometimes went on for months, and in an effort to keep the spectators absorbed in the exhibition, comics were employed to liven things up. Red quickly gained a reputation as one of the best marathon emcee/clowns and, aside from the fact that he enjoyed receiving the much-needed paycheck the Walkathon provided, he also seemed to revel in his total freedom to indulge in pratfalls and high jinks. According to his biographer, Arthur Marx, "Red kept up a running patter of jokes, sang songs, made faces, did imitations, took pratfalls, kissed ladies, crawled under seats, climbed chandeliers, sat on laps, ate neckties, broke plates, undressed, doused himself with soft drinks yanked from customers' hands, walked on all fours, imitated drunks and rubes and 'mean widdle boys,' recited poetry, performed card tricks, rode a tricycle around the ege of the balcony. Once he even stole a mounted policeman's horse from the street and galloped around the auditorium on him, with the gendarme in hot pursuit."[1]

But Walkathons were products of their era, and they soon began to fade in popularity. Red was desperate to make a name for himself in the "legitimate" theater, vaudeville, and he and Edna put together a short act with Edna acting as the stooge. There were more than a few lean times when sneaking out of boardinghouses to avoid the bill and going to bed hungry were the rule rather than the exception. Red was reduced to resorting to some of the tricks he had learned from Doc Lewis; he sold rat poison guaranteed safe for children and pets. Also rats. He also promoted a "Miracle Windshield De-Fogger"—an ordinary bar of soap cut up and wrapped in newspaper. Eventually things began to pick up and the young couple played some of the smaller vaudeville circuits, finally landing an engagement at the prestigious Lido Club in Montreal. After a rocky start because of language differences, the customers warmed to the redhaired comic even if they did not speak English, and by the end of his third week he was a smash. Red became so well-known at the Lido and other Canadian nightclubs that by the time he returned to the United States he was known in the business as "that Canadian comic." It was in Montreal that he and Edna devised his Doughnut Dunkers routine. In this he imitated the various ways people drench their morning pastry: carefully, sloppily, greedily, shyly, etc. The bit became one of Skelton's most famous, and he continued to gobble doughnuts for audiences for the next decade. The only problem was that the more successful he became, the more doughnuts he had to devour. When he was playing the Roxy Theater in New York, for example, in 1938, he did five shows a day, consuming nine doughnuts at each show. That meant 45 doughnuts a day, 315 doughnuts a week! It was no surprise that he put on nearly 35 pounds during this period, and eventually he had to drop the routine for a while in order to drop some weight.

Red himself was more popular with audiences and critics than was his material, which was still pretty corny and unoriginal. *Variety* reported on February 9, 1938:

> Skelton spreads his rich and resourceful reservoir of clowning from the moment the foots first come up until they're finally doused. Of substantial aid to him in a couple of passages is his blonde feed, Edna Stillwell. Skelton calls his initial shots with a row of hoary wife, marriage and mother-in-law jokes, but the folks howl down at 'em as though every one is as crisp and bright as a new banknote. The redhead's parade of stew types socks 'em as soundly as his dunking routine, while the finale baseball-playing bit provides applause of ear-splitting proportions.

It seems that Red may have overdone his reliance on the doughnut dunking sketch. In *Variety*'s review of his show in Chicago on September 6, 1939, he was blasted with "Disappointment is Skelton, with his motheaten vaude routine. The doughnut bit, which used to get laughs, failed to connect at all with this audience."

In spite of his scarcity of material, Skelton's star continued to rise. In March of 1940 he played New York's Paramount Theater with Frank Sinatra and Tommy Dorsey. He continued at the Paramount in April, headlining with the "Mexican Spitfire," Lupe Velez (rumor has it that he and the sexy Lupe shared more than the spotlight). His salary had gradually grown to the point where he could command up to $4,000 a week at the big vaudeville houses.

In 1940 Red added a sketch to his act that became a tremendous sensation, one that audiences would continue to request more than 40 years later. Guzzler's Gin was a take-off on a radio (later tele-

vision) announcer who becomes so enamored of the gin he is hawking that he becomes plastered. Starting out seriously and soberly, the
pitchman describes his product as a "nice, smooth drink." That is, until he tastes it and the paint-removing properties of the potion
become etched on his face. Each time he does his spiel and drinks
more of the gin, the rotgut seems to go down a little easier. His pro-
nouncement that it is a "nice, smoooooooooth drink" gains more "o's"
each time he makes his pitch and drinks another glass. By the end
of the piece, disheveled and sodden, his voice is gravelly and his gait
swaying. Finally he passes out. Ironically, Guzzler's Gin established
Red as one of the great stage drunks, though in those early years the
strongest libation he would enjoy was an ice cream soda.

Red's huge success on the vaudeville stage brought him, almost
inevitably, to the attention of Hollywood's movie studios as well as
to radio producers. In 1938 he appeared as Itchy the M.C. in a forgettable cinematic adaptation of the Broadway play "Having a Wonderful Time," with Lucille Ball. Shortly after making the film he made
his radio debut on "The Red Foley Show," broadcast from Cincinnati,
Ohio, on station WLW. Foley provided the country and western
music on his guitar, and Skelton the laughs. The producer was the
Russell M. Seeds Advertising Company, a Chicago firm headed by
Freeman Keyes, who was to be of invaluable assistance to the comedian's career. Although Skelton's agent by this time was William Morris, it was Keyes who signed him to an exclusive contract for radio
and—with a great deal of foresight—the as-yet-untried medium of
television.

Skelton was a hit on "The Red Foley Show" and was soon starring in his own weekly radio show, broadcast from Chicago on NBC
with the Raleigh Cigarette Company as the sponsor (Red himself
never smoked cigarettes). Edna was in charge of providing him with
enough material to appear week after week, and she accomplished
the job with her usual efficiency, maintaining vast files of jokes tried
and untried. They also hired a fresh young comedy writer after receiving a telegram that read "Dear Red, I heard your show last night.
You need me. Jack Douglas."

On radio Red developed many of the characters that would sustain him for years on television, and none was more popular than the
Mean Widdle Kid. This little brat was every parent's nightmare:
whining, devious, spoiled and uncooperative. Like Fanny Brice's
Baby Snooks, he was perfect for radio; the audience was free to

imagine him as it chose, guided by Red's childishly petulant voice as Junior, who wheedled his way into getting a present, skipping school or going to the circus. He was a pint-sized conniver, telling one adversary "Don't you hit me. You hit me and I'll tell Papa I was twins and you'll have a terrible time explaining what you did with the other one." Junior's motto was his ungrammatical admission of guilt, "I dood it," which became a national password, catapulting Red into the limelight. The slogan became so popular that when the United States bombed Tokyo in 1942, many of the nation's newspapers reported the event as "Doolittle Dood It!"

The Mean Widdle Kid was Skelton's psychological alter ego. Because he had never had a father and had been forced by circumstances to seek employment at an early age, Red's emotional development was stunted. There always remained a childlike, and often childish, facet to his personality. Immature, capable of throwing terrible temper tantrums, Red relied on Edna to play the role of his mother; in fact, he called her Mummy or Mummy Doll and she referred to him as Junior. It was Edna who pushed him into completing his education (he received his high school diploma via a correspondence course in Chicago in 1938), for she knew he felt inadequate to the task of reading his scripts. Having never enjoyed a childhood, the Mean Widdle Kid helped Red deal with the little kid inside him who had never grown up.

In the late thirties and early forties it all seemed to be happening at once for the redhaired comic and his astute wife: radio, film, important stage appearances. In 1940 he signed a seven-year contract with an option to renew with Metro-Goldwyn-Mayer Studios starting at $1,500 a week. Beginning with the inconsequential *Flight Command* in 1940 through *Half a Hero* in 1953, Red made 28 movies for MGM and was twice loaned out to Columbia Studios. His first starring role came in *Whistling in the Dark* (1941), and nearly all the critics hailed him as another Bob Hope, a comparison that was to plague him for some time. He reprised his Guzzler's Gin number (renamed When Television Comes for the film) in the all-star *Ziegfeld Follies* (1946). Red seemed destined to be a latter-day Buster Keaton when he did a remake of that silent film clown's *Spite Marriage*, rechristened *I Dood It* (1943), and *The Cameraman*, which became *Watch the Birdie* (1950). Keaton was an avowed admirer of the carrot-topped comic and according to Keaton biographer Rudi Blesh, he once implored studio boss Louis B. Mayer to "Let me take Skelton

Young Red in his movie star days, a handsome guy who made his share of mischief.

and work as a small company within Metro — do our stories, our gags, our production, our directing. Use your resources but do it our way — the way I did my best picture. I'll guarantee you hits. I won't take a cent of salary until they have proved themselves at the box office."[2] Unfortunately, Keaton was out of favor with the studio and Mayer refused.

Red's movie stardom brought with it temptations and pitfalls. Formerly a confirmed imbiber of nothing more powerful than an ice cream soda, he began to enjoy stuff with a kick to it. Sometimes he enjoyed it too much. He also fell victim to the many ladies in Hollywood who were after a good-looking young comic actor with a flourishing career. He and Edna had been together for so long that they were beginning to relate to each other more as brother and sister (or Mummy and Junior) than as lovers. She continued to be his manager, accountant, head writer, secretary and confidante, but Red was out belatedly sowing his wild oats. More and more frequently he would be out for the whole night with one of the beautiful starlets who populated the MGM lot.

By 1943 Edna could take no more of Red's drinking and womanizing, and she was awarded a divorce in December of that year. It was one of the most amicable splits Hollywood had ever seen. Edna retained a 50 percent interest in all of Red's holdings and continued as the head writer of his radio show (actually her job was not so much being a comedy writer but editing the work of the other writers, and she was extremely proficient at knowing what was or was not right for Skelton). On the very day of their divorce Red and Edna boggled the minds of Hollywood's gossip columnists by leaving the courtroom arm in arm to go to lunch.

Since he was now single, Red lost his draft deferment and entered the Army in June of 1944. He is fond of recalling that he was the only celebrity to enter the army as a private and to leave as one as well. He devoted himself to entertaining the troops in the United States and Europe. He often ended up doing 10–12 shows a day to relieve the boredom of the men on his troopship or those engaged in mopping-up operations after the war's end in Europe. The continual pressure to be funny finally got the better of him, and he relied increasingly on liquor to get him through the day. Eventually he suffered a nervous breakdown and complete physical exhaustion. He was given a medical discharge and a Good Conduct Medal, and said good-bye to the Army in September 1945.

Waiting for him in Los Angeles was his bride of six months, the former Georgia Maureen Davis, a lovely redhaired actress from Colorado whom he had met on the MGM lot. After dating for a year, they were married while Red was home on furlough. Their marriage was tempestuous almost from the beginning. For one thing, Red still relied on Edna as his manager and business partner. It was Edna who decided where Red and Georgia would live and how much spending money they could have each week, hardly a harmonious way for a marriage to begin. "Little Red," as Skelton dubbed his new bride, was not unreasonably unhappy with the arrangement. Red mollified her with expensive presents and promises to break away from Edna's control, but in his heart Edna was still Mummy and he was still tied to her apron strings. Yet outwardly, at least, Red and Georgia were good friends with Edna and her husband (she married director Frank Borzage in 1945, perhaps on the rebound from Red, but the marriage lasted only until mid-1949), and the foursome were often seen lunching or dining together in one of Los Angeles' chic restaurants, astounding the Hollywood crowd with the unorthodox nature of their friendship.

Georgia took a big step towards independence from Edna by presenting Red with two bundles that gave him more joy than any movie script; daughter Valentina was born on May 5, 1947, and son Richard on June 14, 1948. Both were redheads.

During the late forties and early fifties Red made some of his finest films: *A Southern Yankee*, *The Yellow Cab Man*, and *Three Little Words* (with Fred Astaire. The two played composer-lyricist team Bert Kalmer and Harry Ruby; Red's semiserious portrayal of the baseball-loving Ruby surprised many, including himself, by its charm and sensitivity) for MGM, and he was loaned out to do the very funny *Fuller Brush Man* for Columbia.

Red's continued achievement of insuring hit pictures for MGM brought him considerable raises and bonuses. By 1950 he felt financially secure enough to move Georgia and the two children to a huge estate in Bel-Air. The mansion had 27 rooms and four and one-half acres with a swimming pool and a greenhouse. Of its enormous size Red later quipped, "It had 27 rooms. One room had its own room. I planned to have a vacation in the living room—I'd never been there." There were numerous garages to house what would become Red's mini-fleet of seven Rolls Royces, one for each day of the week. The richer Skelton became, the more bizarre his purchases. In

Georgia and Red out on the town. Note the camera Red carries, one of many from his collection.

addition to his fleet of fine cars, he collected a huge selection of movie and still cameras, an antique merry-go-round, circus relics, old Bibles, Lincolniana, and more than 1,000 watches. For years the Hollywood community had been amused by his well-known aversion to talking on the telephone and to fire in any form (the latter phobia apparently caused by a near death in a house fire as a child, and though Red is rarely seen without a cigar, they remain unlit; he chews up 20 expensive House of Windsor cigars a day). He also has a fear of water, never stepping into a full bathtub, always getting into an empty tub and letting the water fill around him. He rarely took advantage of the swimming pool on his estate, taking infrequent dips and never going in above the waist. Having endured the indigence of his youth, he insisted upon wearing nothing but conservative blue suits, white shirts and one of the more than 500 ties he owned, all of which were maroon.

By 1950 all the talk was about the new medium of television. Milton Berle had already captured America's eyes and ears, the Goldbergs caught the heartstrings of the nation's viewers, and "Captain Video" thrilled its audience with trips to outer space. Red Skelton was firmly established as a first-rate radio comedian, surprisingly so in that much of his material was visual. Very often the folks at home were left wondering what the studio audience was laughing at. Because of Red's foresight, his contract with MGM could not restrict his working on television if he wanted to—when he had insisted on this clause back in 1940 the MGM brass thought he had lost his marbles; they knew television was never going to catch on, so they indulged him by acquiescing to his unusual request. Ten years later they were eating their hats, and their profits.

Red held a quaint view of how television was going to affect the nation. In an interview in June 1951 he propounded that

> I consider the television set as the American fireplace, around which the whole family will gather. . . . Socially I think television is going to have a wonderful effect. Families, instead of gadding about, will learn to stay home in the evenings as they used to. That'll give its members an opportunity to know one another again. TV is already taking the kids off the streets, where they get into trouble. . . . I consider the medium so intimate that . . . it'll be like knocking at the doors of strange homes and asking, "May I come in? This is the kind of fellow I am. If you like me, I hope you'll ask me back to your home next week."

Yet Red did not jump straight into the new medium; in fact, he made his entrance sometime after his contemporaries Gleason, Caesar and Berle. Red was afraid of television, afraid of the restrictions of "meeting the mark" for the cameras, memorizing new scripts every week (one of the joys of radio was that it entailed a minimal amount of rehearsing and the performer held the script in his hand), afraid of running out of the material he had so lovingly gathered for years onstage. Yet if he was going to retain an important career in comedy there was no other way to go but towards television. He made his small-screen debut in his 30-minute "Red Skelton Show" on NBC-TV at 10:00 P.M. on a Sunday night in September 1951. This time slot was unfortunate because it cut off his children's audience. The error was rectified the following year when he was moved to the 7:00 P.M. position. It is interesting to note that Skelton was one of the first performers to broadcast from California, having refused to pull up stakes and move to New York where almost all major broadcasting had been done until then. By 1951, however, television technology had advanced to the point where the highly touted "coaxial cable" linking the East and West coasts could be put to use. In Los Angeles, television companies scrambled to locate suitable sites for studio space, appropriating radio stations, former film studios, and legitimate theaters for the new medium, to be used temporarily until new, custom-made television studios could be built, principally in the suburb of Burbank.

For his writing staff Red brought with him the men responsible for making him funny on radio: Benedict Freeman, Jack Douglas and John Fenton Murray (by this time Edna had been completely cut off from her ex-husband, much to Georgia's relief). Over his years on television Skelton gained one of the worst reputations with regard to keeping writers; his staff changed constantly over the next 20 years. Red was fearful and jealous over the writers' positions. He rarely met with them directly, preferring to use his producer Seymour Berns as a go-between, and he always insisted on being given a writer's credit at the end of the show, while his actual contributions to the weekly script are in doubt. At one point, according to Arthur Marx, Red was asked by an interviewer where the inspiration for his sketches came from and the redhaired comic looked up and replied, "God." The writers, having slaved over each joke and sketch without a word of thanks from the star of the show, were naturally irate and resentful over Red's apparent callousness and ingratitude. For the following week's show he was handed a sheaf of empty papers instead of a script with the note, "Please have God fill the empty pages. Thanks. Your writers."[3]

Red's television format was similar to his radio show's. There was a short monologue by Red, a production number with singers and dancers, a pantomime, and a sketch featuring one of his stable of characters, many of whom had begun on radio: Clem Kadiddle-hopper, the numbskulled hick; Cauliflower McPugg, the punch-drunk pugilist; San Fernando Red, Skelton's answer to Senator Clag-horn; or Willie Lump-Lump, the benign drunk, among others. Although Skelton had some celebrity guest stars on his show over the years, at no time were they permitted to eclipse the star himself. In any case, Red's formula for success seems to have worked. For his debut season of 1951/52 he zoomed up to fourth place in the Nielsen ratings, capturing a whopping 50.2 share of the audience.

While Red's professional star was in ascendance, his private life was descending into a shambles. In 1952 he and Georgia went through the first of their several separations. When other Hollywood couples split, it was usually done as unobtrusively as possible, without publicity or fanfare. Not so with Red. After moving into the Beverly Wilshire Hotel, he practically called a press conference to announce his grievances to the world. "She always keeps her bedroom door locked," he moaned. "I just can't take it any longer. I've taken all a man can expect to take. I'm so much in love it's pitiful, but she does not want to be in love." Georgia, however, was standing fast. She told reporters that as she was a Catholic, "A divorce is out of the question. I don't believe in it. I've had plenty of troubles with *this boy* [italics added], only before it just never got into the papers. I'm not going to quit now because we have two wonderful kids. The only reason we're having trouble now is because Red is overworked, because he's artistic, and because he's a high-strung genius."

Georgia knew just how to play her husband. She knew that she would have to supplant Edna as his mother-figure if she was to have any control over him. In 1952 Red was nearly 40 years old and Georgia was referring to him as "this boy." She also knew how much Red doted on Valentina and Richard, and she was not above using them to get their father back. She also knew how to appeal to Red's ego, using descriptions like "artistic" and "genius." She was su-premely confident that Red would return after a few days, like a little boy who had run away from home. And she was not wrong.

Georgia had been tactful in her use of the word "high-strung." Actually Red was not so much high-strung as strung out. By this time he was hitting the bottle very heavily, able to consume a whole bottle of vodka without coming up for air. By his second season on NBC his timing was off, and so were his ratings. The network decided not to take any chances and did not renew him for the following season. As luck would have it CBS was scouting for comic talent and signed him for the 1953 season at $12,000 a week for 39 shows. His show was moved to Tuesday nights, where he stayed, always somewhere between 8:00 and 9:00, for his entire television career.

On occasion his dipsomania would get completely out of hand. When he was irate with Georgia he was known to take a bottle of booze and move into the upper branches of a tree on his estate and refuse to speak or come down. A coworker recalled some hairy times getting Red into the studio when he was stewed:

> We never knew when Red would show up or *how*. . . . Marty Rackin, the movie producer, was Red's writer and director then, and sometimes he had to haul him to the studio in an ambulance or even a hearse, with a tank of oxygen to bring him around. Marty would have to steam him out in the gym . . . and then when he got him to the studio we had to keep buckets and ice water and wet towels all over the place. We also had a doctor who used to give him shots. Red was a pretty good pro, though. Somehow we always managed to get the program on the air.

Red was also known to indulge in some pretty risqué high jinks when drinking. For several nights in a row Beverly Hills police were mystified by reports of porno movies being shown on the wall of an apartment building for the whole world to behold (and nearly causing serious traffic accidents). They never did find out that it was Red entertaining a bunch of cronies with his movie projector, showing stag films onto the side of the building next door.

One of Red's most famous quips was made to Franklin D. Roosevelt during a White House dinner when the President reached for his drink. "Better not drink that," said Red with his hand on Roosevelt's sleeve, "I've been rolled in a place like this."

Part of the reason for Red's heavy drinking, besides his problems with Georgia, was to ease the pain in his abdomen. For some six months he had been suffering from a herniated diaphragm, probably caused by the strain of years of very physical comedy. Shortly after

Red overcame marital and alcohol problems, plus acrimony with his staff, to star in his own comedy show. From 1955 until his departure from CBS in 1970, "The Red Skelton Show" was consistently top-rated.

walking out on his wife he had to be admitted to the hospital for a five-hour operation to correct the condition. His illness was well-timed, however, for it effected a reconciliation with Georgia, who remained steadfastly by her husband's side during his hospital stay. From there he returned to the house in Bel-Air.

Red's switch to CBS did not immediately earn him better reviews or ratings, and his heavy drinking and acrimony with writers, directors, and producers did not contribute to smooth sailing. But he managed to get a handle on his drinking problem and by 1955 "The Red Skelton Show" was in the top 15 according to the Nielsen ratings, with a 32.3 share of the Tuesday night audience. It is a testimony to the endurance and perseverance of the clown from Vincennes, Indiana, that from 1955 till he left CBS in 1970 he remained consistently within the top 20 shows and usually in the top ten. His unique blend of corny jokes and schmaltzy humor endeared him to American hearts.

Though Red today has the reputation of being a totally "clean" comic, never stooping to use four-letter words or sexy situations, it was no always so. As far back as his film *Bathing Beauty* in 1944 with famed swimmer Esther Williams, he was able to shock his innocent co-star so much with his filthy language that she was actually reduced to tears. Red had not changed by the time he was on television. Tuesday afternoon rehearsals at CBS were known as the "Dirty Hour." Employees of the network, from executives to secretaries, would show up at 3:00 to be entertained by Red's X-rated ad-libbing—a voice that on the air wouldn't melt butter. So little work was being done during this period that CBS had to circulate a memo instructing its executives (the secretaries were let off the hook) to remain at their desks. Occasional guest star Martha Raye, in particular, was known to give as good as she got, and together she and Red could have embarrassed a sailor.

Red's use of obscenity was basically a method of letting off steam, reducing tension on show day. Like a teenager discovering the delicious thrill of intoning taboo words, Red delighted in blue material, even (or perhaps especially) if it could never be seen by the television audience. Some might say that Skelton's drinking and use of blue material, countered by his squeaky clean public image and pointedly sentimental farewell to his weekly audience ("Goodnight and God bless"), made him a bit of a hypocrite, but it went deeper than that. There were two sides to Skelton: the religious, conservative (he later became a member of what could have been called the "John Wayne School of Politics" during the Vietnam era) and flag-waving Red and the Mean Widdle Kid trying to get out and raise the dickens, and he has never been able to fully reconcile the two.

Although the ratings on Red's show had picked up considerably, at home the situation was like a bad rerun. He and Georgia continued to fight, split up (Red would move into a hotel) and reconcile so frequently that they could have installed a revolving door in their Bel-Air home. On January 25, 1954, columnist Erskine Johnson of the New York *World Telegram* reported a bizarre conversation he held with the Skeltons when he phoned them for information about an accident Red had had:

Hollywood, January 25 — Comedy falls are Red Skelton's specialty. But there wasn't anything funny about two falls he took over the weekend, even if one left him in stitches.

Friday night he took an accidental fall through a glass shower door, was knocked unconscious and a doctor took 30 stitches in his right arm.

On Sunday afternoon he had what he says is a "final" falling out with his wife of nine years, blond Georgia.

"If Georgia doesn't file suit for divorce by Wednesday," Red told me, "I'm leaving home. My trunks are already packed and downstairs. If Georgia doesn't sue me for divorce, I'll get one when I play Las Vegas in a couple of months." Red gave me both stories when I telephoned him to check on the shower-door incident.

But when he started spilling the news that his stormy marital life was about to end, a tearful-near-hysterical Georgia picked up an extension telephone in their home to tell me: "I won't sign any divorce papers. Red may leave me again but he'll be sorry. He'll come home."

Red snapped back with: "Don't believe her. This is the end — it's final."

What followed may go down in history as the longest three-way telephone family argument ever aired to the press.

For exactly 47 minutes and 18 seconds — I timed 'em — Red and Georgia staged a verbal duel that sounded like a radio soap opera before it's OK'd by the censorship department.

As they battled over the extension phone in their home, I was forgotten as Red and Georgia gave me a strange preview of the charges that will be hurled if their hectic marriage problems are aired in a divorce court.

After one particularly long speech by Georgia, Red finally interrupted to tell me: "I think Georgia's mother was vaccinated with a phonograph needle and her father was a politician. I have the longest long-playing record in the country — my wife."

About that shower door: Red says he was bathing, slipped and fell through the glass. Dr. Stanley Immerman rushed to the Skelton home and took 30 stitches in the comic's right arm. An ambulance was called and then cancelled when Georgia determined that no main arteries were cut.

The fact that Red and Georgia did not seem the least embarrassed to wage war over the telephone with a newspaperman on the line is odd to say the least. It is as though they needed an audience to witness their vitriolic argument; it fueled them up and allowed them to communicate more freely with each other, even if only over an extension phone. In the end, once again, Georgia was proved right, and Red came back to her waiting arms.

Part of their problem over the years stemmed from a continual lack of faithfulness to each other. Red had always had an eye for pretty girls, ever since being thrown off a riverboat for trying to seduce the captain's daughter. Although he seemed devoted to Georgia when they were first married, in time, like Edna, she began to realize that he was sneaking around with a variety of girls, all eager to know and please the big television star. Georgia too, perhaps in retaliation, began a series of escapades with lovers chosen from Hollywood's attractive male population. Red took a cavalier attitude toward his wife's extramarital activities and never bothered to try to keep them secret. Arthur Marx's biography reports one episode that typifies Red's feeling about Georgia's promiscuity:

> Red and Georgia were guests at a fancy party thrown by John Wayne at the Beverly Hills Hotel. Red and Georgia were standing with Humphrey Bogart when an exquisite foreign actress, with whom Tyrone Power was having an affair, passed in front of them, swinging her hips provocatively.
>
> All the men looked at her, and Red asked, smacking his lips, "Who's that?"
>
> "I don't know her name," replied Bogart, "but Ty Power says she's the best cocksucker in town."
>
> Whereupon Red patted Georgia on the head fondly and said to Bogart, "Aw, now you've gone and hurt Georgia's feelings."[4]

It would have taken an event of major proportions to repair the foundering marriage, and, sadly enough, that is what happened. In January 1957 eight-year-old Richard Freeman Skelton (named for Red's benefactor Freeman Keyes) was diagnosed as having terminal leukemia and was given less than a year to live. Richard was a bright, sweet, charming little boy who not only strongly resembled his comic father, but adored him to distraction. He loved to watch Red on television, and the two could amuse each other for hours with jokes and gags. "What are you going to give up for Lent?" the elder Skelton once asked his son. "School homework" was the budding comic's reply, and they would both be on the floor in fits of giggles. The onset of Richard's illness was the beginning of a nightmare for the whole family.

Today, childhood leukemia has a fairly good recovery rate due to advances in research and drug therapy; in 1957 it was almost always a death sentence. It was the hardest thing imaginable for Red and Georgia to see their son suffer fatal illness and feel powerless to help him. Their first decision was to place their son in the care of the established medical profession, not to run off seeking miracles cures or faith healers. They had been informed by Richard's doctors that he was likely to enter and remain in a state of remission over the summer months, at which time he would seem healthy except for occasional fatigue. Red decided to show his son as much of the world as he could in the remaining months. After a short tour of the United States, the Skelton family headed off to Europe, the press on their heels. It was the kind of story no newspaper could resist—a cheerful young boy with but a few months to live, and his father the clown trying to hold back tears. The highlight of their European trip came when they were in Rome and had a private audience with the Pope. "How's your tooth, Pope?" the boy chirped (the Pontiff had recently had a tooth removed) and his Holiness assured the youngster that he had suffered no pain.

The most distressing stop of their tour was in Great Britain, where they were again greeted by hordes of press. A reporter for the London *Daily Sketch*, miffed that he could not get a private interview, reported in his column that Red was using his son's illness to generate publicity for himself. Skelton was understandably hurt and irate, and the family headed home.

Richard knew that he was ill, but his parents did their best to shield him from the knowledge of his impending death. Yet as children often do, Richard seemed to know what was happening to him without being told, and he remained stalwart and hopeful until the end. In April 1958 the boy was readmitted to the hospital for the final time. On May 10, his doctors, knowing that his situation had deteriorated, called Red and his family to the child's bedside. Richard asked each member of the family to kiss him good-bye, and when his ten-year-old sister hesitated for a moment, he snapped "Hurry up, Valentina! I haven't got all day!" A few moments later he uttered his final words: "I can't see. Everything is fuzzy."

The death of their only son devastated Red and Georgia, and the tragedy ultimately affected them in diametrically opposite ways. Red stopped drinking entirely. Richard's death had taught him something about the preciousness of life and how each day should be lived to the fullest. In any case, his alcohol-swilling days were over because he had developed severe asthma that could be triggered by even one small drink; he switched to beer, which, in moderation, did not adversely affect him. Even the fumes of audiences' drinks in the Las

Vegas nightspots he played could assault him badly enough to send him to the hospital and an oxygen tank.

Little Red, on the other hand, fell into a deep depression over the loss of Richard, and in an attempt to obliterate her pain she took increasingly to liquor and prescription drugs. Unlike her husband, she had no career to throw herself into to help her forget her anguish. For a while her grief was exacerbated by Red's insistence on maintaining a shrine, composed of some of Richard's possessions and mementos, in a hallway in their home. Finally she was able to convince him that the shrine was morbid and unhelpful to her and Valentina in coping with their sorrow.

Richard's death also started a downhill slide in Red's business ventures. Perhaps in an effort to be consumed with activity he jumped into a number of ill-conceived enterprises, including buying the former studio of his idol, Charlie Chaplin. Though the studio was on a valuable piece of real estate, as a viable place to make movies or television shows it was an antiquated white elephant. The opportunity to put his feet up on Chaplin's very own desk made the whole deal worthwhile to Red, even if he lost his shirt. The tribute from famed comedian Groucho Marx in *McCall's* magazine in May of 1959 must have thrilled the new proprietor of Chaplin's workplace:

> Red Skelton is the most unacclaimed clown in show business. . . . I think the logical successor to Chaplin is Skelton. . . . I've seen most of the great, legendary clowns of the circus, but I confess I've rarely seen one who could amuse me for more than a minute. There is no one around who can take a comic fall as completely and magnificently as he can. . . . Some day I'm afraid the eggheads will take time up and start reading social significance into his antics. Let's hope they don't because this has ruined many a good performer. And we need all the pure comedians like Red we can get.

Skelton also became involved in a company that provided mobile color television facilities. The idea may simply have been ahead of its time, or else it was badly managed, for it folded—after an expensive investment. Red finally came to feel that he had been continually swindled by a number of lawyers, business managers and partners, and he divested himself of all their services.

If Red and Georgia were not the most social couple in Hollywood before their son's illness, after his death they became virtual recluses. They had few close friends and never attended gala openings, parties or other public events. An uneasy truce was established between them, and there seemed to be a tacit agreement to remain at home with Valentina in order to try to put their lives back together.

Finally the unhappy memories of the house in Bel-Air became too much for the Skeltons, and in 1960 they moved to Rancho Mirage, near Palm Springs in the California desert. Red was also concerned about getting Georgia to a healthier atmosphere to wean her from drink and drugs. A Japanese teahouse and garden were built where Red could work and think. He evolved a strange ritual for dealing with those he found offensive: "When anyone hurts us, my wife and I sit in our Japanese sand garden and drink iced tea. There are five stones in the garden—for sky, wind, water and earth. We sit and think of five of the nicest things we can about the person who hurt us. If he hurts us a second time, we do the same thing. The third time we light a candle, and he is, for us, dead."

The house in Bel-Air was not sold; it was kept for Valentina until she finished school and for Red to stay in when he commuted in for two or three days each week to do his show. Unfortunately the move did not ease Georgia's dependence on alcohol and drugs, and her condition grew worse. Perhaps hoping to spend less time with her, Red developed several hobbies that kept him busy all day. Oil painting, which he had dabbled in for years, became a passion. He often recalls how he originally became interested in the fine arts: "I went into a gallery back in 1943, saw a painting I liked and asked the price. The man said, 'Five thousand wouldn't buy it.' I told him 'I'm one of the five thousand.' Then I went out and bought a 73-cent canvas and some paints." His subjects, however, were limited; they came to encompass 3,000 paintings of ducks and untold thousands of circus clowns, often in the guise of celebrities like W.C. Fields, Emmett Kelly or Carol Burnett, and they began to fetch high prices and were produced as posters.

Red also loved to spend hours at the piano, picking out tunes. Though he was not much of a musician and could not read music, when he created a melody he particularly liked he would play it into a tape recorder and have it professionally arranged. Unlike Jackie Gleason's similar endeavor, Red's tunes never sold millions of records, but several of them did make their way into the repertoires of high school marching bands.

Short stories were another of Skelton's pastimes, though they have never been read by the public. He also wrote daily love letters to Little Red, now that they had achieved a more or less peaceful co-existence. One, written to Georgia on Father's Day 1970, revealed an undercurrent of hostility:

> Is it really love for this guy called Dad
> Of a part of youth's logic so untrue?
> Examine your conscience—he's glad he's a father
> But what kind of child are you?
>
> Lord Baron Von Humpy Doc

Because of the continuing success of "The Red Skelton Show," CBS decided in 1967 to go from a 30- to a 60-minute format. This meant twice as much work for the writers and double the rehearsal time for Red. It also gave the home audiences some in-depth looks at the stable of Skelton characters and his touching pantomimes. Freddy the Freeloader, for example, began to appear more often and was obviously a favorite of Red's. Freddy was a tramp clown in the grand old circus and vaudeville traditions. With his battered top hat, stubby cigar butt and fingerless gloves Freddy, like Chaplin's Little Fellow, always remained a gentleman. And if Freddy did not elicit great sympathy from television viewers as did Gleason's Pour Soul, he did manage to bring forth smiles and an occasional tear.

Clem Kadiddlehopper, having originated on radio, was one of the most enduring of Red's creations. This amiable country boob, too stupid to know how stupid he was, made fun of country rubes without being cruel. Skelton must have met up with dozens of Clems in his early days with Doc Lewis' Medicine Show or while doing Tom shows or minstrel entertainments. Clem always wore a beat-up hat with the side brims folded up, and he displayed an exaggerated overbite—he was the perfect dupe for whatever scam a con man tried to pull.

None of Red's characters could be called overly brilliant. The pugilist Cauliflower McPugg (his name was printed on his sweatshirt with the PU underlined) had had his brains scrambled long ago. George Appleby was the meekest, tamest, most henpecked husband since Caspar Milquetoast. Deadeye the Sheriff was notoriously bad at maintaining law and order in his one-horse town. And San Fernando Red, a cross between Senator Claghorn and W.C. Fields, was all hot air and no more honest than a three-dollar bill.

Red's pantomimes, which he called "the silent spot," were a mixture of slapstick, commedia dell'arte and pure maudlin sentimentality. Some of his most famous pantomimes included a Greek saladmaker slicing his fingers into the bowl; the birth, life and death of a flower; an old veteran watching a parade; and a lonely old man who builds a snowman and brings it inside by the fireplace for companionship on New Year's Eve. Even the most hardboiled cynic may have found himself getting misty over such blatant tearjerkers.

By 1966 Red's marriage again had begun to deteriorate. On July 20, after an argument with her husband, Georgia "accidentally" shot herself in their hotel room while Red was performing in Las Vegas. She either missed or did not miss, depending on how serious she may have been about ending her life, but in any case she was rushed to the hospital where she was found to have a broken rib from the bullet of the .38 Smith and Wesson that Red always kept in his bedside table.

In 1969 Red fell for Lothian Toland, the beautiful, 32-year-old secretary/girlfriend of Broadway composer and fellow Palm Springs resident Frederick Loewe. The middle-aged comic and the daughter of Hollywood cinematographer Gregg Toland (*Citizen Kane*) began a torrid love affair that Georgia could not help knowing about. Two years later Big and Little Red separated for the last time. A tempestuous marriage that had endured more than its share of heartbreak and acrimony had irrevocably broken down. The divorce was made final in 1973, and in October of that year Red and Lothian were married. Georgia remained in the Palm Springs house, alone; her ex-husband and his bride lived a few miles away. The second Mrs. Skelton was in and out of the hospital with various illnesses, as well as for drying out periods. She was never reconciled to losing control over Red, and her grief over Richard's death never abated. On May 11, 1976, Georgia made another attempt at suicide, and this time she did not miss. By putting the gun to her head and pulling the trigger, this sad, lonely and desperate woman sent a clear message to the world: It was 19 years to the day since the death of her young son.

The Skelton show on CBS eventually ran its course, and Red's last season with that network was in the spring of 1969. For the 1970–71 season he returned to NBC, but after an incredible 20 years on television the handwriting was on the wall—television audiences were looking for fresher, hipper kinds of comedy, and Red did not even make it to his customary place within the top 20 in the ratings.

After a long career in comedy, Skelton still goes for the laughs, performing at Las Vegas nightspots and county fairs across America, and occasionally doing television specials.

"Rowan and Martin's Laugh-In" was all the rage that year; there was no room for the corny antics of Clem Kadiddlehopper or Gertrude and Heathcliff, Red's lively seagulls who loved to drop mementos of their flight upon the deserving below.

Skelton continues to perform at Las Vegas nightspots and at county fairs across the land. On March 12, 1977, he did two sold-out, one-man shows at Carnegie Hall and received standing ovations, even for his very un-urbane interpretation of the Pledge of Allegiance (giving an explanation of each word in the oath) before the crowd of normally jaded New Yorkers. He continues to do television specials, usually for HBO, featuring his favorite characters and mime routines, and occasionally resurrecting Doughnut Dunkers and Guzzler's Gin.

One of the most hard and fast rules in comedy is that a comedian must not laugh at his own jokes. Red was the first to make a career of breaking that edict, to prove that when it comes to comedy there simply are no hard and fast rules. His insane giggle proved to audiences that he loved making them laugh—why should the clown be the only one who is not having any fun? Red once explained what made him tick before a crowd:

The absolute terror is the clown's secret. Terror of the Clem Kadiddlehoppers who won't laugh. When the flop sweat comes, the comedian's got to be a warrior. A lot of comedians give up on audiences. You can't. You break them and then you own them if only for a few seconds. It is enough. . . . *I'm nuts and I know it. But as long as I make them laugh, they ain't going to lock me up.*

Dick Van Dyke

Dick Van Dyke is a rubber-faced, angular comedian who was probably born too late for his talents. Had he lived during the era of silent films, he may well have rivaled the great movie clowns for a place in film history. As it was, he has performed admirably on the modern-day equivalent of the local nickelodeon: television.

Van Dyke is one of those clowns whose every emotion can be read in his face. Backed up by an agile, expressive body, he can make the audience feel like laughing or crying through corporeal expression. A true product of television, he came into our homes in a role as the world's most beloved comedy writer, and it is as such that he will remain in our hearts.

Dick Van Dyke was born in West Plains, Missouri, on December 13, 1925, to Loren W. and Hazel Van Dyke. His father was a public relations man for a freight line, and he moved the family to Danville, Illinois, when Dick was a child. His younger brother, Jerry, born on July 27, 1931, also grew up to enter show business as a comedian.

Dick's childhood was uneventful, and though he participated in school productions, there was no indication that performing would become his life's work. Not until he entered the Army Air Corps during World War II did his talents start to emerge. It was in the Air Force that he became a radio announcer and took part in a special services show. Also while in the service, he met Byron Paul, who would remain his lifelong friend as well as business partner and producer.

Upon his discharge from the Army Air Corps, Van Dyke returned to Danville to start up an advertising agency. Fortunately for future television viewers, the agency failed, and Dick teamed up with his friend Phil Ericson to form "The Merry Mutes." Their act consisted of pantomime and lip-synching to records. From 1948 to 1954 they toured nightclubs around the country, such as the Last Frontier in Las Vegas and they were eventually known as "Eric and Van."

When they split up, Dick took a job as an emcee of a local show in Atlanta, Georgia. In 1955 he moved to New Orleans where he hosted "The Dick Van Dyke Show," a talk and variety program for WDSU-TV. Soon after that his old Army Air Corps buddy, Byron Paul, got him an audition at CBS in New York, where Paul was a director. Dick was hired to replace Jack Paar as host of "The Morning Show" and occasionally filled in for Garry Moore. He continued as host of daytime shows with "The Morning Show" in 1958, a panel talk show for housewives, and with "Laugh Line," where Dick made his first real contribution to comedy as an emcee of a variety show featuring such guests as Nichols and May and Orson Bean.

On November 2, 1959, Van Dyke opened as one of the supporting cast in the revue "The Girls Against the Boys" starring Bert Lahr and Nancy Walker. The show, with music by Richard Lewine and Albert Hague and sketches and lyrics by Arnold B. Horwitt, ran for only 16 performances at Broadway's Alvin Theater. Van Dyke made a favorable impression on the critics (the *New York Times* called him "an amiable performer"), particularly in a sketch about a drunk husband returning home late who manages to act stone-cold sober whenever his wife is looking. It was a sketch that he would reprieve on the premiere episode of "The Dick Van Dyke Show" on October 3, 1961, when as Rob Petrie he entertains at a gathering at the home of his boss, Alan Brady.

Van Dyke continued to expand his talents by playing a dramatic role on the U.S. Steel Hour's production of "Trap for a Stranger" in February 1959. He also began a radio career as the host of "Flair," a daily show on ABC beginning in October 1960.

On February 12, 1948, Dick married his childhood sweetheart, Marjorie Willett. They had four children: Christian, Barry, Stacy and Carrie Beth. Van Dyke had a reputation as a clean-cut, upright member of the community and was an elder in the Presbyterian church and taught Sunday school.

On April 14, 1960, Dick had a chance to show off his musical abilities for the first time. "Bye, Bye, Birdie," with music by Charles Strouse, lyrics by Lee Adams and libretto by Michael Stewart (the last being a former writer for Sid Caesar), opened at Broadway's Martin Beck Theater and was an immediate hit. The musical co-starred Chita Rivera, Dick Gautier, Michael J. Pollard and Paul Lynde, with Dick Van Dyke as Albert Peterson, the agent and songwriter for rock star Conway Birdie. His big song was "Put on a Happy Face," and the role served as a showcase for Dick's singing and dancing abilities. Some years later famed director/choreographer Michael Kidd said of Van Dyke (while they prepared a tour of "The Music Man"): "He's the best natural dancer I know, and he's never taken a lesson in his life."

His success on Broadway brought him to the attention of Hollywood's television producers. Carl Reiner, who had been a fine straight man (and writer) for Sid Caesar in "Your Show of Shows" and "Caesar's Hour," was looking for someone to play the lead in his forthcoming situation comedy. The format of the show, originally entitled "The Head of the Family," was to feature the life of the head writer of a popular television comedy show, the star of which was the brilliant, if tyrannical, Alan Brady. Obviously Reiner drew for inspiration upon his years with the brilliant (if occasionally tyrannical) Sid Caesar, as well as his years in the frenetic, pressurized environment of the writers' room.

The show, written by Bill Persky and Sam Denoff, premiered on October 3, 1961, as "The Dick Van Dyke Show," with Van Dyke as comedy writer Rob Petrie. Mary Tyler Moore, who had formerly played Sam, the secretary (whose shapely legs were the only part of her seen by the audience) on "Richard Diamond, Private Detective," was cast as his wife, Laura Petrie, and Larry Mathews was seen as their son, Richie. Reiner took over the role of the egomaniacal Alan Brady, and Richard Deacon played the show's producer (and Alan's brother-in-law) Mel Cooley. Morey Amsterdam as Buddy Sorrell and Rose Marie as Sally Rogers rounded out the cast as Rob's fellow writers.

The interesting part of the show's premise was the dichotomy between Rob's normal life in the suburbs (the Petrie's resided at 485 Bonnie Meadow Road, New Rochelle) of New York with his attractive wife, young son and friendly neighbors, and his crazy existence at work, writing sketches and jokes for Alan Brady and his guests.

Van Dyke was brilliant, especially when he was acting out a sketch for that week's "Alan Brady Show." Often his physicalization was eerily reminiscent of Sid Caesar himself, particularly when portraying an inanimate object. Van Dyke as Rob Petrie also nicely dealt with the problems of being husband and father, especially when his wife, in the Lucille Ball mode, was wont to cook up some outrageous schemes. Probably one of the best loved episodes took place, in flashback, on the night of their son's birth. Van Dyke's hilarious im-

Mary Tyler Moore, Morey Amsterdam, Dick Van Dyke and Rose Marie on the set of "The Dick Van Dyke Show." This immensely popular situation comedy ran for 158 episodes in the sixties and has been widely syndicated.

pression of an expectant father so nervous about the imminent birth that he keeps his hat on his bedstead (and then leaves for the hospital *sans* wife) was one of the funniest moments in television.

After 158 episodes "The Dick Van Dyke Show" came to an end on September 7, 1966. In syndication it has entertained millions as an example of situation comedy at its best. Van Dyke had made several fine films, including the movie version of "Bye, Bye Birdie"

(1963), as well as the box-office smash *Mary Poppins* (1964). After the demise of his television show, Dick went on to star in *Divorce, American Style* (1967) with Debbie Reynolds, and the popular children's film *Chitty Chitty Bang Bang* (1968). In 1969 he made *The Comic*, a charming, little-known film about a silent film comedian, with Carl Reiner.

A few years later Dick was back on television, this time as the star of "The New Dick Van Dyke Show," which premiered on CBS on September 18, 1971. The first version of the show ran until September 3, 1973, and featured Hope Lange, Marty Brill, Nancy Dussault and Fanny Flagg. Carl Reiner was once again aboard as creator and executive producer. The action was set (and filmed) in Dick's new hometown, Carefree, Arizona, and it featured the trials and tribulations of Dick Preston, host of "The Dick Preston Show," a 90-minute talk/variety show produced by KXIU-TV, Channel 2 in Phoenix (Van Dyke really did own an AM radio station in Phoenix, KXIV). The show had its high spots, but generally audiences were disappointed by the absence of a spark comparable to what there had been on the original Van Dyke show.

The second version of "The New Dick Van Dyke Show" ran from September 10, 1973, to September 2, 1974. Once again Hope Lange played Dick's wife, with Dick Van Patten, Richard Dawson and Chita Rivera as the supporting cast. Set in Tarzana (Van Dyke had moved back to California), its hero was once again Dick Preston, this time as an actor who portrays Dr. Brad Fairmont, a surgeon at Pleasant Valley Hospital on the television soap opera "Those Who Care." Byron Paul took over for Carl Reiner as executive producer.

By this time Dick's battle with alcoholism was in full swing. As he reported to *TV Guide* some years later:

> I was into the loss-of-control stage. I suddenly found I couldn't decide when and if I was going to have a drink.
> My excuse for drinking was the pressure of my career. I tried to tell myself that I was a passive person, that this business was too difficult for me. I told myself I wasn't an alcoholic because I didn't drink in the morning or at work. I had all the excuses in the world, and they were all baloney. It took me a long time to prove to myself that I couldn't drink. I just wouldn't admit it could happen to me.
> I was an alcoholic drinker for five years. It's funny, I didn't drink at all until I was in my 30's. That was ordinary Saturday night

Pressures of a show-business career finally caught up with Van Dyke in 1972, forcing him to seek treatment for alcoholism. Two years later he received an Emmy nomination for his role as a recovering alcoholic in the made-for-television film *The Morning After*.

drinking. In my 40's, it became a problem. Finally one day I said, "I've got to get help for myself."

My wife began drinking to keep me company. We'd sit up until three or four in the morning, talking and drinking in the bar at our home. We both became alcoholics. . . .

In August 1972 Dick Van Dyke entered the alcohol rehabilitation program at St. Luke Hospital in Phoenix, Arizona. After he left the program, his wife entered. In 1974 Dick starred as a recovering alcoholic in a television movie, *The Morning After*, for which he won an Emmy nomination.

Van Dyke made a short comeback on television as the host and star of "Van Dyke and Company," a 60-minute comedy show on NBC, with Andy Kaufman and the Los Angeles Mime Company. Although Van Dyke engaged in some wonderful pantomime, much of the show was corny and sentimental. It ran from September 20 to December 30, 1976.

In 1979 Van Dyke gave a stirring performance as a priest on trial for murdering the nun he loved, in Stanley Kramer's *The Runner Stumbles.* At the time Kramer said of his star, "Damn the man, he has so many phobias and complexes, he's scared of his own shadow."

Unfortunately, Dick and Marjorie's marriage broke up after many years. He later married Michelle Triola Marvin, of the famous "palimony" suit.

Dick Van Dyke has made his mark on television comedy and provided many hours of warm laughter for his viewers. The rubber-faced, bulbous-nosed, thin-as-a-rail clown has proved to possess wonderful comic timing and a superbly expressive body. Stan Laurel once told Van Dyke that he was such a wonderful visual comedian that it was a shame he was born 30 years too late for silent films. Van Dyke has carried something of the magic of those early silent comedies to the small screen, and over the years he has gained a wide and appreciative following.

Flip Wilson

"The devil made me do it!" entered the American lexicon with the advent of Flip Wilson on the television screen. Wilson ingratiated himself to audiences both black and white by gently satirizing racial prejudices and caricaturing black stereotypes. His expert use of drag to comic effect had not, at least in recent memory, been seen performed by a black artist, and certainly not on television.

Flip began his life as Clerow Wilson, one of 18 children of an alcoholic janitor in Jersey City, New Jersey, on December 8, 1933. The large family was desperately poor, and their problems worsened when the parents divorced when little Clerow was seven years old. He then spent some time in foster homes (running away 13 times), as well as in reform school, and later was returned to the care of his father.

When Flip was nine, history foreshadowed itself when the future Geraldine made his stage debut in the class play—as Clara Barton. It seems the little girl who was cast in the part suddenly fell ill, and the budding comedian stepped into her white nurse's shoes.

In an effort to escape his family's poverty, at 16 Wilson lied about his age and enlisted in the Air Force. It was there that he earned the moniker "Flip," owing to his flippant sense of humor.

When he left the Air Force at age 20, Flip became a bellhop in a San Francisco hotel. There he got his first break as a professional entertainer, doing a drunk act in the hotel's floor show. From then on he was on the road, performing at every small nightclub across America that catered to a black clientele. Along the way he met, married and divorced (the marriage lasted less than a month) a dancer from the Bahamas named Peaches. Later his union with the former Blondell Pitman produced four children; they were divorced in 1976. His third wife was Tuanchai (Cookie) Wilson.

Flip's big break came in 1965 when he broke up host Johnny

For a while, Flip was flying high. In its first season, 1970/71, "The Flip Wilson Show" ranked second in the Neilsen ratings and won an Emmy for Outstanding Variety Series.

Carson on the "Tonight Show." Following this appearance he was a popular guest on "Laugh-In," the Carol Burnett and Dean Martin shows, as well as returning many times to the "Tonight Show."

In 1969 he did his first solo show, an NBC special where he introduced the character Geraldine, complete with high heels, fishnet stockings and false eyelashes. Actually, Flip possessed a pair of gams that many women would not mind having. Geraldine was saucy and outspoken as she strutted her stuff and tossed her wig. "What you see is what you get!" was her motto, and none dared to cross her. Unlike Jonathan Winters' Maude Frickert, or Berle's grotesque dressing up, Geraldine was flirtatiously sexy, a fine example of drag, which has been a tradition in the theater since the caveman first learned to tell stories.

On September 17, 1970, "The Flip Wilson Show" debuted on NBC, a 60-minute variety show that featured Wilson, singers and dancers, and guests. In addition to Geraldine, there were other

Wilson characters. There was Reverend Leroy, known as Rev, hip-talking minister of The Church of What's Happening Now, where a sermon might be "On the Creation of the Hilton Hotel." Freddy the Playboy was on hand, with his fine eye for the ladies and a smooth tongue to go with it. There was also Sonny, the White House janitor, the only sane voice in the mad upper realms of government.

The show ran until June 27, 1974. During its first two years, "The Flip Wilson Show" placed second in the Nielsen ratings, by the third year it was still doing well in twelfth place, but by the fourth year it did not place in the top 20. The show had been nominated for a number of Emmys, winning in 1971 for Outstanding Variety Series.

After the demise of his show, Wilson went back to entertaining in clubs and ran into a few rough years, including two arrests on drug charges in 1980 and 1981. In 1985 he returned to television for one season with "Charlie and Company," a clone of the immensely popular "Bill Cosby Show." Hopefully, America's first black superstar will again return to our home screens.

Jonathan Winters

Jonathan Winters has the reputation of being a crazy man. His is a wild, uncontrollable talent that spews forth like a freshly dug oil well. There has certainly been no one like him during his all-too-brief stay on the television airwaves, and not until someone thought to invent another whirlwind of inspired talent, named Robin Williams, was there anyone with his brand of chaotic comedy.

A master of voices and characters, Winters has seen his most popular creations assimilated by other, more successful comedians, as well as absorbed into public vernacular. A gentle man who seems to have been haunted by the products of his own, overly vivid imagination, he developed a large, devoted following of those on the same feverishly funny wavelength.

Jonathan Harshman Winters III was born in Dayton, Ohio, on November 11, 1925, the only child of Alice Bahman and Jonathan Winters II, an investment broker. Young Jonathan spent much of his youth in the company of his grandfather. "My grandfather was my greatest inspiration," he has said. "His name was Valentine Winters and his one frustration was that he could not get into show business. Once, Grandpa was introduced to a noted actor of the day, and he was so elated that he would not leave the actor alone. Finally, my grandfather asked how it felt to be a great actor. The man, who was really annoyed, looked at my grandfather and smugly said: 'You'll never know.' Grandpa always told me to remember that line so I could tell it to someone when I was famous."

Apparently Grandpa Winters was a rather flamboyant bank president. He was known to greet Orville Wright on the streets of Dayton by flapping his arms wildly and shouting, "How's the airplane today, Orville?" As a child, Winters remembers his grandfather ordering roast beef in a restaurant and then demanding of the waiter, "Is the chef on vacation?" "No sir," the waiter replied. "Well, he should be," countered the elderly Winters. "The only thing this lacks is a zipper."

When Jonathan was seven years old his parents divorced, and his father moved to Florida and went into real estate. His mother took him to Springfield, Ohio, where she worked in a factory and eventually had her own radio show for women.

The future comic did not always aspire to show business. He showed talent as an artist and studied commercial art at Kenyon College in Gambier, Ohio, and at the Dayton Art Institute. He also served with the Marines in the Pacific during World War II, enlisting while still underage at 17. He manned an anti-aircraft gun aboard the carrier *Bon Homme Richard,* and he fought in battles in Japan and Okinawa.

Back in Ohio, he met an attractive college student, Eileen Schauder, and they were married the following year. It was actually his love for his bride that led him to take his first stab at performing. At Eileen's urging he entered a local talent contest, in which he won her a wrist watch. The contest was sponsored by a Dayton radio station, and he was soon offered a job as a disc jockey for the 6:00–8:00 A.M. shift. When there was no one for him to interview he would make up a character and interview himself in two voices. "I'd make up people like Dr. Hardbody of the Atomic Energy Commission, or an Englishman whose blimp had crash-landed in Dayton."

It was evident, at least to Winters, that his unusual talents could not be contained in the small state of Ohio, and soon he moved East to try to land a job as a disc jockey with one of the networks. Leaving his young wife back in Ohio, he moved into an apartment on 13th Street in New York City. His Ohio friend Mickey Spillane got him his first paying job in the city. "I sat on a stool and did the sound effects for Spillane's new movie, *I the Jury,* while he described the plot," he recalled.

Soon Winters was making guest appearances on such television shows as "Omnibus," "Today," "Tonight," "Comedy Hour," "The Garry Moore Show," "The Jackie Gleason Show," "You Are There," and "Studio One."

But the show that undoubtedly had the greatest influence on the budding comedian's career was Jack Paar's. In 1956 Paar was one of the hosts of "The Morning Show" on CBS, a two-hour news and entertainment program designed to compete with NBC's popular "Today Show." Paar became Winters' greatest champion, exclaiming,

"When the wind is right and the moon full, Jonathan can be a genius." Paar assumed the mantle of "The Tonight Show" in 1957, and Winters became a frequent guest during his reign there over the next five years.

In October of 1956 Winters was given his own, if rather short, television show. "The Jonathan Winters Show" was a 15-minute enterprise which ran from 7:30 to 7:45 on Tuesday evenings on NBC. Fifteen minutes did not give the star much time to develop characters or sketches, especially since several precious minutes had to be given over to that week's guest star. But Winters and his writers Larry Markes, Jack Crutcher, Jim Lehner and George Atkins came up with the unique Winters-style characterizations that left the audience wanting more.

Elwood P. Suggins, for instance, was an amiable hick, a typically Midwestern individual, the type that Winters saw plenty of in Ohio. As his portrayer describes him: "Elwood is trying to better himself. He represents some kind of fundamental common sense—you're laughing at him, but with him at the same time. He's a square—an innocent guy—a diamond in the rough. . . . He's grass roots. He's '76." Elwood used to be "Far chief a while back, until they found out who was setting the fars."

This Midwestern, all–American quality marked all of Winters' characters. He has never used ethnic or political humor, preferring instead to draw the many personalities he has created from his own, small-town experiences.

Granny Hopps also made her debut on this show. Granny, a forerunner to Maude Frickert, was a little old lady who discovered her talent for painting late in life, à la Grandma Moses. But Granny Hopps was no docile sweetie: "I'm just knocking out these stupid pictures and the suckers are still buying them."

Another feature of the show was a segment titled "Person to Personage," where, as in his radio days, he interviewed himself as such august personalities as Henry VIII, Anne of Cleves, or Santa Claus.

After the program's demise in June of 1957 Winters continued doing his act in nightclubs across the country, including appearances at New York's Ruban Blue and Blue Angel and Chicago's Palmer House. By then he had moved his family, including son Jonathan IV, known as Jay, and daughter Lucinda, into a large house in Mamaroneck in suburban Westchester County.

Apparently the endless nightclub tours and the pressure to be continually funny overloaded Winters' psyche, for while performing at the hungry i club in San Francisco he lost control. During the act he began rambling about Alcoholics Anonymous (he had joined the organization in the previous year), and about a broken cigarette holder someone had given him. When the audience walked out, the distraught comedian began to cry. By the end of the evening he was in the grips of a full-fledged nervous breakdown. On May 14, 1959, the *New York Times* reported:

JONATHAN WINTERS ILL

Jonathan Winters, comedian, under overnight observation in a psychiatric ward, will need further care and treatment, the hospital's superintendent said today.

"Mr. Winters is quite disturbed," said Dr. T.E. Albers, superintendent of San Francisco Hospital, a city institution. "He is definitely in need of further care and treatment."

Mr. Winters was taken into custody late yesterday at Fisherman's Wharf, after he insisted, officers said, on climbing the rigging of an old-time sailing ship and declared he was "a man from outer space." The comedian had been appearing here in a night club.

After his breakdown Winters spent eight months recuperating in a California sanitarium. A troubled and sensitive man had been overtaken by his inner demons and had to struggle to conquer his anxieties. The pressure of working in nightclubs in particular had taken its toll, and Winters did not return to them until 1971.

In 1964 Winters moved his family out to California to a home in Toluca Lake. He was cast in the dual roles of funeral director– brothers in the film *The Loved One*, and he went on to do several other movies, including *It's a Mad, Mad, Mad, Mad World* (1963), *The Russians Are Coming, The Russians Are Coming* (1966), and *Viva Max* (1970), in which he played a bumbling general. He also played Rosalind Russell's late husband (in flashbacks) in the film version of Arthur Kopit's *Oh Dad, Poor Dad, Mama's Hung You in the Closet and I'm Feelin' So Sad* (1965).

On February 2, 1964, Winters returned briefly to television with his special "A Wild Winters Night," with guests Art Carney and the New Christy Minstrels. In one of the evening's sketches, Winters plays the indomitable oldster Maude Frickert, who is given a surprise party by her young friends to mark her 100th birthday. She is so over- come by emotion that she has to turn away to "shed a tear," when in fact she takes a quick swig from her flask. Some of the young people present take the opportunity to ask Maude a few questions about growing older:

> QUESTION: Granny, how does it feel to be 100 years old?
> MAUDE: I kiss a lot slower.
> QUESTION: What was your fondest experience?
> MAUDE: I used to go out on a summer's night and throw mixed fruit at the Northern Lights. Or sticking marshmallows in the ground.
> QUESTION: What's the most terrifying experience you've ever had?
> MAUDE: When the fourth mister took me out one day, it was a hot summer day, pushed my face down on the hot highway. Made me sing "Tenderly" out of the side of my face. He had a warped sense of humor. Don't ever let that happen to you. Never, never, never.
> QUESTION: Granny — who's the most unforgettable character you've ever met?
> MAUDE: Florence Nightingale. Yes, she fixed a robin's wing in flight. I used to shine Teddy Roosevelt's glasses, just before he'd say "Charge!" and go up San Juan. Long before your time, my child.
> QUESTION: Granny, could you let us know your formula for living to a ripe old age?
> MAUDE: Oh yes child — I remember you, you're the boy that's down at the grocery. Remember I used to come in, you were just about that high. And I used to sneak one into you [a punch]. Drive one into your face. You just smiled and became a preacher. Bless you my boy.

Winters was always honest about the direction of his comedy. "I suppose you might say I direct my humor at the Babbitts, the bores and the phonies in the world," he has stated. "I can say a lot through my characters. Maude Frickert's a dirty old lady who thinks sex is okay. She calls a 27-year-old boy 'a gas.' She's a wild old broad." Winters also thinks that "She's a hip old chick, a kind of worldly gal. A little malicious, caustic, bitter. But there's a lot of life in her, in a wild way. She loves life. She refuses to adjust to age. She's a kind of DAR type, but not all the way. There's a tremendous pioneer spirit. She's a fighter. . . . She's a fun person but she's grass-roots. Down deep inside she's a Puritan. She's the Plymouth Rock, 'The Star-Spangled Banner,' Valley Forge — she's American history. She's the gal on the white horse, and yet there's a lot of the Tom Sawyer and Huck Finn in her. She shoots out of church because she can't stand the preacher — he's a bore. She has a place down by the stream and she may go fish or just lie around and go skinny dipping."[1] Maude also

Jonathan Winters entertained with his own brand of zany humor in "The Wacky World of Jonathan Winters," a half-hour comedy series syndicated in 1972.

had a weak-minded brother named Maynard, who tried to emulate Icarus: "He went up to Willard's Bluff and Scotch-taped 146 pigeons to his arms, and flew just fine for maybe 20 seconds, when a kid came out of nowhere and throwed a handful of popcorn inta the stone quarry, and poor Maynard's brains was bashed out."

Johnny Carson became such a fan of occasional guest Jonathan Winters on his "Tonight Show" that he created his own Maude Frickert–style old lady, known as Aunt Blabby. Though it was obvious that Aunt Blabby was a blatant imitation of Maude, Winters retained his equanimity. "I work with Johnny and enjoy him very much. People have said it's a copy. But, as they say, imitation is the highest form of flattery. Anyway, when you get to be my age, a lot of things don't bother you."

In December of 1967 Winters starred in his own television show, again titled "The Jonathan Winters Show," a 60-minute production that was aired on Wednesday nights at 10:00 on CBS. The show's regulars included Paul Lynde, Alice Ghostley and Cliff Arquette. Once again the whimsical Winters characters were around, including those with such improbable names as Chester Hunihugger, Maynard Tetlinger, Winslow G. Flydipper and Lance Loveguard. One overseas visitor, Winters explained, was "King Kwasi from Kwasiland, which is 200 miles long and two feet wide, [who] is always after 'money for me and my people.' If he doesn't get it, he threatens to turn Communist."

Lamar B. Gumbody was a retired United States Army general: "Last year I'll bet I painted the house a half-dozen different colors just to keep from going crazy. . . . What this country basically needs is a good five-year war." Seventy-three-year-old former football star Piggy Bladder was coach for the State Teacher's Animal Husbandry Institute for the Blind: "We beat the Deaf and Dumb in our big game this year. They couldn't give or get signals. Our boys could hear all right but had trouble with passes. It made for a whale of a game." And spaced-out Luna Moon was not always in touch with reality: "All the scientists and hepcats are going celestial, man. Back to the mother ship!"[2]

Winters' humor may have been too unusual, too manic for the average Nielsen viewer: in any case the show was cancelled in May 1969. In 1972 Winters tried a return to the medium in "The Wacky World of Jonathan Winters," a 30-minute show that ran in syndication. The show was largely unrehearsed in order to utilize Winters' gift of improvisation.

In 1981 Winters joined the cast of "Mork and Mindy" as the extra-terrestrial son of Robin Williams' zany Mork. The combination of Winters and Williams was as exciting as it was apt, for Williams freely admits that he is the direct comic descendant of Winters, whom he venerates.

Jonathan Winters continues to create comic fantasies out of the most mundane American realities. "There isn't anything I do, or any place I am," he says, "that doesn't provide me with material. I've found characters and situations I could use when I'm collecting antiques, which is one of my hobbies, and when I'm fishing, which is another. The only place where I draw the line is on a long plane trip, say to the West Coast, which I make from time to time. On a plane, you're a captive audience, and it's impossible to escape. I've thought often that the only way out is for me to announce loudly, when I get on that plane, 'My name is Oscar Mitnick, and I am going to be met in Los Angeles by two men in white coats, and they are going to take me to the Glendale Rest Home for a good long rest.' But I probably never will."[3]

A painter of verbal pictures, adept at capturing the intrinsically American personas and eccentricities of life in the small towns of the Midwest, Jonathan Winters has maintained a loyal following among his many fans. A sensitive, troubled individual, he has dared to seek his own way to comedy without being derivative. He is certainly unique, and the history of television comedy certainly would have been poorer had he not appeared on our screens.

Ed Wynn

In the very early days of television, stars were culled from Broadway and vaudeville to bring their already well-known talents to the small screen. Many found the adjustment disconcerting, if not insurmountable. Ed Wynn was one of them.

In a class with such great vaudeville comedians as Fanny Brice, Eddie Cantor, Al Jolson and W.C. Fields, Wynn came to television prepared to repeat the wild success he had maintained for more than 40 years on the stage. Known as the "Perfect Fool" (a sobriquet he earned by appearing in a 1921 show of the same name, a take-off on the Norma Talmadge/John Gilbert vehicle "The Perfect Lovers"), he was, with his face of oversized features, bizarre costumes and high-pitched cackle such a distinctive figure that he became instantly recognizable to American audiences.

Wynn was born Isaiah Edwin Leopold (his stage name derived by splitting up the two syllables of his middle name) on November 19, 1886, to Joseph Loeb, a millinery manufacturer, and his wife, Minnie, in Philadelphia. He entered vaudeville at age 16 as half of a double act with partner Jack Lewis. In the early days of his career he was known as The Rah Rah Boy, the Boy with the Funny Hat, King's Jester, and finally as The Perfect Fool. His preeminence grew, and soon he was the star (and occasional writer or lyricist) of such Broadway shows as "The Ziegfeld Follies" (1914 and 1915 versions), "The Passing Show" (1916), "Doing Our Bit" (1917), "Sometime" (1918), "The Ed Wynn Carnival" (1920), "The Grab Bag" (1924), "Manhattan Mary" (1927), "Simple Simon" (1930), "Laugh Parade" (1931), "Hooray for What!" (1937), "Boys and Girls Together" (1940) and "Laugh, Town, Laugh" (1942).

On October 6, 1949, Wynn began his own 30-minute variety show on NBC. It was the first show to be broadcast live on the West Coast and filmed on two 16mm cameras for Eastern audiences to see

237

Ed Wynn, for more than 40 years a successful vaudevillian comedian, had difficulty adjusting his talents to the small screen in television's early days.

two weeks later. He brought with him all the accoutrements that had sustained him in the theater: the outrageous puns, the fluttering hands, the pursed lips, the trademark lisp, the cartoonish backdrops. What he could not bring was the spark, the intimacy or the relaxed mastery of timing that was second nature to him on stage. Publicly, he did not seem worried about transition to the new medium. He told *TeleVision Guide* on November 25, 1949:

> For the artist, television is the stage, pure and simple. Or perhaps not so simple; it's not the movies. It's the stage . . . . I have

found it necessary to make only one change from my stage technique to fit the TV camera: I must make my hand gestures above
my waistline so that the movement of my fingers won't be out of
the picture on close-ups.

Privately, he was not so sanguine, moaning "You just can't get laughs
out of the cameramen's asses."[1] The show's run ended on July 4,
1950.

In 1950 Wynn joined the roster of rotating hosts on "The Four-
Star Revue," a 60-minute variety show on NBC. The following year
the show was retitled "The All-Star Revue" when more hosts were
added. "The All-Star Revue" continued to air until April 1953.

It was not until some years later that Wynn returned to television, this time in a half-hour situation comedy. This "Ed Wynn Show"
cast him as a retired widower struggling to raise his two orphaned
granddaughters. The NBC show ran from September 25, 1958, to
January 1, 1959.

Ed Wynn was married three times: to Hilda Keenan, daughter
of famed actor Frank Keenan and mother of their son Keenan Wynn,
who became a well-known actor in his own right; to Frieda Mierse;
and to Dorothy Nesbitt. Although Wynn was never able to match the
heights of popularity that he had attained on the legitimate stage, he
continued to be an American institution until his death on June 19,
1966, at the age of 79.

Chapter Notes

Lucille Ball

1. Bart Andrews. *The "I Love Lucy" Book.*
2. *TV Guide.* September 5, 1964.
3. New York *Post.* February 18, 1985.

Milton Berle

1. Milton Berle and Haskel Frankel. *An Autobiography.*
2. Milton Berle. *Laughingly Yours.*
3. Ibid.
4. Milton Berle at seminars sponsored by the Museum of Broadcasting, April 17–18, 1985.
5. Ibid.
6. Ibid.
7. Ibid.

Sid Caesar

1. *Colliers.* November 11, 1950.
2. For an excellent and heartrending account of Sid Caesar's struggles and eventual triumph over alcohol and drugs, see *Where Have I Been* by Caesar and Bill Davidson.
3. Ted Sennett. *Your Show of Shows.*
4. *Comedy Magazine.* Vol. 1, no. 1, Summer 1980.
5. Ibid.
6. Ibid.

Imogene Coca

1. Interview with the author, October 22, 1984.
2. Ibid.
3. Ibid.

4. Ibid.
5. Ibid.
6. Ted Sennett. *Your Show of Shows.*
7. Ibid.
8. Ibid.
9. Idem.
10. Idem.
11. Idem.

Jackie Gleason

1. *People* Magazine. November 3, 1980.
2. Steve Allen. *The Funny Men.*
3. Jim Bishop. *The Golden Ham.*
4. Ibid.
5. Donna McCrohan. *The Honeymooners' Companion.*
6. *Sunday News.* October 8, 1953.
7. *Liberty Magazine.* February 1955.
8. New York *Journal-American.* April 8, 1962.
9. *The American Weekly.* April 8, 1962.

Danny Kaye

1. Arthur Marx. *Goldwyn.* W.W. Norton & Co. N.Y., 1976.
2. *Pictorial Review.* April 27, 1941.

Ernie Kovacs

1. David G. Walley. *Nothing in Moderation.*
2. Frederic Morton. *Holiday* Magazine. October 1961.

Red Skelton

1. Arthur Marx. *Red Skelton.*
2. Rudi Blesh. *Keaton.* Collier Books. New York, 1966.
3. Idem.
4. Idem.

Jonathan Winters

    1. *TV Guide.* March 8–14, 1969.
    2. Peter Maas. *Esquire.* May 1959.
    3. *Pictorial TV.* February 3, 1957.

Ed Wynn

    1. Max Wilk. *The Golden Age of Television.*

TV-ographies

(Does not include guest appearances, specials, or game shows, unless noted.)

Lucille Ball

"I Love Lucy" 30 mins., CBS. October 15, 1951–September 1956.
"The Lucy-Desi Comedy Hour" 60 mins. October 1957–April 1, 1960 (once a month).
"The Lucy Show" 30 mins., CBS. October 1, 1962–September 16, 1968.
"Here's Lucy" 30 mins., CBS. September 23, 1968–September 2, 1974.
"Life with Lucy" 30 mins., ABC. September 20, 1986–November 15, 1986.

Milton Berle

"Texaco Star Theatre" 60 mins., NBC. September 21, 1948–June 9, 1953.
"The Milton Berle Show" 60 mins., NBC. September 29, 1953–June 14, 1955.
"The Milton Berle Show" 60 mins., NBC. September 27, 1955–June 5, 1956.
"The Kraft Music Hall" 30 mins., NBC. October 8, 1958–June 13, 1959.
"Jackpot Bowling" 30 mins., NBC. September 19, 1960–March 13, 1961.
"The Milton Berle Show" 60 mins., ABC. September 9, 1966–January 6, 1967.

Carol Burnett

"Toyland Express" (with Paul Winchell) 30 mins., ABC. November 7, 1955–December 12, 1955.
"Stanley" 30 mins., NBC. September 24, 1956–March 11, 1957.
"The Garry Moore Show" 60 mins., CBS. October 19, 1959–June 1962.
"The Entertainers" 60 mins., CBS. September 25, 1964–March 27, 1965.
"The Carol Burnett Show" 60 mins., CBS. September 11, 1967–March 29, 1978.
"The Carol Burnett Show" 60 mins., ABC. Summer 1979.

Sid Caesar

"The Admiral Broadway Revue" 60 mins., NBC & Dumont. January 28, 1949–June 17, 1949.
"Your Show of Shows" 90 mins., NBC. February 25, 1950–June 5, 1954.
"Caesar's Hour" 60 mins., NBC. September 27, 1954–May 25, 1957.
"Sid Caesar Invites You" 30 mins., ABC. January 20, 1958–May 25, 1958.
"As Caesar Sees It" 30 mins., ABC. September 19, 1963–March 14, 1964.

Imogene Coca

"The Admiral Broadway Revue" 60 mins., NBC & Dumont. January 28, 1949–June 17, 1949.
"Your Show of Shows" 90 mins., NBC. February 25, 1950–June 5, 1954.
"The Imogene Coca Show" 60 mins. October 2, 1954–June 25, 1955.
"Grindl" 30 mins., NBC. September 15, 1963–September 13, 1964.
"It's About Time" 30 mins., CBS. September 11, 1966–September 3, 1967.

Tim Conway

"The New Steve Allen Show" 60 mins., ABC. September 27, 1961–December 27, 1961.
"McHale's Navy" 30 mins., ABC. September 11, 1962–August 30, 1966.
"Rango" 30 mins., ABC. January 13, 1967–June 25, 1967.
"The Carol Burnett Show" 60 mins., CBS. September 11, 1967–March 29, 1978 (semiregular).
"Turn On" 30 mins., ABC. February 5, 1969.
"The Tim Conway Show" 30 mins., CBS. January 20, 1970–June 19, 1970.
"The Tim Conway Comedy Hour" 60 mins., CBS. September 20, 1970–December 28, 1970.
"The Tim Conway Show" 60 mins., CBS. March 1980–?
"Ace Crawford, Private Eye" 30 mins., CBS. March 1983–June 1983.

Jackie Gleason

"The Life of Riley" 30 mins., Dumont. October 4, 1949–March 28, 1950.
"Cavalcade of Stars — The Jackie Gleason Show" 60 mins., Dumont. January 7, 1950–September 13, 1952.
"The Jackie Gleason Show" 60 mins., CBS. September 20, 1952–June 18, 1955.
"The Honeymooners" 30 mins., CBS. October 1, 1955–September 22, 1956.
"The Jackie Gleason Show" 60 mins., CBS. September 29, 1956–June 22, 1957.
"The Jackie Gleason Show" 30 mins., CBS. October 3, 1958–June 1959.

"You're in the Picture" 30 mins., CBS. January 20, 1961–March 24, 1961.
"Jackie Gleason and His American Scene Magazine" 60 mins., CBS. September 29, 1962–June 4, 1966.
"The Jackie Gleason Show" 60 mins., CBS. September 17, 1966–September 12, 1970.

Danny Kaye

"An Hour with Danny Kaye" 60 mins., CBS (three specials). October 1960, October 1961, November 1962.
"The Danny Kaye Show" 60 mins., CBS. September 25, 1963–June 7, 1967.

Ernie Kovacs

"Deadline for Dinner" 30 mins., WPTZ, Philadelphia. March 20, 1950–April 18, 1952.
"Three to Get Ready" 90 mins., WPTZ. October 27, 1950–March 28, 1952.
"It's Time for Ernie" 15 mins., NBC. May 14, 1951–June 29, 1951.
"Now You're Cooking" 30 mins., WPTZ. May 15, 1951–June 12, 1951, and September 18, 1951–October 16, 1951.
"Ernie in Kovacsland" 30 mins., NBC. July 2, 1951–August 24, 1951.
"Kovacs on the Corner" 30 mins., NBC. November 1951–March 1952.
"Kovacs Unlimited" 60 mins., CBS. April 21, 1952–December 26, 1952.
"The Ernie Kovacs Show" 60 mins., CBS. December 30, 1952–April 14, 1953.
"The Ernie Kovacs Show" 30 and 60 mins., Dumont. April 12, 1954–April 7, 1955.
"The Ernie Kovacs Show" 30 mins., NBC. December 12, 1955–July 27, 1956.
"The Ernie Kovacs Show" 30 mins., ABC. 1958–1959.
"The Dutch Masters Specials" 30 mins., NBC. May 22, 1959–January 13, 1962.
"Take a Good Look" 30 mins., ABC. October 22, 1959–July 21, 1960, and October 27, 1960–March 16, 1961.

Olsen and Johnson

"The Olsen and Johnson Show" 60 mins., NBC. Summer 1949.
"Fireball Fun for All" 60 mins., NBC. 1949–1950.
"Five Star Comedy" 30 mins., ABC. May 18, 1957–June 15, 1957.

Martha Raye

"The All-Star Revue—The Martha Raye Show" 60 mins., NBC. 1951–1952.
"The Martha Raye Show" 60 mins., NBC. December 26, 1953–May 15, 1954.
"The Martha Raye Show" 60 mins., NBC. September 20, 1955–June 29, 1956.

Soupy Sales

"Soupy's On" 30 mins., Detroit. 1953–1960.
"The Soupy Sales Show" 30 mins., ABC. June 4, 1955–August 26, 1955.
"The Soupy Sales Show" 30 mins., ABC. 1960–1964.
"The Soupy Sales Show" 30 mins., WNEW-NY. 1964–1965.

Red Skelton

"The Red Skelton Show" 30 mins., NBC. September 30, 1951–June 1953.
"The Red Skelton Show" 30 and 60 mins., CBS. September 22, 1953–June 1969.
"The Red Skelton Show" 30 mins., NBC. September 14, 1970–August 29, 1971.

Dick Van Dyke

"The Morning Show" 120 mins., CBS. January 20, 1956–April 5, 1957.
"The Chevy Showroom" 30 mins., ABC. July 3, 1957–September 25, 1958.
"Mothers Day" 30 mins., ABC. October 3, 1958–January 2, 1959.
"Laugh Line" 30 mins., NBC. April 16, 1959–June 11, 1959.
"The Dick Van Dyke Show" 30 mins., CBS. October 3, 1961–September 7, 1966.
"The New Dick Van Dyke Show" 30 mins., CBS. September 18, 1971–September 3, 1973, and September 10, 1973–September 2, 1974.
"Van Dyke and Company" 60 mins., NBC. September 20, 1976–December 30, 1976.

Flip Wilson

"The Flip Wilson Show" 60 mins., NBC. September 17, 1970–June 27, 1974.
"Charlie and Company" 30 mins., CBS. September 1986–December 1986.

Jonathan Winters

"Here's the Show" 30 mins., NBC. July 9, 1955–September 24, 1955.
"The Jonathan Winters Show" 15 mins., NBC. October 2, 1956–June 25, 1957.
"The Jonathan Winters Show" 60 mins., CBS. December 27, 1967–May 1969.
"Hot Dog" 30 mins., NBC (educational). September 12, 1970–September 4, 1971.
"The Wacky World of Jonathan Winters" 30 mins., syndicated. 1972.
"Mork and Mindy" 30 mins., ABC. September 14, 1978–August 12, 1982.

Ed Wynn

"The Ed Wynn Show" 30 mins., NBC. October 6, 1949–June 4, 1950.
"The Ed Wynn Show" 30 mins., NBC. September 25, 1958–January 1, 1959.

Bibliography

Allen, Steve. *The Funny Men.* New York: Simon and Schuster, 1956.

_____. *More Funny People.* Briarcliff Manor, N.Y.: Stein and Day, 1982.

Andrews, Bart. *The "I Love Lucy" Book.* Garden City, N.Y.: Doubleday, 1985.

_____, and Thomas J. Watson. *Loving Lucy.* New York: St. Martin's Press, 1980.

Arnaz, Desi. *A Book.* New York: William Morrow, 1976.

Berger, Phil. *The Last Laugh.* New York: William Morrow, 1975.

Berle, Milton. *Laughingly Yours.* New York: Samuel French, 1939.

_____, and Haskel Frankel. *An Autobiography.* New York: Delacorte Press, 1974.

Bishop, Jim. *The Golden Ham.* New York: Simon and Schuster, 1956.

Blesh, Rudi. *Keaton.* New York: Collier Books, 1966.

Burnett, Carol. *One More Time.* New York: Random House, 1986.

Caesar, Sid, and Bill Davidson. *Where Have I Been?* New York: Crown Publishers, 1982.

Campbell, Robert. *The Golden Years of Broadcasting.* New York: Charles Scribner's Sons, 1976.

Freedland, Michael. *The Secret Life of Danny Kaye.* New York: St. Martin's Press, 1985.

Gregory, James. *The Lucille Ball Story.* New York: Signet, 1974.

McCrohan, Donna. *The Honeymooner's Companion.* New York: Workman Publishing, 1978.

Marx, Arthur. *Goldwyn.* New York: W.W. Norton, 1976.

_____. *Red Skelton: An Unauthorized Biography.* New York: E.P. Dutton, 1979.

"Milton Berle Mr. Television." New York: Museum of Broadcasting, 1985.

Morella, Joe, and Edward Z. Epstein. *Lucy: The Bittersweet Life of Lucille Ball.* Secaucus, N.J.: Lyle Stuart, 1973.

Parish, James Robert. *The Slapstick Queens.* New York: Castle Books, 1973.

Sennett, Ted. *Your Show of Shows.* New York: Collier Books, 1977.

Stein, Charles W., ed. *American Vaudeville as Seen by Its Contemporaries.* New York: Alfred A. Knopf, 1984.

"The Vision of Ernie Kovacs." New York: Museum of Broadcasting, 1986.

Walley, David G. *Nothing in Moderation: A Biography of Ernie Kovacs.* New York: Drake Publishers, 1975.

Wilk, Max. *The Golden Age of Television.* New York: Delacorte Press, 1976.

Index

Names of comedians featured in individual chapters appear in **boldface**.